Philosophy, Religion, and the Question of Intolerance

We wish to express gratitude to all who helped make this volume possible, in particular President William M. Anderson, Jr. with the administration of Mary Washington College, and our colleagues in the Department of Classics, Philosophy and Religion. We owe special thanks to Cindy Toomey, Charlotte Itoh, and Stephanie Barnes for their valuable assistance in the final preparation of the manuscript.

Philosophy, Religion, and the Question of Intolerance

Mehdi Amin Razavi
and
David Ambuel
Editors

State University of New York Press

Published by
State University of New York Press, Albany

For information, address State University of New York Press,
State University Plaza, Albany, N.Y. 12246

Production by E. Moore
Marketing by Nancy Farrell

Library of Congress Cataloging-in-Publication Data
Philosophy, religion, and the question of intolerance / Mehdi
    Amin Razavi and David Ambuel, editors.
        p.   cm.
    Includes bibliographical references and index.
    ISBN 0-7914-3447-8 (alk. paper). — ISBN 0-7914-3448-6 (alk.
paper)
    1. Toleration.   I. Amin Razavi, Mehdi, 1957–   . II. Ambuel,
    David.
    BJ1431.P47   1997
    179'.9—dc20   96-46170
                                                          CIP

10 9 8 7 6 5 4 3 2 1

Contents

Introduction

PHILOSOPHY AND THE QUESTION OF INTOLERANCE

Were we to compile a late twentieth-century list of virtues, tolerance would equal or surpass in prominence the more ancient and traditional, such as justice or wisdom. But we will not find the word or any approximate synonym on any lists dating from a time when it was more common for philosophers to compile them.

Although the technical terms may fill only a small space in the Western philosophy of the past two centuries, the problems are problems of the human condition. They have been and continue to be encountered by our kind and to be dealt with—not always very successfully—in all times and places. And the ongoing practical problems are ongoing problems of reflection, not resolved by the mere recognition of toleration as a positive value.

Toleration works its way into the vocabulary of ethics in early modernity, around the time of Locke's often cited *Letter concerning Toleration*. The first recommendations to be tolerant are negative ones. The word's Latin root is *tolero*, to bear, endure, sustain; it is cognate to *tollo*, to lift up or carry, and derived from the Indo-European root *tela*, to lift or weigh. To tolerate is to endure, to put up with the objectionable, to bear a burden. One tolerates as one shoulders a burden. Like the burden, the persons or actions tolerated are neither pleasant nor welcome. Consequently, toleration is valued only as a means, not an end. Even as a means, toleration, negatively conceived, is not, like a vaccination, the painful means to a future good, but rather a means to accomodate the least objectionable among objectionable alternatives. Thus, for example, Locke does not endorse toleration because toleration is good in itself, but only because the consequences of intolerance are a greater evil than the evil that is tolerated. Even so, toleration is construed narrowly: Locke, for example, extends tolerance to those whose faith requires different practices, but not to atheists, who have no faith. Only recently has it become common to find toleration as the principle of mutual acceptance and the embrace of diversity represented as intrinsically desirable. Although Locke's and other writings of his period on toleration were confined to a religious context, his argument embraces at least two principles central to later less restrictive and more positive conceptions of toleration. Locke's advocacy of religious tolerance is closely tied to his epistemology with its critical emphasis, anticipating Kant, on the limits of human knowledge—because of those limits, unshakable confidence in one's own faith does not grant the epistemological certainty to justify persecuting another. It is also closely tied to the modern conception of society as modeled on a contract, viewing the structure of society as the coordination of atomic individuals, whose interests may overlap, but who are essentially separate and private. Insofar as a person's religion is a private matter, it is to be tolerated, since one person's private errors are not another's concern. However, if that faith requires foreign allegiance, then it is in Locke's view a public concern that need not be tolerated.

In the present-day West, the question of intolerance is, of course, much broader and of greater scope than the question of religious tolerance alone. In many parts of the world where distinctions between the public and the private and between the sacred and the secular are not drawn as in the West, the suffering inflicted by religious conflict is a frightening reality. In the secular West, too, the problem of religious tolerance has not vanished, nor have episodes of violence, although the outbreak of religiously motivated warfare seems remote. More common are tensions and conflicts short of war, even if wistfully dubbed by some "culture war." Yet this is indicative that even matters of religious toleration are much connected with secular affairs in the contemporary West. In such situations, proponents of more liberal and of more conservative sides of an issue generally share a view that certain matters of belief and of behavior fall under private concerns but are at odds over where that line between private and public concern is to be drawn. And this is a concern to religious and nonreligious alike.

Insofar as religion per se still occasions questions concerning toleration specific to religion, it has become to a great extent not a problem of public action, but one of private religious conception: how can the individual reconcile faith in the absolute truth of her own tradition with her acceptance of the proposition that one should be tolerant; how can one remain religious while being tolerant, not whether one can remain tolerant given the truth of religion.

That questions of religious toleration often take this form in the West is a manifestation of the scope of concern for intolerance. It is generally accepted as a good that one should be tolerant not only of the faith of others, but of all other varieties of cultural and social activity. With the uncritical assurances of the brief overview, we might say that the Lockean principle that private matters are private matters has contributed significantly to secularizing and broadening the understanding of questions of intolerance in the West.

The broadening includes its extension from something negatively defined—toleration as enduring bad because it is worse to oppose it—to something positively embraced—toleration as embracing what is different and finding intrisic value in diversity. Nevertheless, the broadening in our conception of toleration even to the extent of embracing toleration as a positive good does not resolve the fundamental problems. The line dividing private and public realms is fuzzy and floating; it is highly culturally dependent, constantly being redefined in public discourse, and consequently perceived differently from one individual to another.

Even if one uncritically accepts the principle that private matters are not the concern of another, the question of how to determine what is private still must be answered. Likewise, if we accept Locke's other principle that our knowledge remains severely limited even at its best, the principle still demands that we define the limits. The seemingly benign comfort of supposing otherwise can ease the path into further manifestations of intolerance, as a more specific form of intolerance gives way to a more general yet kindred form.

The more specific form, intolerance born of unquestioned and resolute faith, one might say, manifests a certain mental sloth. This is the complacency of the intolerance that rests in the self-assurance of the finite person's infallibility. Not only does this trespass on private ground, but it violates the principle of imperfect knowledge by taking the assurance of one's own beliefs as reason enough to act against another's, whether it be the demolition of a temple in India or the harrasssment of a child not wanting to pray in public school in Mississippi.

The mirror image of the intolerance of faith is an intolerance of indifference, reversed left to right, but not top to bottom. It, too, one might say, is born of unrealistic and self-serving complacency, the self-asurance of the finite person's fallibility: another way to release oneself from real and critical engagement in the society, and a way that may lead to analogous consequences.

One possible response to the principle demanding that we recognize limitations to our knowledge is the assertion that since no standards are infallible, at least not to the best of human knowledge, no standards apply. The rejection of all standards as anything but subjective may translate into a principle that any moral agent's wishes must be tolerated. While not practicable in this form, the proposition may be turned into the assertion that no judgements should be made or at least acted upon, that no action be taken against anything that can be construed as private or against any desires that do not interfere with the desires of others. However, this is a principle without grounds. If we would not acknowledge standards for action, then on what footing do we assert the standard that one person's pursuits are tolerable as long as they interfere with no other person's? It is perhaps at best an uncritical remnant from social contract theory. However, if there are grounds for this principle of toleration, on what grounds do we demur from passing judgement on human end and purpose, both one's own and those of others?

Perhaps, one might continue, this principle has no grounds, but so what? Neither does any other principle, and, besides, is this not the essence of toleration? Two avenues lead on from this mental detachment, depending on how we draw our vague line between public and private. Perhaps we are called upon to tolerate everything, and, if we are to enforce absolute toleration, then we must curtail any beliefs or practices that can be construed as intolerant in any sense. This road circles back to absolute intolerance. Alternatively, one may under the guise of utter tolerance adopt the pretence of living in a vacuum—a tolerant monad of private interests, neither affecting nor affected by others. All of the cases converge in the refusal of considered and reflective engagement with differing ideas. If one dogmatically asserts infallibility, one asserts power without justification; if one rejects any legitimacy whatsoever, one implicitly acknowledges no other basis for action than the assertion of power. It is no accident that the contemporary West is so gripped by the discourse of power, nor that the discourse is so empty.

We are left with a situation reminiscent of the vying of dogmatism and skepticism described (in another context) by Hume:

> The sceptical and dogmatical reasons are of the same kind, tho' contrary in their operation and their tendency; so that where the latter is strong, it has an enemy of equal force in the former to encounter; and as their forces were at first equal, they still continue so, as long as either of them subsists; nor does one of them lose any force in the contests, without taking as much from its antagonist. 'Tis happy, therefore, that nature breaks the force of all sceptical arguments in time, and keeps them from having any considerable influence on the understanding. Were we to trust entirely to their self-destruction, that can never take place, 'till they have first subverted all conviction, and have totally destroyed human reason.[1]

This is a natural conclusion, if, like Hume, one is persuaded that no moral distinctions derive from reason. However, it is not an agreeable conclusion, since it condemns us, helpless against our own nature, to living in the balance of opposing forces of intolerance.

Still, the awareness that our human meagreness, with all its limitations is assurance enough that we will never exhaust the supply of problems to solve, does not directly lead to the narcisisstic inference that we cannot meaningfully and rationally address those problems. Blind faith and simple indifference are two forms of complacency, whereas genuine respect for differing standards implies not uncritical acceptance, but awareness of the limitations of one's own insight and awareness of the necessity to continually re-examine one's own standards.

We may continue to debate the utility of talk about virtues and debate whether toleration should be counted as one. Yet perhaps, though the term *toleration* is a relatively recent entry into the vocabulary of ethical discussion, its essence is captured by Plato's Socrates, who was so concerned with virtue: "The unexamined life is not worth living." What follows in this volume is an excursion into that examination.

RELIGION AND THE QUESTION OF INTOLERANCE

Is it in the nature of religious truth to be intolerant? This is one of the central questions which has been examined extensively in the religion section of the present work. Whereas various perspectives have been presented by different authors, we would like to argue that tolerance, and the attainment of an "appreciative mind" regarding those values that are different and often threatening, requires an ongoing rational discourse and engagement with an alien value system. Also, we would like to argue that a rational approach to the question of religious truth allows a person to maintain the integrity of his belief in a religious truth while allowing for various other religions to make truth claims of a different nature. Whether religious beliefs are rationally justifiable is not the aim of this inquiry.

Religions in and of themselves produce neither tolerance nor intolerance; it is how one encounters religious truth which determines the outcome. Let us examine the following three mind sets and their respective outcomes as a starting point: (1) intolerant, (2) tolerant, (3) appreciative.

The intolerant mind is convinced that it knows the truth and is certain that this truth is obvious and self-evident. Those who do not share this self-evident truth, according to the believer, are naturally wrong for refusing to accept the obvious. The intolerant mind whose "faith" makes the content of his belief self-evident then is angered by those who "choose" not to see "the truth." The anger is directed toward the person who does not want to be a conformist and submit to someone else's perception of reality, as well as her underlying principles and belief system. The intolerant mind, convinced of the evil intention of those unlike itself, rejects the person as much as his "false religion," a classical case of *ad homenum*. The rejection of the message and the messenger partially stems from the insecurity and vulnerability of the intolerant person who is intimidated by nontraditional values. Religious truth, for the intolerant mind, therefore not only is absolute in a personal sense but also is universal in nature. It is not sufficient for a person to know the truth, according to the intolerant person, but everyone else must accept his world views as well. In fact, the obsession to convert others and the intellectual imperialism resulting from certainty becomes the salient feature and the focal point of an intolerant mind. The intolerant person lives for his cause.

Although tolerance compared to intolerance is a virtue, since it implies enduring an undesirable phenomenon, it falls short of being an inherent virtue. For a tolerant individual, religious truth even if it is held in an absolute sense for the individual who adheres to it, does not necessarily entail intolerance. All it does claim is that this truth for me is a binding one whereas others need not follow it. The problem occurs when one claims that religious truth not only is true for him but everyone else ought to accept it as well.

Tolerance, though it is the necessary condition for having a civil society, does not go far enough. It remains passive and accepts reluctantly what is different. It is this passivity of tolerance which, while acceptable, is not sufficient. Enduring and tolerating is different than being actively engaged in what is different, foreign, alien, and therefore threatening to one's *weltanschauung*.

It is therefore reasonable to infer from the above that there are two senses of tolerance; passive and active. In the passive sense, the tolerant individual maintains that although his position is true, he chooses to ignore those concepts and values that are different or even contrary to his. It can be said that a tolerant mind is one which affirms the truth of his own views but holds a noncommitted view regarding those of others. Since for the tolerant person the focus is on himself and not others, he does not engage in value judgments.

What distinguishes the two types of individuals is precisely the position each one maintains with regard to her engagement with what is threatening to the order of her world view. Whereas the intolerant individual rejects the other and their notion of truth (for him there is only one Truth, that of himself), the tolerant mind holds a position of neutrality and makes no value judgment regarding it. In this regard, the tolerant person is halfway between the intolerant individual and the individual who appreciates what is different.

An aspect of the tolerant mind is closely connected with what is known as the "perennial view." Perennialists argue that all religious traditions are manifestations of the same Truth and their apparent differences are merely indications of their relative ignorance of Truth. Only the Absolute knows the

Absolute absolutely perennialists argue, the knowledge of all other beings of the absolute is only relative.

The model offered by the perennialists indeed does provide a framework within which one can be tolerant and appreciate other religions even if they are contradicting hers, since religions emanate from the same Source. The problem is that although such a model which has functioned in the traditional world—where most, if not all people have had a religion—is no longer able to respond to the challenges of the modern world. What would the perennialists say about the secular humanists, Universalist Unitarians, existentialists, atheists, and even those with a secular or nontheistic interpretation of a religious tradition? Perennialism, which in the traditional world was inclusive of almost everyone, in the secular world excludes a great number of people.

The remedy to this problem is to widen the ontological domain of the "acceptables" to the "untouchables" and that requires an *appreciative mind*, one that is willing to be open to all but not necessarily accepting all. Tolerance, in its authentic and positive sense, therefore, is opening oneself to the unknown abyss of the other. *Appreciation* is a better term to describe this mind-set than *tolerance* since it denotes the active role of the individual in the process of tolerance. Tolerance in its positive sense goes further to be engaged actively with despised values. The appreciative individual chooses a path of engagement and a constructive discourse with the foreign and alien world view and the values it espouses. From this active engagement and critical self-examination comes an inner enrichment of the appreciative individual. In this case, the person in question need not fear "conversion," since examination of and being receptive to a different notion of truth can only stimulate a hermeneutical process resulting in a deeper understanding of one's own religious tradition. The basis and the criterion for this engagement however, should be none other than the fruit of human wisdom, a rational process of discourse and reflection.

The person with an appreciative mind may argue that his views are correct, but he does not negate that others may be right as well regardless of how far apart they might be. In fact, he would go so far as to say that truth is not and cannot only be an exclusive property of a select number of people. Therefore, an appreciative mind would want to explore other traditions of wisdom either to choose amongst them the superior tradition or to enrich his own views. Such a view demands that the appreciative mind be in a constant dialogue with and in search of what is different and challenging to one's intellectual and religious perspectives.

It should be noted that this type of relativism does not negate the truth of the individual traditions but can regard them as manifestations of a process of rationalization, intellection, reflection, and contemplation. The central message, and the *core* of many religious traditions which have survived the test of history, contains a great deal of human wisdom which is not necessarily inconsistent with the principles of rationality. The subsequent development of religions has added layer upon layer of rituals and beliefs which ought to be weeded out by the sword of rational reflection in order to separate the wheat from the chaff.

One's active and rational engagement with other traditions and value systems does not have to take place to verify one's philosophical validity or to falsify one's claims. The purpose of such inquiry should be to understand alien values and concepts in a clear manner and in comparison to one's own tradition. A rational discourse can be more beneficial if it is not intended to examine whether religious claims can or cannot survive the scrutiny of reason. If this were the case, then once again truth becomes an enterprise exclusive to a select number of people, that is, rationalistic philosophers. Rationality in this sense only assumes that values different than mine have something inherently worth cultivating and therefore should be respected and explored.

It is only reasonable to conclude that, throughout millenniums, every society has had the opportunity to discover, develop, and cherish ideas, concepts, and values that are essential for the vitality and spiritual health of that society. However, maintaining a healthy society is only possible through a rational and critical examination of its underlying values. This necessitates that "our" value system be compared and contrasted with "theirs," a process that requires adoption of a rational framework within which there is room for truths, not only one Truth.

OVERVIEW

The body of questions mentioned above, together with its cultural, social, religious, and philosophical implications are addressed in the following chapters. Despite the inevitable overlaps that defy ordering, the contributions to this volume are arranged into four sections: philosphical roots of intolerance, religion, politics, and ethics. Earlier versions of each chapter were among the papers presented at the conference Intolerance and Toleration, held at Mary Washington College in November 1994.

The first section presents three contrasting perspectives on the conceptual roots of intolerance. In "Bayle, Locke, and the Concept of Toleration," J. B. Schneewind gives a historical account of the period of Locke's *A Letter concerning Moral Toleration,* the document to which we usually date the entry of the term *toleration* into the vocabulary of philosophical ethics. Schneewind makes the case for paying greater attention to Locke's contemporary Bayle, and he concludes with an argument defending a Rawlsian model of toleration.

In "Aristotle and the Metaphysics of Intolerance" John McCumber spans thinkers from Aristotle to the present to advance the claim it is not metaphysics that encourages or precludes intolerance, but the kind of metaphysics. In McCumber's account, Aristotelian substance metaphysics as defined by a dominant and dominating form determines a structure within which intolerance becomes inevitable.

Finally, Robert Cummings Neville argues in "Political Tolerance in an Age of Renewed Religious Warfare" that this "transcendent orientation" of religions can contribute to the passion that leads to religious warfare. To acknowledge that religious passion can lead to violence is not to say that religion is inevitably intolerant. On the contrary, Neville claims that the transcendent orientation, as a ground of obligation, is essential to tolerance, and he calls for development of a public theology, for which he draws upon elements of Buddhism and Confucianism.

The second section further examines the confrontation of religion and intolerance. It opens with Seyyed Hossein Nasr's "Metaphysical Roots of Tolerance and Intolerance: An Islamic Interpretation." Nasr argues that intolerance is a manifestation of human imperfection and is therefore an undesirable element of human existence that can be overcome only by the spritually accomplished. Although among us at all times, intolerance may be more severe or less severe, and Nasr goes on to argue from an Eastern perspective that a secular and individualized society like that of the West exacerbates intolerance. Far from a cause of, religion is a limitation of, intolerance, and without a traditional metaphysics that is the underpinning of religion, excessive intolerance is unavoidable.

David Cain, Edwin C. George, John Donovan, and William O'Meara express four views on how religious faith can be tolerant in light of the diversity of religious committment. In "An Elephant, an Ocean, and the Freedom of Faith," Cain, drawing upon Kierkegaard, presents "faithful appreciation" as a challenge of the freedom of faith. George, also drawing on Kierkegaard, claims that Christianity as conceived by Kierkegaard, far from being a source of intolerance, provides a foundational principle for toleration. Donovan's "Faith and Intellectual Fairness" comments on Aristotle and Charles Taylor in developing a conception of toleration as a virtue particular to religion, one that might be called a "self-regarding" virtue of religion. O'Meara's "Beyond Toleration" focuses in particular on the relation of Christianity to other religions.

The third section turns to politics and intolerance. In "Disagreement: Appreciating the Dark Side of Tolerance," Edward Langerak focuses on the fact that toleration involves enduring what is distasteful. He makes a case for toleration as a kind of respect or open-mindedness that does not extend to the elimination of this negative aspect and does not "delight in diversity."

Gordon Graham, in "Toleration and the Idea of Progress," confronts the apparent paradox between the emergence of a value of toleration in an age that embraced the idea of moral progress and the ensuing connection of toleration with moral relativism, which, by denying objectivity in morals, denies the possibility of moral progress as well. Graham argues that the connection is a misplaced one, that toleration need not lead to relativism.

"The Justification of Toleration," by Richard Dees, turns to the long association of a principle of toleration with political liberalism. Arguing that the traditional positions from Locke to the present do not furnish adequate justification for the adopted principle, Dees attempts to revise their interpretation to solidify the justification without having to reject liberalism.

The final two articles of the section, Gertrude D. Conway's "Differences: Indifference or Dialogue" and Henry Ruf's "Radicalizing Liberalism and Modernity," deal with contemporary philosophers. In developing her ideas, Conway directs some attention to Gadamer and Rorty, while Ruf turns to Habermas and Foucault. Both Conway and Ruf focus on the issue of toleration in the light of postmodern philosophical thought and its criticisms of the conception of toleration as developed from the ideals of political liberalism, which were defended in a number of chapters of this volume.

The final section is devoted to ethical theory. Robert Paul Churchill gives a masterful analysis of the concept of 'toleration' in his article "On the Difference between Nonmoral and Moral Conceptions of Toleration." In doing so, he argues that much recent debate has been fundamentally confused, and he concludes by offering a new defense of toleration as a moral virtue.

Jeff Jordan's chapter, "Concerning Moral Toleration," raises a conceptual paradox. If toleration is a positive moral virtue, it might follow that one is morally correct to tolerate a moral wrong. Addressing this "conceptual puzzle," Jordan examines the limits of moral toleration.

In "Toleration as a Form of Bias," Andrew Altman looks at one "pervasive feature of human life," which is group bias. He proceeds to analyze possible strategies for making toleration work, short of unrealistically utopian appeals.

Evelyn M. Barker, in "Socratic Intolerance and Aristotelian Toleration," provides an analysis of ethical attitudes relevant to toleration found in Plato's *Republic*, while taking a critical look at the *Republic*'s detractors from Aristotle to I. F. Stone.

Stephen F. Barker, in "Carnap's Principle of Tolerance," addresses the moral claims of a philosopher who denies the meaningfulness of all philosophy beyond logical analysis. Carnap develops a principle of tolerance that issues from his understanding of logical and linguistic rules.

As it should be, the argument and analysis that follow neither resolve the questions raised, nor present one unified view on intolerance. However, the chapters do present the coherence of penetrating debate. The attentive reader will find debate, balance, and complement not only within each section but also across the sections. Brief introductory remarks cannot disclose the richness of the selections. May they serve instead as a quick guide to the reader and the incentive to read on.

NOTE

1. David Hume, *A Treatise of Human Nature,* I.IV.1.

I

Philosophical Roots of Intolerance

1

Bayle, Locke, and the Concept of Toleration

J. B. Schneewind

In the spring of 1993 the great Czech leader Vaclev Havel spoke on "The Post-Communist Nightmare" at a graduation ceremony. One of the ghastly things about communism, he says, was "its tendency to make everything the same." It hated liberty, and so hated all that liberty brings— "individuality, variety, difference." Communist buildings, parades, state administrations, popular festivals were all the same. "This vast shroud of uniformity," Havel continues, "stifling all national, intellectual, spiritual, social, cultural, and religious variety, covered over any differences and created the monstrous illusion that we were all the same." With the collapse of communism, which Havel thinks is equal in significance to the fall of the Roman Empire, there came a burst of assertions of difference and uniqueness, every ethnic and religious and regional group rejoicing in its freedom to express its own identity. Havel plainly welcomes this, and his reminder of the grim uniformity imposed by Communist regimes encourages us to join him in rejoicing.[1]

Why, then, is postcommunism a nightmare? Not only because of the grave economic and political problems it poses, but more deeply because its opening of spirit toward the assertion of difference may lead to endless racial and cultural struggles, possibly even to another world war. Havel is fully aware of the gravity of our situation. It calls, he says, for "a new type of self-understanding . . . and a new type of politics that should flow from that understanding." He says that first we must "liberate ourselves from the captivity of a purely national perception of the world" and try to understand people of different cultures. But we must do more. Havel thinks we must "discover a new relationship . . . to the universe and its metaphysical order, which is the source of the moral order."

I find Havel's analysis both perceptive and moving, but I am not as convinced by his positive suggestions. Of course we must try to understand one another better, and we may have to come to a new understanding of ourselves as well. But I do not see that the need for a new self-understanding requires us to seek for a new relation to the universe. For those concerned with the problems Havel so eloquently presents, such a search would be a complete waste of time. It is not clear why Havel thinks otherwise. What does he suppose the discovery of a metaphysical order underlying moral order might do for us? The suggestion that agreement on metaphysics is what would bring peace to society sounds ominously like a hope for uniformity. If Havel wants to see difference flourish, as I do, then he must have some other idea of what metaphysical foundations could give us. He must think they can ground peace with disagreement, and I do not understand what metaphysics has to do with this aim.

I

However, peace with disagreement is precisely the aim of religious toleration. A society that is religiously tolerant is one in which the religious beliefs, or rejection of religion, of the citizen are not allowed to affect their legal right to live, marry, raise children, worship, pursue careers, own property, make contracts, participate in politics, and engage in all the other activities normally open to citizens in that society. Where religious toleration is the public policy, the power of the state allows religious groups to set their own criteria for membership. It may or may not use public funds to support some religious groups and not others. What matters is only that religious belief and disbelief are not allowed to count as reasons for asserting or denying people the rights generally allowed to citizens.

Religious toleration seeks peace with disagreement because people tend to disagree on religious matters. The centuries of warfare following the Reformation that split Western Christianity into Catholic and Protestant versions taught a harsh lesson. Without compulsion there will never be uniformity in public religious profession, and even with compulsion there will never be agreement in belief. Persuasion never convinces everyone, and compulsion, it seems, does not work in the long run. Toleration as I have explained it seems to be the only way to avoid constant warfare.

In Western liberal democratic societies toleration is now accepted as a basic condition of life. Havel leads us to consider whether anything other than further slaughter will bring the rest of the world to seek peace amidst disagreement.[2] I do not know what might lessen ethnic and religious strife, but I do not think that philosophical arguments can do the job. It may well take a collapse like that of Soviet communism, or exhuastion after mutual slaughter, to bring those who believe in ethnic cleansing and the killing of secularists to an admission that somehow we must all live together in one world. Philosophy will not hasten the day when everyone agrees that the bloodshed has to stop.

What philosophy might do is to help us to understand what is involved in that agreement. What exactly are we committed to in accepting toleration as a basic principle? In what follows I will look at several theories of toleration, asking which, if any, we should now accept. We cannot confine our concern to differences about religion. We know that ethnic and cultural differences can generate conflicts as durable as those involving religious belief; and yet with Havel I hope we can create a world in which such differences can be preserved.

Because I value differences, the question I wish to ask is this: If we are prepared not to use force to produce uniformity and agreement, what must we think about the different views—our own included—that we tolerate, protect, and perhaps welcome? Do we have to require everyone to change their comprehensive views in order to accept a positive principle of toleration and be willing to refrain from the use of force? If we do, what changes must we ask ourselves as well as others to make? It seems obvious that the fewer changes we must ask everyone to make, the better chance we have of getting toleration accepted. The most acceptable theory will be that which supports toleration while interfering as little as possible with existing comprehensive views. I will use this principle to examine two seminal theories of toleration, those of Bayle and Locke, and will end by sketching a view that I think better satisfies the principle than they do.

II

The first major attempt to offer a philosophical warrant for toleration was offered by a thinker famous for his skepticism, but his skepticism was not directed at the content of his religion. He made an effort to find a new level from which competing religious views could be considered and their implications held in check. Pierre Bayle was an erudite and prolific scholar and controversialist of the late seventeenth century. Born a French Protestant, his passionate search for religious truth led him first to convert to Catholicism and then to revert to his original faith. Under the laws of the time he was subject to the severest penalties for these waverings and had to live in exile, never wholly safe from persecution. Bayle's argument for toleration was an argument against persecution. One of his important assumptions emerges in his defense of the thesis, which shocked everyone at the time, that a society of atheists might be not only viable but decent as well.

One of the chief rationales for persecution was that atheists are necessarily immoral. People are atheists, it was widely held, only because their corrupt desires lead them to live such criminal lives that they cannot abide the thought that there is a just God who will eventually judge and punish them. Bayle rejects this view of atheism. It supposes that without fear of punishment after death, people will live vicious lives of uncontrolled sensuality. But, in fact, says Bayle, belief in God does nothing to control vicious desires.[3] People do not really live according to the principles they profess. Our "unregulated desires" are what win the day. If people lived by their beliefs, he asks, how could we understand Christians? They have an unmistakable revelation supported by miracles and taught by marvelous preachers, but they live "in the most enormous disorder of vice."[4] On the other side, people can completely disregard the morals taught by Christianity while still believing in God. To give just one of Bayle's many examples, the Crusaders were not atheists, but they committed, he thinks, unspeakable crimes.[5]

We should not allow Bayle's deliberately provocative examples to distract us from the assumption that gives its point to his theory that no one acts according to their beliefs. Bayle has no doubt that conscience shows clear moral principles to everyone, to atheists as well as to believers. Whether atheists are less or more virtuous than Christians, they do not need religion to teach them what virtue is.

The assumption that morality is separable from religion underpins Bayle's attack on intolerance. His most important work on the subject was stimulated by the notorious retraction of religious liberty in France: the revocation in 1685 of the edict of Nantes, allowing the Huguenots some religious liberty. His fellow worshippers were thereafter subjected to appalling pressure to convert to Catholicism. The "converters" appealed to the words of Christ, "Go out into the highways and hedges, and compel them to come in, that my house may be filled."[6] In his *Philosophical Commentary on these Words of Jesus Christ* (1686)[7] Bayle argues strongly that persecution cannot bring about the sort of inner religious devotion that would alone be pleasing to God,[8] but for us the most significant part of his argument concerns the proper way of interpreting the text used to justify persecution.

He announces at the opening that his mode of interpreting the text is entirely new.[9] Leaving textual criticism, philology, history, and mysteries entirely aside, he bases his reading on just one principle: "Any literal interpretation which carries an obligtion to commit iniquity is false."[10] The result of applying to Christ's words "Compel them to come in" the principle that the Scripture could never command what is immoral is striking in its simplicity. Christ must have meant, Bayle says, that unbelievers should be given arguments and evidence that would compel them on rational grounds to assent to the truth. No use of force is warranted by the words. To read them as allowing physical threats and violence would be to make Christ condone iniquity. And if unbelievers or misbelievers will not listen to reason, Bayle implies, there is nothing more we can do about it. After all, their mistaken beliefs are not apt to make them behave any worse than anyone else does, so after we have tried our best we must let them go on their erroneous way.

Bayle is quite clear about the broader implication of his insistence on using moral standards to judge the meaning of Scripture. It is that "reason, speaking to us by the axioms of the natural light . . . , is the supreme tribunal . . . Let it nevermore be said that theology is the queen and philosophy only the handmaiden."[11] Reason shows us undeniable principles of morals. God has allowed us this insight into his mind to guide us in understanding his written message. Without such a test we cannot know whether an alleged revelation comes from God or from the devil. Morality must tell us what religious doctrines to accept, not the other way around.[12]

Here, then, is an understanding of toleration that does not assume a position that is simply one among the warring religions. Atheists, Huguenots, Catholics, even pagans, Bayle thinks, can tell what is or is not morally iniquitous and use that as a test of what religion can require. Because we have a common morality, there is a vantage point from which everyone, whatever their religious views, can see the justification for toleration.

Bayle's moral interpretation of toleration gives us an answer to the question What do we make of the beliefs we tolerate? So long as those beliefs require nothing contrary to morality, we do not need to have any view about their truth or their knowability. Where they require anything against morality, we do not allow them to be true or valid. We either give them a morally acceptable interpretation or we dismiss them as false.

Nowadays we are apt to overlook the truly radical nature of Bayle's move. He is forcing into two quite separate domains what for most people formed the seamless whole of a comprehensive view. Most people could not imagine morality as something separate from religion, or virtue as quite distinct from piety. Christianity teaches that the love we are required to feel toward others is an offshoot of God's love toward us. Consequently our conduct toward humans, most people believed, is a part of our relations with God. If our moral convictions form an important part of our own identity, then Bayle in his time was calling for what Havel thinks is necessary in ours: a deep revision of our self-understanding. Bayle asks his readers to think of themselves as united with others by something they have hitherto thought of as one aspect of what divided them from exactly those others.

III

In 1689, only a few years after Bayle's great work on interpreting Christ's words "compel them to come in," John Locke published his *Epistola de Tolerantia*, promptly translated as *A Letter concerning Toleration*. In it he gives a powerful defense of toleration on grounds quite different from Bayle's. Like Bayle, Locke tries to find a standpoint outside the waring factions from which toleration can be made acceptable to those who hold the contending views. However, he has a broader problem in view than Bayle had. While he is opposed to persecution, his concern is less with the consequences to individual victims than with the threat intolerance poses to the continued existence of society itself. He had lived through the midcentury civil wars in Britian. Hatred of Protestants for Catholics and of Protestant sects for one another continued to rend his country after the civil war, and he himself had to flee for his life after the failure of a revolutionary plot in which he was deeply involved. He was no atheist, but he thought that unless religion was excluded from state affairs there was no hope for the survival of the commonwealth. Moreover, he had a good reason for looking for some other understanding of toleration than the moral interpretation of it that Bayle offered.

Morality, for everyone in Locke's time, was a matter of conscience. And conscience, in one common Protestant view of it, was God's voice speaking within the individual. As the Puritan divine William Ames put it, conscience is "a man's judgment of himself, according to the judgment of God of him." Conscience tells us not only about how we ought to treat our neighbor in the ordinary affairs of life, but also about how to worship and how to govern one's church. Piety is as much its domain as virtue. Ames along with many others held that even if conscience is erroneous, it must be followed. Otherwise one is showing disregard of what one believes is God's direct command.[13] Demands for liberty of conscience were thus demands for freedom of worship, and in England some of the fiercest sectarian battles were occasioned by disagreements about the way religious services were held and churches administered.

This fact shows why a defense of toleration as liberty of conscience runs into a problem—a problem Bayle saw, and for which he had no ready solution. Consciences simply do not agree. Suppose one of Bayle's converters has a conscience that tells him to persecute those who do not agree with him. He will not think persecution iniquitous, and it is hard to see how Bayle's appeal to his own conscience can alter his view.

Locke does not treat conscience as the voice of God within. He defines it simply as "our own opinion of the rectitude or pravity of our own actions."[14] Despite this reductionist account, he thinks no one should be forced to worship in ways her conscience forbids. But in arguing for toleration he makes no appeal to conscience. He begins by asking us simply to distinguish between a commonwealth, or what we might call a "civil society," and a church. A commonwealth is "a society of men constituted only for the procuring, preserving, and advancing of their own civil interests."[15] A church is also a society, "a voluntary society of men, joining themselves together . . . in order to the publick worshipping of God, in such a manner as they judge acceptable to him and effectual to the salvation of their souls."[16] The aims of each society point to certain limits to their rightful power.

The ruler of the commonwealth, the magistrate, may act only in what concerns the civil interests of its members. A church may act only in matters concerning what it takes to be proper worship and whatever else is needful for the salvation of its members. Locke's view is that these two sets of concerns do not overlap at all. Consequently, there is no call, as there is no right, for either society to meddle with the concerns of the other. The magistrate must leave religion alone. He can make people comply with the law only by threats of force; but, Locke says, "true and saving religion consists in the inward persuasion of the mind, without which nothing can be acceptable to God. And . . . the understanding . . . cannot be compell'd to the belief of anything by outward force."[17] Since a church is a voluntary society, its rulings bind only its own members, and its clergy have no authority over nonmembers. Anyone, Locke says, "may employ as many exhortations and arguments as he pleases toward the promoting of another man's salvation," but no other means of compulsion may be used.[18] Churches may not, for instance, deprive nonmembers of any rights they are allowed by the commonwealth. As to the doctrine and the practices churches think necessary in worship, the commonwealth can have nothing to say about them.

Well, not quite nothing. Locke thinks the magistrate should not allow anyone to teach "opinions contrary to human society." But this does not seem to him a serious danger. No sect, he optimistically thinks, will be so insane as to preach "such things as manifestly undermine the foundations of society."[19] As for controlling church practice, Locke thinks anything that the magistrate finds allowable in terms of the good of society outside a church should be allowed within a church, and what is not legally permissible in general cannot become permissible by being done in church. Thus ritual murder of people would be forbidden not because it is against some religious doctrine of the magistrate's, but because it is against a law necessary for the security of society. Similarly wearing a hat while praying, or sacrificing a living animal, would be allowable, because wearing a hat when you please, and killing animals, are allowed outside the churches. Yet if there were some social reason to end the slaughter of animals—Locke imagines a disease dangerously depleting the stock of cattle—the magistrate could order a stop to ritual sacrifice, not, again, on religious grounds, but for the good of the commonwealth.[20]

Locke notoriously does not extend the protection of toleration to everyone. Jews, Muslims, and religious pagans are to be tolerated, but not Roman Catholics, because they owe political allegiance to a foreign prince. Nor are atheists allowed—Locke is no follower of Bayle—because morality only controls behavior through our fear of divine punishment, and atheists have no such fear.[21] In these restrictions of the scope of toleration, he simply draws some implications from his view of its purpose.

Toleration is a policy necessary for the public good, and the magistrate decides what that is. How are we to view the religious beliefs—our own always included—that are thus tolerated? It is clear throughout the *Letter* that Locke thinks there will never be agreement about them, and he knows this might lead to skepticism. He neither adopts it nor asks us to. What we must think is simply that our religious convictions have no bearing on the public good. They are a matter of concern only to us individually and to the groups we voluntarily form for public worship.

Once again, this may seem a point so obvious that it raises a yawn, not an objection. Yet like Bayle's separation of morality from religion, acceptance of it would have required most of Locke's convictions. The Protestant Reformation shattered Christendom, but it did not do away with the idea of a Christian commonwealth. Sectarians of every shade of opinion believed that if heretics, Jews, and pagans were given the same public status as true believers, it would be an offence to God. Their ideal required a unified community of the faithful, informed and guided by the true religion and therefore necessarily excluding those who did not believe it in their hearts and make their belief evident in their behavior. Believers took their own views to unite them with fellow believers. Nonbelievers must be either converted or excluded so the community was conceived in terms that did not include its being in a proper relation to God. In saying that the commonwealth seeks the good of secular society and churches the salvation of their members, Locke was quietly rejecting this view of community. His thesis that the magistrate is to act for the good as he sees it and is not to determine that good by appeal to any particular religious doctrine was a revolutionary departure from accepted opinion.[22] But precisely because of that, it required a deep change in the comprehensive views of those to whom it was addressed.

IV

Bayle and Locke tried to reply to two different views about toleration as impermissible. Bayle combatted the view that error about religion is necessarily a cause of vice and crime, Locke the view that a society that allows those with the wrong views to be citizens is displeasing to God. Each tried to defend toleration by basing it not on any religious view but on a nonreligious principle that would at the same time leave people free to hold their own religions as firmly as they wished. Bayle appealed to morality, and Locke to public utility. To many citizens of modern Western democratic societies, these will seem obviously quite different from religion. I have suggested that to contemporaries of Bayle and Locke both views called for drastic rethinking of the content or extent of their religious commitment. In the terms I used earlier, my suggestion is that both Bayle and Locke are proposing comprehensive views that are in fact alternatives to exactly those warring comprehensive views to which they hoped to bring external peace.

For this reason, neither Bayle's account of toleration nor Locke's goes very far toward satisfying the principle I suggested earlier, that our theory of toleration should support a principle that makes only minimal demands on the comprehensive views of those called upon to tolerate one another. For similar reasons, we cannot try to explain toleration as respecting a human right to diversity of opinion, since some comprehensive views do not work with notions of rights at all, still less with that particular right. And we cannot appeal to an appreciation of the marvelous diversity of human communities, because there are comprehensive views according to which some human communities are offenses to God or ethnically impure or built on acceptably distorted constructions of human nature.

We might get toleration in practice if the warring defenders of conflicting comprehensive views simply became exhausted and agreed to a truce. But this would not get us a very stable acceptance of toleration. Any group's assessment of its chances for power might shift, encouraging it to repudiate the agreement. And if one group did indeed become so powerful that its hegemony could not be challenged, there would be no argument the others could use for allowing them to live in its own way. We would therefore prefer to have a basis for toleration that convinces everyone concerned that it is reasonable for them to accept it for itself. The third view of toleration offers such an option. It is the view suggested by John Rawls in his 1971 book *A Theory of Justice* and developed since then in some of the articles now collected and revised in his *Political Liberalism.*

It is the way Rawls argues for and interprets his view of justice that is pertinent to toleration. Rawls addresses his theory to people who are willing to think of themselves and others as free and equal members of an ongoing venture in social cooperation. Each person has a set of interests, in what she takes to be her own well-being or success of the people or causes to which she is committed. Each is presumed to recognize that others have similar broad interests, and each is willing to make accommodations to them that can be recognized to be fair—to demand no more of one than is demanded of others, to give each as good a chance of success in society as is given to others.

We can think out what is implied by our willingness to accept a fair scheme, Rawls says, by a special way of imagining ourselves deliberating about the conditions under which we would be willing to spend our lives in the same society. We need only suppose that in these deliberations we do not know very much about ourselves. We put a veil of ignorance around us as we talk matters over. We do not know our actual social position: how wealthy, how privileged in education, or how talented we are. Neither do we know our age, face, gender, religion, or ethnicity. We know that we have interests, some broad, some narrow. We know we need material and social resources to achieve what we want. We know that these are in short supply, so that there will be competition for them. What we want is to reach agreement on a set of institutions that will ensure, as far as possible, that the competition be fair.

Rawls argues that rational deliberators behind a veil of ignorance would come to a unanimous conclusion about the principles that should govern the basic aspects of the society in which they are going to live. The veil ensures that no one can take advantage of any special power he has over others to force acceptance of principles that favor him or his group. Hence the outcome of the deliberation will itself be fair. And among its outcomes there will be a principle of toleration.[23] Each deliberator behind the veil of ignorance knows that he has some view of the good life, one that may well center on religion or ethnicity, and that is likely to diverge from the views actually held by others. Each will wish to protect the possibility of living as his vision of the good life directs. Because of the veil no one will know what actual power he has to protect that possibility. Hence each will conclude that the best option is to accept a principle that protects everyone's right to pursue his own vision of the good. If everyone must be allowed that right, then everyone's comprehensive views about the good life, religious or secular, must be treated as irrelevant to his or her possession of the full rights of citizenship and the full protection of the law. The government must never use force to make people accept one comprehensive view rather than another.

This sounds just like the modern liberal democratic view of toleration as involving a society in which we are each equally free to pursue the good life as we see it. How, then, can the Rawlsian position fail to be one more comprehensive view competing with other comprehensive views? Is not the Rawlsian principle of liberty of conscience just a liberal moral principle rejected by numerous groups? Indeed is not the whole device of the veil of ignorance itself just a disguise for the morality of liberalism?

I think it is not. Rawls is trying to step back from the comprehensive views, religious or secular, whose conflicts threaten to cause a nightmare world. In doing so he, like Bayle and Locke, is asking us to come to a new understanding of ourselves in relation to our most deeply held convictions. But he is not seeking a metaphysical foundation for the position, as Havel thinks we must. He is in fact trying to find a way to cut us loose from the need for philosophical bases or underpinnings or foundations of any sort. His theory of toleration is what he would describe as "political." What does this mean?

Rawls calls his view of justice and toleration "political" because he thinks it is independent of any moral or religious or philosophical theory. It presents what free and equal agents who are willing to live together can agree to if they can agree to anything about the basic institutions of their society. We have seen how a reasonable principle of toleration emerges from the ideal deliberations behind the veil. Now we do not have to ask why actual people will in fact agree to the principle of toleration. Given their varied comprehensive views, they may have different reasons for accepting it. Revulsion at continued bloodshed, belief in a right to form one's own religious opinion, appreciation of diversity, the thought that God leads us by different paths—any of these reasons might move people toward acceptance. We need no agreement on reasons for accepting the principle. What we ask of those who accept toleration is only a public political commitment. We ask that regardless of their actual power, they commit themselves to the principle and make not violating it a basic constraint on their actions. Rawls assumes that people have the ability to make such a commitment and honor it. He thinks this ability does not depend on the comprehensive views people hold. He himself offers no general theory of human nature to explain how it is possible for people to accept the constraint of toleration, because any such theory would be part of a comprehensive view. And he does not invoke one.

Precisely because the Rawlsian theory makes no claims of a comprehensive sort, it requires no agreement about the different comprehensive views with which we are trying to deal. As long as they overlap enough to lead to a consensus on the principle, we can get the political agreement we need. The Rawlsian view, then, seems to make no demands at all on the content of the varying comprehensive views we happen to hold.

In fact, however, it does make one demand. It requires that each of us should take it, for political purposes, that people with different views are capable of honoring the principle of toleration. For purposes of living with others, we have to act as if we think that those who hold different views are not fanatics who stop at nothing, but reasonable people who see the point of toleration and act appropriately.

It is part of this requirement that we must think that people can be reasonable in holding a view which other reasonable people do not accept, even though they know all the reasons for it that the believers have. And of course we must be able to see ourselves in the same way. Even if I believe that I have utterly compelling grounds for my comprehensive view, I must allow that many reasonable people will not accept them as compelling. I need not feel my own position threatened by this fact; and the explanation of how others can be so blind may vary from one person to another. So may the accounts people give of how it is possible to take such a dual stance toward one's own comprehensive view—how I can remain convinced of its reasonableness while allowing that equally reasonable people, knowing my reasons, can remain unconvinced. As long as our differing views overlap enough, we will have a consensus on toleration. We need make no other adjustments to our basic beliefs.

I think the Rawlsian theory of toleration comes closer than any other theory we have to giving a rationale for a principle of toleration making minimal demands for change in conflicting comprehensive views. It requires no substantive change in anyone's views because it makes no claim at all about the truth or reasonableness or certainty of such views. It requires us only to allow that reasonable people can disagree reasonably about the hardest questions in life. This is not a call for skepticism, and it does not require decreasing the variety of comprehensive views that people hold. It seems to me, therefore, to offer more room for divergence than any other theory of toleration. There are doubtless many people who would not accept even the minimal change in their comprehensive view that Rawlsianism requires, people who think that those who disagree must be vicious or diabolical and cannot be trusted. Philosophy, as mentioned earlier, can do nothing to change such beliefs. Rawls proposes principles he thinks we can agree on if we can agree on anything. Some people hold comprehensive views so forbidding that there may be nothing they and we can agree on. They are the stuff of which Havel's nighmare is made. We can only hope that their number will diminish.

NOTES

1. Joseph Brodsky, review of "The Post-Communist Nightmare," by Vaclav Havel, in *The New York Review of Books* (May 1993). Joseph Brodsky comments on this talk, and Havel replies, in the same journal, Feb. 17, 1994.

2. For a reminder, here is a statement from a leading Egyptian Islamic cleric: "A secularist represents a danger to society and the nation that must be eliminated. It is the duty of the Government to kill him" (*New York Times* (New York), 18 August 1993).

3. *Oeuvres Diverses*, introduction Elisabeth Labrousse, vol. 3 (1727) reprinted Hildesheim, Olms, 1966, 86–87a.

4. Ibid., 3:88a.

5. Ibid., 3:89b. 90a.

6. Luke 14.23.

7. I cite page numbers from the translation by Annie Tannenbaum 1987, followed by the page reference to the *Oeuvres Diverses*.

8. E.g., Tannenbaum, 35–37, 2:371–72a.

9. But Walter Rex has shown that in fact the principle was used in Protestant apologetic writings to defend Protestants against persecution from Catholics. See his *Essays on Piarre Bayle and Religious Controversy* (The Hague: Martinus Nijhhoff, 1965).

10. Tannenbaum 28; 2:367a.

11. Ibid., 2:368a.

12. This is not meant as an effort to present the whole of Bayle's thought. His skepticism must be taken into account.

13. William James, *Conscience with the Power and Cases Thereof* 1.1 1.3.2 1.2.4.

14. John Locke, *An Essay concerning Human Understanding*, ed. Peter Nidditch (Oxford Clarendon Press, 1975), 70.

15. John Locke, *A Letter concerning Toleration*, ed. James Tully. (Indianapolis: Hackett Publishing, 1983), 26.

16. Ibid.

17. Locke, *Letter,* 27.

18. Ibid., 47.

19. Ibid., 49.

20. Ibid., 41–42.

21. Ibid., 50–51.

22. See Kirstie M. McClure, "Difference, Diversity, and the Limits of Toleration," *Political Theory* 18, (August 1990):361–91, to which I am indebted.

23. John Rawls, *A Theory of Justice* (Cambridge Mass.: Harvard University Press, 1971), section 33.

2

Aristotle and the Metaphysics of Intolerance

John McCumber

Tolerance and intolerance can be viewed from a variety of angles and seen correspondingly as different kinds of things: as psychological traits, or as political, social, and ethical issues. But wherever and however we look, we find one disenchanting fact: intolerance seems to be the factual norm, and tolerance an ideal for which we must strive. Intolerance, in other words, seems to have a certain unfortunate *priority* over tolerance. It seems to be a pervasive given, while tolerance is merely a hoped-for, even utopian, imperative. When something is so pervasive as to approach universality, we are tempted to view it as natural. What if intolerance were a fact of *nature*? What if it were, say, a phenomenon of physics? Would it be illuminating to say that positive and negative charges cannot "tolerate" each other or that the North Pole of a magnet cannot "tolerate" the South?

What if the factual priority of intolerance went even beyond physics to infect *all* that is: what if intolerance were an *ontological* phenomenon, one inscribed in the nature of Being itself, so that to be is to be intolerant? The thought not only is disenchanting; it is depressing indeed. For absolutely everything, of course, *is*; if to be is somehow to be intolerant (or to be untolerated), then we can never escape intolerance, no matter how hard we try.

Such, I believe and hope, is not the case. But it suggests a different question: what if there were a culture which believed, however falsely and unconsciously, that intolerance were such an ontological phenomenon? And which then set out to eliminate it? Would not that culture be in a very precarious position—setting itself at war with what it takes to be Being itself?

How could that culture ever succeed—how could it even go on—unless its inscription of intolerance into Being itself were overcome? And how can that fateful inscription be overcome unless it is understood?

I believe that there is indeed such a culture; that it is our own "Western" culture; and that the understanding of intolerance as an ontological phenomenon was instituted by the very thinker who founded that genre of ontology which has now fallen into various sorts of disrepute under the name *metaphysics:* Aristotle. Intolerance, then, is not accidental to the Western tradition, but inheres in it—philosophically—almost from the beginning. In what follows, I will outline how the structure of Being, for Aristotle, is understood as a certain sort of domination which amounts to intolerance. This is evident in Aristotle's account of his own key ontological concept, that of substance, οὐσία.

SUBSTANCE[1]

According to Aristotle's *Metaphysics* (7.1), substances alone, and nothing else in the world, exist καθ' αὐτό, or "according to themselves." A substance is not merely itself, then, but accords with itself. It has a reflexive structure: it does not merely exist (the way a heap or grain exists) but exists *in virtue of* something: of itself. And this means that a substance is in a peculiar way distanced from itself. It sets a standard according to which it exists, and that standard is (somehow) itself.

Aristotle also tells us that a substance in at least two ways is "separable."[2] First, nothing in the other categories can be "separated" (χωρίζεσθαι) from substance. For everything nonsubstantial inheres in a substance: a substance can walk or not walk, it can "separate" itself from the activity of walking. But walking has to be the movement *to* something, from which it is therefore inseparable: the movement of a substance. When we say, "it walks," we have implicitly said "a substance walks." All the other Aristotelian categories are smilarly inseparable from substance. It follows, though it is not stated explicitly, that substances are separate from each other as well. For if to inhere inseparably in a substance is the prerogative of what is in the other categories, of nonsubstances, then no substance can inhere inseparably in another substance. A substance is separable, not only from other kinds of thing, but also from other substances.

A further implication is that if a substance is separable from other substances, but the properties it exhibits are inseparable from it, then no such property can inhere in more than one substance. For if some property inhered in two things which could be separated from each other, then it could be separated from itself.[3] So substances individuate properties: the color of this particular object, as a quality of it, can never be identically the same as the color of another object. It can only resemble it.

In this we see terse, minimal hints of two traits of Aristotelian substance, which I will call boundary and disposition. By "boundary" I mean that a particular instance of some property, inseparable from its underlying substance, cannot inhere in two substances at once. It follows that any individual quality, quantity, and so on is either inside or outside some individual substance, which therefore has very definite boundaries.

"Disposition" (διάθεσις) (at *Metaphysics* 5.18) refers to the arrangement of the parts of a thing.[4] In a substance, the parts of a thing are or ought to be arranged, or disposed, by its underlying nature. *Metaphysics* (7) presents this view in quite general and indeed abstract form: the other qualities a substance has exist only in virtue of its underlying nature and have their being through it alone, they are "inseparable" from it. This too, as will be seen later, is enriched by Aristotle, so that the parts of a thing will receive from its underlying form properties far more complex than mere being.

In any substance, that is, in anything that truly is, something underlying thus sets up boundaries and disposes everything that happens within them. If the substance in question is a human being, then nothing "horsey" can come to be within it; everything that comes to be within it must come to be from its human form. Nothing opposed to the basic nature of the substance can come to pass within its boundaries. Indeed, nothing "other" than that basic nature, that is, not derived from it and corresponding to it, can come to pass within those boundaries. Intolerance, the inability to sustain otherness, is thus inscribed in the nature of Being itself.

THE STANDARD

When (*Metaphysics* 7.4) Aristotle takes up the question of substance as related to the concept of essence, the first thing we are told about the latter notion is that the "essence" of a thing is "what it is said to be according to itself," καθ᾽ αὐτό. If, then, a substance is something which exists "in accordance with itself," or in accordance with a certain standard which it, itself, is, then its essence is that standard as linguistically expressed. The essence of a thing is that in it which is most basic and can be put into words, the *primum significatum:* the point at which being and language meet. And so we arrive at the view that the formula for the essence of a thing must contain a set of predicates that are ultimate; each must be needed; and all together suffice for the existence of the thing. Such a formula is a "definition" (ὁριζμός). The "essence" of a thing, then, is that particular subset of its properties which is expressed in the predicates included in its definition. As *Metaphysics* (7.10–12) tells us, the essence of a thing is its "form." And that in the thing which does not meet this standard, which is other than it, is "matter."

That element in the thing, that basic nature which sets the standard to which it and all its contents must conform if it is to "be" at all, is then its essence or its (substantial) form. What such form shapes, in accordance with the standard that it itself sets—indeed, is—is the "matter" of the thing. Let us look at this binary opposition for a moment. Form is "the responsible factor" (αἴτιον) by which matter comes to be a "this."[5] If matter comes to be a "this" only by being brought together with form, then matter in itself has no form of its own, is wholly un-formed. Hence the negativity of Aristotle's most attentive definition, here, of matter: "By matter I mean that which in itself is neither a particular thing nor of a certain quantity nor assigned to any other of the categories by which being is determined."[6]

Matter so viewed is somehow outside being, and Aristotle goes on to say that it is neither positive nor negative with respect to the categories: quantity, quality, and the rest can no more be denied of it than they can be asserted of it.[7]

Matter is thus other than all predicates. As *Metaphysics* (7.3) tells us, if all predicates (all forms) are stripped away from a particular quantity of matter (including, of course, predicates in the category of quantity itself), then there is no way whatsoever to identify the subject of the predication: there is nothing left which is definite enough to be separate from anything else, no "this," no subject for a possible sentence, and hence no predication. Indeed, it is doubtful whether there is such a thing as truly formless matter, or prime matter.[8] Thus escaping all predicates, matter is unknowable according to itself (ἄγνωστος καθ' αὐτήν); only form has a knowably determinate nature.[9] Having no such nature or properties, matter can itself only be indirectly known: through the constraints it places on the composite's form.

To sum up: substance is not only the most basic kind of thing in Aristotle's cosmos; any substance exhibits a further hierarchy of basicality within itself. Most basic is the essence or form: a complex but determinate set of predicates denoting a complex but unified activity whose different aspects are always found together in anything of that particular species. This form is the "standard" that the thing seems to set for itself: when it exists according to its essence, it exists "according to itself."

Beneath this, beneath essence and being themselves is the passive, posterior, unspeakable, unknown, unknowable; communicating its unknowability upward almost to the level of essence itself; abasing the pristine universality of Form into the random and defective uniqueness of the Individual; supporting all characteristics, while exhibiting none; lurking in the lowest depths—the shrouded alpha from which all things come, and the dark omega into which they must return: the Dionysian ancestress of the id and of the proletariat, and of power and *différance* and of all that seeks liberation: matter.

Because the form, or essence, of a thing is to have total disposition over whatever happens within the boundaries of that thing, it is *intolerant* in a double sense. First, it will not tolerate the disposing activity of other essences within its own boundaries: no alien essences allowed. Second, it will not tolerate even its own matter, except as something passive and indeterminate (which means, for Aristotle, wholly bereft in itself of form, the principle of activity and determination).

This view of being, abstract and theoretical, does not remain so for Aristotle. The middle term between his theoretical account and the various concrete ethical and social phenomena it will structure is intelligibility. For substance—actually form—is what is knowable.[10] We think we know a thing best when we know its substance, rather than when we know its quality, quantity, or other characteristics.[11] Knowledge of other kinds of characteristics is not separable, then, from knowledge of substance, while knowledge of substance can be had without knowledge of other characteristics.

Because substance (as form) is what is knowable, anything is intelligible only insofar as it approximates the structure of a substance. Since Aristotle's own discourse is an "intellectual" exercise in right knowing, substance gains and exercises the power to structure and orient further Aristotelian discourses. And since human life itself is, for Aristotle, largely a matter of right knowing, substance comes to play this structuring role not only in his own discourse, or even in philosophy in general, but also in his accounts of nondiscursive practices that traverse the entire spectrum of human activity. What we can deal with intelligently is what is intelligible, and what is intelligible is what has an essence, that is, structured like a substance. Hence (to anticipate much of what will follow), if we want our marriages, alliances, families, societes, states, religions, and works of art—among other things— to be intelligible, we must see to it that they embody substantial structures. I will now give some examples of how Aristotle's account of substance structures his talk about ethical and social issues.

SUBSTANCE AND ETHICS

A key feature of Aristotle's ethical thought is the moral hierarchy that, in his view, spans the realm between the gods and the beasts—a hierarchy which encompasses, that is, the human realm itself. At the beginning of *Nicomachean Ethics* (7.1), two of the most important terms on that hierarchy are *continent* and *incontinent*. They are important because they mark the line between the good and the bad: the continent man is the lowest form of good man, while the incontinent man is the highest form of bad man. Aristotle's words for these moral exemplars are, respectively, ἐγκρατης and ἄκρατης: the man "in" dominance and the man "without" it. But it is not strictly the "man" who has mastery here. As Aristotle tells us, "the continent and the incontinent man are so called because in them reason dominates or does not, *reason considered as being the man himself.*"[12]

The echoes of *Metaphysics* 7 are clear: reason is the essence of man; like all things, men "are" the same as their essence, which is reason. So each man is the same as his reason. If reason is not in control of our lives, then "we" are not in control of our lives; but if reason dominates, then "we" dominate.

The general model for such domination is sketched in *Nicomachean Ethics* 1.13, together with its metaphysical backdrop. The soul, like the body of which it is the form, is complex. In addition to the nonrational "vegetative" soul, which handles nutrition and growth, it contains another part "which is by nature opposed to reason, fights against it, and resists it."[13] In spite of this antagonism to reason, the soul's irrational part—which is desire—is, in a passive sense, rational. For it is able to go along with reason, to be persuaded by it. When it does, we have the virtuous man, in whom desire "speaks with the same voice" (ὁμωφῶνει) as reason. When desire opposes reason, and the man nonetheless acts as his reason advises, he is continent. When a man follows his desires, though reason tells him not to, he is incontinent. And when his reason chimes in with desire, telling him that whatever he happens to want is what, in fact, he should do, then he is unhindered (ἀκολαστός) in his evil. The whole of *Nicomachean Ethics* 1.13, in fact, trades on various analogies between reason's rule over desire and the soul's rule over the body. Reason, then, either is the ethical form of human life, with desire as the ethical matter, or is something very akin to this.

In sum, in the incontinent man, and even more so in his unhindered colleague, reason does not *dispose* desires. Desires resist and oppose reason in chaos and commotion. And because these desires, though "within" the moral agent, are for Aristotle provoked by external objects, the *boundary* of the person is continually transgressed. To be unethical is thus to violate both boundary and disposition.

The good man, by contrast, possesses boundary and disposition in their plenary human form. His ultimate desire is not for external objects but for the well-being of his own rational principle—of what he himself most is—and so he is not determined from outside.[14] The boundary of his body is in good order, as witness his relative imperviousness to eros[15] and his attention to diet—it is no accident that the *Nicomachean Ethics*'s main example of moral deliberation concerns whether or not to eat "dry food" (bread) rather than "wet" (porridge).[16] His desires, unlike the incontinent man's, are, as I have noted, at the disposition of his reason to the point of "homophony." Any other voice would be intolerable.

The good man does not have to tolerate either the activity within him of alien forms, or the cacaphony of his own ethical "matter," his desires. Implicit in this account is the view that substance, with its structure of domination and intolerance, is not actually descriptive of the human world: not everybody behaves as if he or she were a substance. But those who do not behave that way are both evil and irrational. Where it fails descriptively, the concept of substance becomes normative. In such cases, the gap between substance and one of its defective instances is to be narrowed or even closed by remodeling the instance. When it structures ethical discourse in this way, the concept of substance affects a discourse which, in turn, is meant to structure our lives: "We are inquiring, not in order to know what virtue is, but in order to become good."[17]

SOCIAL STRUCTURE

The same intolerance of polyphony can be found on the level of the household. Bad men are not the only humans whose human form cannot play an effective, disposing role: "For the slave," Aristotle writes, "has no deliberative faculty at all; the woman has, but it is without authority; and the child has, but it is immature."[18] The anomalies that the concept of 'substance' encountered in the ethical realm are thus reproduced on the social plane; but these deficiencies are not strictly moral because they cannot be made good by action. (In this respect, young males are in a slightly different situation than girls, slaves, and women, because they will one day be moral agents; but that comes about only after decades of maturation and instruction, not by mere decision or action.)

Since members of these groups cannot acquire active reason, or cannot acquire it soon, they cannot exhibit the structure of a substance within themselves. What they must do—for their own good—is participate in reason in the only way open to them, by adhering to a structure in which a single active reason informs, not merely its own soul, but several others as well. This is the household with a mature male at its head.[19] Certainly the family—and particularly the ancient one—exhibits the two traits of an Aristotelian substance discussed here. Its *boundaries* are secure, for there are only three ways into a family: by purchase, by marriage, or by birth. Since the *pater familias* not only buys the slaves but approves the marriages of his children and (technically) has the right to have them exposed at birth, he is able to establish and secure the family's boundaries. His wife and children, to say nothing of slaves, must obey his orders and heed his advice as a matter of course; they are at his disposition. Independent action will not be tolerated, and the Aristotelian family has, strictly speaking, only one moral agent: the *pater familias*.

Within Aristotle's thought, the organizing power of the concept of substance is thus extraordinarily wide. It serves not merely to render things readily comprehensible, but to provide scientific comprehension of what they truly are—or, in the case of ethics, of what they truly should be. The scope of this concept is apparent, not only on the level of the individual organism in fields such as cognition, biology, and ethics, but both in Aristotle's politics and in his theology. The *Politics*, for example, like politics since, is structured on the following principle:

> In all things which are composed out of several other things, and which come to be some single common thing, whether continuous or discrete, in all of them there turns out to be a distinction between that which rules, and that which is ruled; and this holds for all ensouled things by virtue of the whole of nature; and even in non-living things there is a sort of ruling element, such as harmony.[20]

Or, in the famous closing words of *Metaphysics* 12—themselves quoted from an even more ancient authority, Homer—"The rule of many is not good; one ruler let there be."[21]

CONCLUSIONS

It must be recognized that this inscription of intolerance into the heart of being remains enormously influential, even today. The modern subject, for example, can be viewed as an Aristotelian substance inhabiting a desubstantialized nature, one composed strictly of matter.[22] It is no accident, I take it, that in his opening characterization of one of modernity's most gigantic projects—that of colonialism—V. Y. Mudimbe says it aims at "the domination of physical space, the reformation of *natives's* minds, and the integration of local economic histories into the Western perspective."[23] The colonial imperative, in other words, is to draw boundaries so as to dispose of minds. The current debate between "modernists" and "postmodernists," I think, largely concerns the issue of whether the structures of substance are to be ejected, at long last, from the human world as well as from nature.[24]

But what are the lessons of this for the present issue of intolerance? Three come to mind. First, intolerance is always domestic: I can only tolerate, or fail to tolerate, that with which I share a common space. Second, intolerance postulates a uniformity to that bounded space: it is to be structured in certain sorts of ways—if a political space, by a certain set of ideas and practices, customs, and traditions. Those formative structures must be evidenced in (have disposition over) every point in that space. In virtue of this, any attempt to do things differently will be regarded in one of two ways. Either it will be viewed as an upsurge of matter trying to act as form, like a slave trying to be master, or it will be viewed as the intrusion of an alien form, like someone else ordering my slaves about. In either case, it will be regarded as irrational and unethical, all at once.

Finally, there seem to be only two strategies for dealing with intolerance: to contest the boundaries or to contest the disposition. The former has been adopted by all those liberals, from Mill to Lyotard, who assert the right of an individual (or discourse) to determine her own conduct by her own lights, to be autonomous within the boundaries of her own life or language-game, so long as she does not affect others. The danger, of course, is loss of community, that the boundaries between such individuals will become so absolute that nothing—no shared activities, interests, or even mutual comprehension—can cross them.

The other alternative is to contest the capacity of a particular form to structure or dispose of a particular space. This cannot mean delimiting that space while leaving the form in control of part of it—for such a strategy would, obviously, collapse into the first approach. Rather, the *entire* dominance of the form is what is to be contested—an undertaking of all those who, honorably or not, have thought of themselves as "revolutionaries." Here, too, there is a danger: that the revolution will succeed and thereby insitute a new and perhaps more repressive form in place of the old. So understood, revolution becomes a contest for time—for the future—just as the "liberal" alternative contests space (boundaries).

One result of seeing the contemporary relevance of Aristotle's account is that we uncover the inner complicity of two of our more hallowed ideal political types, the liberal and the revolutionary. They represent, in fact, the two complementary approaches possible to a single problematic: that of overcoming the intolerance of substance by contesting either boundary or disposition. As long as we have either, we will have both. Current wisdom seems to have it that the foreseeable future will consist in more or less judicious applications of these two strategies: of narrowing boundaries around the intolerant until the only people they have left to be intolerant of are their own inner circles, and of "displacing" confrontations which result, not in new regimes, but in what Jacques Derrida calls the "shaking" of the old.[25]

But I wonder if a third way is not possible: one which contests, not merely the boundary and disposition of the form, but its very existence. This way would view the "center" of the entity in question—a state, for example— not as a finished form, but as a sort of dynamic emptiness. To put this in a more down-to-earth way: we would look upon our social and political domesticity as structured, not by a set of well-defined practices and ideas, but by a set of vaguenesses which precisely as such amount to incitements to creativity and and opportunities for action—what I have elsewhere called "poetic elicitors."[26] I will not go into further detail about this proposal here, except to note that it leaves us with a final lesson—one of which Aristotle, who was at such pains to preserve an orderly and static cosmos in the face of his eminent predecssors Heracleitus and Plato, was fully aware—that the greatest nemesis of intolerance, when this is understood in terms of its ontological roots, is not tolerance but *innovation*.

NOTES

1. The present analysis begins from certain passages of Aristotle's *Metaphysics*, in particular the treatise on substance that stretches through books 7 through 9. I translate its opening words as follows:

Being is said in many ways, as we have enumerated previously in our considerations on the different senses of words. For in one sense it means what a thing is, a "this"; and in other senses it means quality or quantity or any of the other categories thus predicated. But, even though "being" has all these senses, it is obvious that the first of them is "being" in the sense of the "what-it-is", i.e. which signifies substance.

"Substance" is thus the primary *significatum*, the first thing signified. There are other kinds of things signified: for example, categories such as quality and quantity. When we say *what* a thing is, we state, not its size, or color, or activity, or the disposition of its parts, but its "basic what," its substance, as in: "This is a horse." And this kind of predication is prior to predication in any of the other categories.

2. Separability and self-accordance are related at Aristotle's *Metaphysics* 7.18: while in most senses to exist "in accordance with self" is to have an essence, it can in one sense be said that any property a thing has when it is considered as existing by itself, separately, from other things, it has "according to itself."

3. To take this out of the language of "separability" and put it in the more perspicuous vocabulary of "being in" or "inhering" (ἐγγίγνεσθαι) found in the *Categories*, (1.1a.22f): if property F inheres in some substance S in that it is incapable of existence apart from S; and if S and some other substance S' are capable of existence apart from one another; then F cannot inhere both in S and in S', for then S could go out of existence and F would still exist, which would mean that F is capable of existence apart from S, is separable from it, and so cannot have inhered in it.

4. Hence, I do not use this term in the sense of *Categories* 8b.28f 36ff., in which it refers to a temporary quality of a thing, as opposed to "habit," the more permanent possession by a thing of some quality.

5. Aristotle, *Metaphysics* 1041b.7f.

6. Ibid., 1029a.19–21.

7. Ibid., 1029a.23–26.

8. Ibid., 1049a.23–26.

9. Ibid., 1036a.8f; 1037a.27f.

10. To know is to know form, and Aristotle's whole account of the knowing soul is structured by this association of form and knowability. At *de Anima* II, sensation is the reception of form into the soul (as opposed to nutrition, which is the reception of matter into the living thing, (*de Anima* 3.12.424a.17f). Reason, for its part, is the actualization of such sensible forms and of their generalized derivatives, images and νοητά which are themselves forms within the soul (*de Anima* III.4.429a.14–17). (It is because the objects of reason do not come directly from without that reason is a "higher" activity than sense (cf. *de Anima* II.5.417b.19–25). Once a perceptible form has crossed the material boundary of the body and has become lodged in a sensory organ, it becomes an object of the imagination (φαντασία), the faculty intermediate between sense and reason. Objects of imagination are under the control of the soul—at its disposition (*de Anima* (III.3.427b.18–22). Indeed, the objects of active reason, itself the highest stage of the intellect, are not merely controlled by but in a sense identical with reason (*de Anima* III.5 *passim*). Inference, too, starts from substance, from "what a thing is": syllogisms begin with the definition of a substance, a procedure which reveals its essence; and their purpose is to prove what other attributes inhere in a thing in virtue of that essential nature. (Hence, as *Metaphysics* VII.10 has it, "As in syllogisms, substance is the start of everything" [*Metaphysics* 1034a.30ff; also cf. *Posterior Analytics* 90b.31]. For equation of substance with *logos* itself, see *Metaphysics* 1035b.27f, 1039b.20f). To know an individual thing is to know the form in it. To cognize that form as operating in a particular quantity of matter is to know it as essence and is to know the thing itself as οὐσία.

11. Indeed, we cannot know those characteristics without knowing what they are—e.g., what their "substance" is. For, in general, anything that has a "what," for Aristotle, has a substance, but only certain basic things *are* substances, see *Metaphysics* 1030a.18–1030b.13.

12. Aristotle, *Nichomchean Ethics* 1168b.31–1169a.1, italics added.

13. Ibid., 1102b.16f.

14. Ibid.,1139b.4f; see also John McCumber, *Poetic Interaction* (Chicago: University of Chicago Press, 1989), 225f.

15. Aristotle, *Nicomachean Ethics* 1156.b2 1167a.3–12 1171b.29f.

16. Ibid., 7.3 1147a.5ff.

17. Ibid., 2.2 1103b.27–29.

18. Aristotle, *Politics* 1.13 1260a.13–15.

19. The structure of the household is, like that of the relation of reason and the soul, very similar to the relation of form and matter articulated in the *Metaphysics*:
And it is clear that the rule of the soul over the body, and of the mind and the rational element over the passionate, is natural and expedient. . . . Again, the male is by nature superior, and the female inferior; and the other is ruled; this principle, of necessity, extends to all mankind. Where then there is such a difference as that between soul and body, or between man and animals, . . . the lower sort are by nature slaves. (Aristotle, *Politics* 1245b.5–18.)

20. Ibid., I.4.1254a.28–32.

21. Aristotle, *Metaphysics* 1076a.4; quoted from Homer, *Iliad* 2.204.

22. I argue this point more fully in my *Diakena: Metaphysics, Oppression, and Heidegger's Challenge*, forthcoming.

23. V. Y. Mudimbe, *The Invention of Africa* (Bloomington: Indiana University Press, 1988), 2.

24. This point is also argued for in my *Diakena: Metaphysics, Oppression, and Hiedegger's Challenge.*

25. Jacques Derrida, "Force and Signification," in *Writing and Difference*, trans. Alan Bass (Chicago: University of Chicago Press, 1978), 6.

26. See John McCumber, *Poetic Interaction* (Chicago: University of Chicago Press, 1989).

3

Political Tolerance in an Age of Renewed Religious Warfare

Robert Cummings Neville

In this brief chapter I want to speak to five theses concerning political tolerance of diverse religions. First, the widespread renewal of religious warfare in our time refutes the secular modern belief that religion is only private and can be marginalized in public life. That belief is empirically false.

Second, to improve upon the modern secular approach to religion we need to look at religion's positive contribution to culture, its function as civil religion, which has to do with demonstrating that the human condition is to be under obligation; religion's special obligation to culture consists both in culture-building and in culture-criticizing institutions regarding obligation.

Third, religion's essential character is not its contribution to culture, important and necessary as that is, but its orientation of people to the ultimate, which itself is the ground of culture's obligations. Religion's essential character cannot be reduced to social roles but indicates that people in some respects transcend their society. This transcendent orientation is one of the important factors that provokes the passions that might lead to religious wars.

Fourth, a principle of tolerance of diverse religions needs to respect both the rights of religions to flourish, with qualifications, and religions' responsibilities to the culture. These rights, qualifications, and responsibilities can be specified.

Fifth, a public theology is needed that can adjudicate issues of conflict regarding both the tolerance of religions in their diversity and the social demands that they fulfill their own responsibilities regarding obligation.

AN AGE OF RENEWED RELIGIOUS WARFARE

The title of this chapter expresses an interpretation of our situation, which is that we live in an age of renewed religious warfare. Without putting too fine a point on the meaning of religious warfare, consider some of the current conflicts important enough to be examined in the *New York Times*. In Europe of course there is the war between Roman Catholic Croats, Christian Orthodox Serbs, and Muslims in Bosnia; the simmering conflict between Catholics and Orthodox in Croatia; the ongoing battles between Protestants and Catholics in Northern Ireland; the intermittant violence in Germany between right-wing Christian Germans and the Muslims and Orthodox from Bulgaria, Romania, the Balkans, and Turkey; the conflicts in Romania of the Orthodox with the Catholic ethnic Hungarians and the Gypsies; the conflicts in Russia between the Orthodox and the Muslims in Chechenya and Ingushetia, and between the Orthodox and the secular heirs of communism; the continued fighting in Georgia between Muslims and Orthodox.

In Africa, the Muslim government of Mauritania has been violently suppressing groups protesting the expulsion and oppression of black Christians and traditionalists; in Senegal also the Muslims are in violent struggle with Christians and traditionalists; in Nigeria, the Muslim Hausas are in constant struggle, often violent, with the Christian Yorubas. Muslim fundamentalists in Egypt, Algeria, and elsewhere are in violent struggles with nonfundamentalist or secular governments.

In Asia, the Communist military in Tajikistan has killed 25,000 Tajik Muslims and displaced 500,000 since 1991 to suppress Islamic power. Both Pakistan and India are caught up in conflicts between Muslims and Hindus. In Sri Lanka the Hindu Tamils are at war with the Buddhist Sinhalese. In Bangladesh the Muslim majority is threatened by the insurgency of the Buddhist Chakmas. Muslims are now fleeing Myanmar claiming that they are harrassed by the Buddhist majority. The Buddhist Tibetans struggle for independence from Communist China. Muslims of Turkish descent in China's Xinjiang province have been suppressed with violence. One to two hundred thousand Roman Catholics in East Timor have been killed by the Muslim government of Indonesia since East Timor was taken over by Indonesia in 1975. Fiji remains on the brink of violence between the Christian native Fijians and the Hindu Indians who have dominated the government.

In the Middle East, the tensions between the Sunnis and the Shiÿites have often been violent. The struggle between the Israelis and the Arabs of Muslim and Christian faiths has had an important dimension of religious conflict.

In addition, there are many conflicts based on tribal or clan disputes that are classed as ethnic conflicts but where religion also plays a role in defining ethnic identity. These include the barely settled conflict in Cambodia, the revolt of ethnic Nepalese in Bhutan, the tribal conflicts in Afganistan, Angola, Zaire, Kenya, Burundi, Rwanda, Uganda, Togo, Liberia, Chad, Mali, Moldova, the Basque independence movement in Spain, and of course Somalia.

The *New York Times,* to be sure, did not describe these conflicts as religious wars, rather as ethnic conflicts. The reason is the resolutely modern secular character of the *Times* which insists that religious matters must be private and not publicly important. Ethnicity is the closest notion to religion acceptable to the modern secular world view, and conflicts thus must be either ethnic or economic. Ethnicity is extremely difficult to define in any sweeping way; surely religion plays important roles in nearly all ethnic definitions, and in the self-definitions of people in ethnic terms. There is usually an economic dimension to most conflicts as well. But the focal point of the conflicts mentioned above is not so much economic nor even ethnic in the sense of racial membership; the focal point is defined by religious differences.

Modern secular inability to appreciate the public force of religion is perhaps an unconscious but willful policy lying in the origins of modernity. The modern nation-state was a polity developed in the seventeenth century in Western European lands to end the devastating wars of religion. The posture toward religion in the modern nation state was to privatize it, establishing rules of minimal religious tolerance, and causing policy and the shape of public life to turn on other, mainly economic, concerns. Religion is supposed, in secular modernity, to be a private matter, to be tolerated so long as others are not hurt. And as private, it is supposed not to be important for determining public matters such as insurrections and wars.

The secular nation-state is not without its critics in our time. While suppressing, at least temporarily, the power of religions to cause violence, the secular nation-states in their turn give rise to economic wars. The economic wars of the twentieth century have been as devastating as the religious ones of the seventeenth, indeed far more so because of the perfection of what Edith Wyschogrod calls the instruments of mass death.[1]

But more to the point, the very occurence of the religious wars in our time, even in Europe, proves the secular assumption, that religion is private, to be mistaken. Religious concerns do shape public life to the point of violence and war. For secular modernity to assume or urge that religion is or ought to be private does not to make it so, at least not for very long. If there is to be tolerance of religious differences in our time, it cannot be on the assumption that religions are treated as private matters. This is my first thesis. We must therefore look to amend the modern secular approach to religion.

RELIGION AND OBLIGATION

The first step toward a better approach to religion is to ask about the cultural function of religions as such.

Of course it is not obvious to modern secularists that religions have a positive cultural function. They might argue that the tolerance of religion as such needs to be challenged. Given the social evils of religion, their oppressions, dogmatisms, and restrictions of liberty, not to speak of their wars, perhaps even one religion is too many and the question of religious diversity is misplaced. This was an understandable reaction in the seventeenth century, and the privatizing of religion was a compromise to allow for the continuance of religion as a kind of detoxified virus. But, as renewed religious warfare shows, religion cannot be detoxified the modern secular way.

The answer to this objection to taking political tolerance of religious diversity seriously has to do with religions' positive contributions to culture, what Robert Bellah and others have characterized as civil religion.[2] Although there are many dimensions to civil religion, attention needs to be called here to the religious functions regarding obligation in society. Every religion, I believe and have argued elsewhere, depicts the human condition as lying under obligation.[3] To be human is to be obligated in important ways, says religion. The obligatedness of human life is a part of the universal religious dimension.

There is no universal religion, of course, only particular religions. The claim that religion as such presents human life as obligated is therefore on one level an empirical generalization. A rough survey can indicate its plausibility. The religions of India—Hinduism and Buddhism—depict human life as such that people ought to be enlightened and from enlightenment gain freedom. Where people lack enlightenment they fail at something obligatory for humanity, which is different from failing to have good health, lots of money, or victory in battle. The religions of China—Confucianism and Taoism—depict human life as such that people ought to be in attunement with reality, primarily with persons and institutions in the case of Confucianism and with nature in the case of Taoism. The religions of Near Eastern origin—Judaism, Christianity, and Islam—depict human life as such that persons are obligated to justice in the social order. Failure to be righteous is not merely to have worked the particular evil at hand but is to be in contradiction to one's essential nature. This rough sampling of major religions lacks nuance and distinction, but I believe more detailed study would reinforce rather than dilute the point. My own language of obligation here betrays the Western origin of my metaphors.

In any of these religions, or in religiousness generally, human life is depicted as standing under norms. What we are, actually and concretely, is normatively measured by what we ought to be, with regard to enlightenment, attunement, justice, or a host of alternative prescriptions. Different religions have different metaphoric systems for expressing this, and cultures differ in many details as to the content of the basic human obligations. With respect to the general religious dimension, however, the fact that religions present humanity as lying under obligation should be seen as performing at least two related cultural functions.

The first is to awaken and habituate people to living in a state of obligation, and to provide the symbols for grasping what it means to be obligated. All of the various norms that might be relevant in a society, norms for moral, political, and economic life; for physical and psychological health; for arts and literature, take their content from their particular circumstances and traditions but take their obligatoriness from the religious dimension of life. Religion builds the habits of taking obligation seriously as it affects language, social practices, imagination, and institutions, as well as its own practices and conceptualities.

When secularism marginalizes or privatizes religion, it undermines the obligatoriness of all the other norms. As the residual cultural effects of powerful civil religion diminish, cultural sensibilities turn to relativism. Despite the passionate intensities of particular groups for their causes, the obligatoriness of the good in those causes fades into mere interest and the pursuit of power. Because the first cultural function of religion is to institute obligatoriness in culture, without religion, or with only its fading detritus, cultural life lacks a bone-marrow recognition of norms and lapses into relativism. Such is a frequent complaint about contemporary Western culture. The point suggests indeed that secularism itself cannot function as a viable civil religion and that some one or several "real" religions are needed.

The second cultural function of religion is to serve as a watchdog critic of how well a given society lives up to its obligations. Religion is not alone in being a moral critic, but it is the major institution articulating and sponsoring such criticism. Not only does religion establish social obligatoriness, the culture-building function, it also assesses social performance. Whereas the first function of religion indicates that religion is a fundamental constitutive component of human culture as such, the second function tips religion over against any particular positive culture. Religions cannot let themselves become too identified with a culture, or to be defined too much in cultural terms, if they are to perform their critical or prophetic function. No religion can be wholly outside culture, of course. For that reason, this second function of religion needs to be aimed self-referentially at each religion's own cultural expressions. In its critical mode, a religion strains for distance from its culture, for objectivity, for appeals to higher norms, for a looseness of cultural embodiment. Religion's critical moment is at least potentially subversive, and insofar as religions can partially institutionalize the critical function in the persons and offices of prophets and jestors, religions are always slightly subversive.

The culture-criticizing function of civil religion is as important as the culture-building function. When secularity marginalizes or privatizes religion, fundamental criticism is easily diminished to the shrill cries of self-interest of particular groups, again a kind of relativism evading obligation.

Needless to say, any religion has a devil of a time balancing its culture-building and culture-critical functions, pun intended. One of the most frequent and understandable corruptions of religion is when it forgets that it is supposed to be "in the world but not of it," to use the Christian language. In our time, some religions have become radicalized in devotion to the critical function and forget the more conservative culture-founding function; fundamentalisms are of this sort. But surely the most frequent corruption is when the critical function fades into a solid identification with a particular culture, blessing its interests and wars. Nearly all religious wars are fought under the guidance of corrupt religions that have allowed themselves to become simply identified with some national, ethnic, or political interest. While we must admit that many of the current conflicts in the world are motivated primarily by genuine religious counterclaims, we do not need to say that the religions involved are faithful to their own principles. When the Buddhists of Sri Lanka, whose religion is supposed to be that of quiet enlightenment, battle with the Hindus whose slogan is Shanti! Shanti! Shanti! they both are making profound mistakes about the implications of their own religions. When Christians, whose God is love, bomb and snipe at one another in Northern Ireland, the forms of Christianity at hand are corrupt.

If it is true that human life does indeed lie under obligation, so that being human as such means that we have obligations to one another, to nature, and to the institutions that shape our habits and relations with one another and nature, then religions need to be performing both of their cultural functions. These two cultural functions regarding obligation are among religions' own obligations to human culture. This is my second thesis.

RELIGION AND THE ULTIMATE

An approach to religion that improves upon that of modern secularity cannot rest with appreciating religions' contribution to the wider culture. It must also attend to what is essential to religions as such. Most religious leaders and theologians indeed would be dismayed at the depiction of religion primarily in its civil functions. Religions rather define themselves in relation to what they take to be ultimate, to the source of the obligations, to the transcendent relative to which it is possible to stand in a partially external critical stance toward society. This abstract way of putting the point is perhaps alien to every particular religion. The theistic religions make the point in popularly understandable terms: religions are essentially defined by the God who acts to found them, who commands their practices and in turn judges the religions and their roles in society, by the God who creates the world with its obligations. With appropriate shifts in metaphors away from agency, similar points could be made, I believe, about the transcendent normative reality of the Tao, of Brahman, of the Original Buddha Nature, and of other religious candidates for ultimacy. Without understanding the orientation to ultimacy, it is impossible to grasp religions in their depth, or to see how they can function with regard to obligation in the human condition.

While acknowledging the essential and primary orientation of every religion to what it takes to be ultimate, we should also note the historical specificity of each religion. Not only are all interpretations and expressions of the ultimate historically conditioned, the religious practices that effect the civil functions of religions have specific histories. Sometimes these histories are associated with racial, national, or ethnic groups. Other instances of religion encompass diverse cultural communities worldwide. In each particular instance of a living religion, however, there is a particular historical connection with the society at hand, and with the history of the religion's development from its founding to its practice in this place.

There is a deep connection between the essential orientations of religions to the ultimate and their civil contributions to society as culture builders and culture criticizers regarding obligation. From the religions' standpoint, their civil functions are mere consequences of the primary religious orientation, which is to the ultimate or transcendent whence derives the obligatoriness of the human condition. From the religions' standpoint, the historical expressions of the ultimate and the historical religious and social practices embodying those expressions are normative ways to salvation and social life. Some religions conceive their way of salvation and life to be transferable from one culture to another, changing so as to be appropriate to different cultural and social conditions but maintaining historical continuity with the normative source of obligation. Buddhism, Christianity, Hinduism, and Islam are great missionary religions, and Confucianism, Judaism, and Taoism have adapted themselves to many different cultural forms outside the places and times of origin. So from the side of the religions, each demands the political tolerance to flourish and to have a chance to determine the civil functions of religion in the society in which it finds itself, at least for the people to whose history it is appropriate if not for the whole to which it can adapt. Some religions demand the right to exclusive tolerance in both respects.

The conception of religions advocated here attempts to harmonize two points in one approach. On the one hand, religions are to be understood in terms of their obligatory contributions to culture, their civil functions. On the other hand, they are to be understood in terms of their essential character, which is an orientation to the ultimate that transcends the particularities of history, however particular and historical that orientation is expressed. Both the essential nature of religion and its contributory nature are necessary. The essential orientation toward the ultimate is necessary for the authority to define obligatedness and engage in fundamental criticism. The cultural engagement of civil religion is necessary if the essential orientation to the ultimate is to find historical expression. The modern secular approach privatizes the contributions of civil religion and hence undermines the sense of obligatedness necessary for social life, leading to relativism. The modern secular approach also simply fails to register the orientation to the ultimate because it has no way of acknowledging ultimacy, or divinity, or infinity, or any of the fundamental symbols that point to the source of reality and its obligations. An improved approach to religion deals with both sides.

Acknowledging the essential orientations of religions to the ultimate allows us to appreciate the passions of religion, which Kierkegaard characterized as infinite. It is easy to see how these passions might easily lead to war if some historical culture or goal is confused with the ultimate. It is also easy to see how historically different particular religions might come into conflict concerning the framing of the obligatoriness of the human condition and assessing how societies measure up to various obligations. Because there are many religions, each with a claim to represent the ultimate and each with implicit if not explicit programs for culture, the question of political tolerance of religion, indeed religious diversity, is urgent. This is my third thesis.

POLITICAL TOLERANCE OF RELIGIONS

If the above characterizations of religions are generally on the mark, then consideration of political tolerance for a diversity of religions needs two sides. On the one hand, there needs to be a principle expressing the conditions under which religions have a right to flourish, a right to be protected politically. On the other hand, the political order itself has the right to call religions to account regarding their civil functions. Let us consider first the conditions under which religions have a right to flourish.

I propose, as a principle of political tolerance, that individuals and groups have a prima facie right to the practice of a religion of their own embrace wherever they live. This principle is far too complicated to defend in detail here and in some respects it is so customary and banal as to be offensive if it were argued at length. But certain explanatory comments can be made. The words *prima facie* signal some qualifications that will be mentioned shortly. The phrase *their own embrace* is used rather than *their own choice* to indicate that people hold to their religions by many forms of identification other than and in addition to personal choice, which might be peculiar to only certain cultural conditions. Individuals and groups are both mentioned in order to indicate that religions are practiced in communities such that the tolerance of religious practice by a lone individual is a rare abstraction; most of the time, questions of tolerance deal with individuals as members of religious communities. The language of rights is used to indicate that freedom of religion is a subclass of human rights.

To appeal to human rights is not necessarily to suppose that rights are "natural" in any of the senses defended by "natural rights theorists." The appeal can also rest upon arguments that the contents of the rights have been shown to be so valuable that political structures ought to guarantee that all people ought to be able to enjoy those contents. In respect of the prima facie right of people to practice the religion of their embrace wherever they live, the relevant values include three considerations.

First, although always historically particular in expression and practice, as argued above religions involve the orientation of people to the ultimate which transcends historical particularity and grounds the obligations that define cultures as such. Part of human reality consists in this relation to the ultimate or transcendent however particularly embodied. Therefore, even though the political structures of a society often legitimately might have to regulate religious practice, the political dimension lacks the comprehensive authority to define people's relation to the ultimate. For a political agency, then, to deny or prohibit a religion, within the limits of the prima facie right, is for it to overstep its scope into a dimension of the human to which it is not relevant. For people who are attentive to the ultimate, there is a point at which goverment is simply irrelevant. Good public theology urges that this be respected, for otherwise something importantly human is denied.

Second, although it might seem paradoxical, the very political vitality of a society depends on religion functioning precisely with reference to the ultimate source of obligation, both in culture-building and in culture-criticizing functions. Therefore the political dimension undermines itself if it fails to respect the rights of a religion to live out its relation with the ultimate.

Third, the political realm now recognizes the fact that peoples are culturally different and yet live together. Without suggesting that all cultures are of equal value or that moral and political judgments should not be made, different cultures, including different religions, should be respected within the same body politic. The costs and pains of tolerance are outweighed by the sufferings of ethnic cleansing that attempt to eliminate cultural and religious diversity within the same country. Therefore, good cases can be made for a prima facie right of individuals and groups to practice the religion of their own embrace wherever they live.

What are the qualifications contained within the phrase *prima facie*? They stem from the need of the religions themselves to embrace the political right of religious freedom.

The first qualification is that individuals and groups need to respect the prima facie right of others to practice different religions. Thus, although a religion might believe that it alone is the true religion, it cannot express or institutionalize that belief in ways that inhibit other religions and still claim its own right to exist in the society. Exclusivism, therefore, must be privatized, and those religions that do not do so need not be tolerated; this is the truth in the modern secular perspective.[4]

The second qualification is that where different religions come into conflict with one another over obligation, either as to what habits of obligation need to be instilled or as to what critical judgments to make, the case needs to be argued publicly with the recognition that the ultimate source of obligation transcends each religion. This is to say, religions need to recognize their own particular fallibility. They need to be able to present their insights and traditions of argument as historically valuable but vulnerable to correction in the public debates about obligation. Although recognition of fallibility might be difficult, especially for some religious traditions, that fallibility expresses the ancient theme of the condemnation of idolatry. Exclusively to substitute a historically particular religious expression of the ultimate for the ultimate itself is idolatry. The public debate about a matter of obligation is inclusive of religions but larger than any one because it needs to make reference, if only in deference, to the fact that obligation is grounded in that which transcends any and every religion.

These two qualifications require, as conditions for tolerance, that religions have a modern historical sense of their own particularity relative to other religions and their own finitude and fallibility. This is not to say that traditional religions, in contrast to those religions modernized, were always exclusivistic and dogmatic in asserting their own authority. Perhaps those attributes characterize the theistic religions originating in the ancient Near East more than the religions of Asia or the primal religions. Whatever the historical case, the claim to the right to flourish in the modern world, I believe we have learned, requires of religions that they claim only their own salvific and culture-forming validity, leaving the question of other religions open to discussion and allowing that their own expressions can themselves be subjected to further religious judgment.

The other side of the issue of political tolerance, according to the understanding of religion advocated here, is that the political order can call religions to account regarding their civil functions. Of course, no political order can demand that civil religion be successful. To the extent the theistic rhetoric expresses a basic point, much of the time the human predicament waits upon God. But the political order can indeed test the genuineness of putative religions by asking how they articulate the fundamental obligatedness of the human condition, and how they can stand both within and without a society in order to gain critical purchase. Where religions do not perform, or do not attempt to perform, these civil functions, their case for tolerance is weakened if they come into conflict with other religions or with other cultural projects. The political order cannot judge a religion's essential orientation to the ultimate; but it can judge whether that orientation yields fruit in civil religion.

That individuals and groups have a prima facie right to the practice of a religion of their own embrace wherever they live and that they also have an obligation to civil religion constitute my fourth thesis.

RELIGION AND PUBLIC THEOLOGY

The fifth thesis is that no formal definition of religion or procedure of due process can handle the issues of political tolerance of religious diversity and that continuing assessments of the claims of religion to the rights of tolerance will have to be made. For this purpose it is necessary to revive and develop the discipline of public theology.[5]

Public theology in this sense is public discourse that is able to make discriminating judgments both about the civil dimensions of religion and about their institutionalizations of their essential orientation to the ultimate. These judgments will be necessary to determine both whether religions meet the conditions for tolerance and whether they are addressing their civil obligations.

Modern secular culture has tended to say that all theology is private. But theology cannot be private only. That religions become corrupted so as to identify too much with a culture and go to war in its defense is a theological mistake and can be recognized publically as such. That religions can become so enamoured of social criticism that they fail to build cultural habits of obligatoriness relevant to the conditions of the modern world is a theological mistake and can be recognized publicly as such. These judgments are theological in the sense that they have to do with the faithfulness of religious practices to their ultimate commitments. They are public both in the sense that everyone who thinks hard about the issues can understand them, whether or not the thinkers belong to any of the religions involved, and in the sense that they deal with the publicly important aspects of religious expressions. Whereas these judgments about religious practices living in contradiction to the ultimate commitments of the religions are easy to make, public theology about matters of political tolerance of religious diversity are more difficult. Whatever the degree of difficulty, the criteria for the validity of the public theology consist in the cases that can be made for the theological judgments.

Although there have been in the past many times when public theology flourished as an articulate discipline, especially in Confucian China and in medieval Europe, there are few models for public theology in the contemporary context of sharp religious diversity. Therefore, the task of theology in the present time requires imagination and innovation. The general form of public theology, like any kind of theology or even plain political discourse, is that of simply making a persuasive case that is vulnerable to correction.

My remarks conclude with a nearly mute appeal for the development of public theology to define the shape of political tolerance of religious diversity. Public theology would be easy if it could limit itself to that upon which everyone already agrees. But religions cite obligations that challenge the lowest common denominator of agreement, and rightly so. Public theology would still be easy if it could limit itself to the social and cultural roles of religions; but then it would not engage the passions essential to religions' orientations to the ultimate. If we are to recognize both the civic dimensions of religions and their essential orientations to the ultimate, as we must if we are to understand religions as public phenomena, then we must enter into public theology that engages religions in their full reality, my final thesis.

NOTES

1. The core of this list comes from the *New York Times,* international section, p. 14, for Sunday, February 7, 1993. At the time of the final revision of this chapter in March 1994, nothing much had changed in that list save that a tentative alliance between the Croats and Muslims in Bosnia against the Serbs seems to be holding. See Edith Wyschogrod, *Spirit in Ashes: Hegel, Heidegger, and Man-Made Mass Death* (New Haven: Yale University Press), 1985.

2. See Robert N. Bellah, *The Broken Covenant: American Civil Religion in Time of Trial* (New York: Crossroad, 1975); Bellah with Richard Madsen, William M. Sullivan, Ann Swidler, and Steven M. Tipton, *Habits of the Heart* (Berkeley: University of California Press, 1985); and Bellah, *The Good Society* (New York: Knopf, 1991).

3. See my *Behind the Masks of God* (Albany: State University of New York Press, 1991) and *A Theology Primer* (Albany: State University of New York Press,

1991). See especially *The Highroad around Modernism* (Albany: State University of New York Press, 1992), chapters 8, 10–11.

4. The term *exclusivism* is widely used in discussions of relations among religions to denote the claim by a religion that it and only it is valid. Alternative positions are inclusivism, which claims that the truths of other religions can be included within the truth of one's own, and pluralism, which claims that different religions have different truths of their own, not necessarily about the same topic. See, for instance, *The Myth of Christian Uniqueness: Toward a Pluralistic Theology of Religions*, edited by John Hick and Paul F. Knitter (Maryknoll: Orbis, 1987), and *Christian Uniqueness Reconsidered: The Myth of a Pluralistic Theology of Religions*, edited by Gavin DíCosta (Maryknoll: Orbis, 1990).

5. See the instructive discussion of public theology in Linell E. Cadyís, *Religion, Theology, and American Public Life* (Albany: State University of New York Press, 1993). On how to make theology public rather than restricted to confessional commitments, see my 1992 presidential address to the American Academy of Religion, "Religious Studies and Theological Studies," *Journal of the American Academy of Religion* 61, no. 2 (Summer 1993), 185–200.

II

Religion

4

Metaphysical Roots of Tolerance and Intolerance: An Islamic Interpretation

Seyyed Hossein Nasr

Before discussing Islamic attitudes toward intolerance and tolerance, it is necessary to deal with the metaphysical roots of these attitudes manifested everywhere in human life and search for their meaning in the context of the existential reality both of ourselves and of the whole of creation. It can be asserted categorically that from the metaphysical point of view, only the Supreme Principle, the Ultimately Real, or what in the climate of monotheism is usually referred to as the Godhead, the Divine Essence, or the Divine Ground has no opposite, for it transcends all duality. The very act of creation or the cosmogenic process implies of necessity duality and opposition. Even in the Divine Order which embraces not only the Supreme Essence or the One but also Its Energies, Hypostases, or what in Islam is called the "Divine Names and Qualities," where already the domain of relativity commences, one can observe duality, multiplicity, and also the roots of opposition. The manifestation of all things in this world issuing from the Divine Nature is furthermore through their opposite, a principle which has been immortalized in a Persian poem by the fourteenth-century Sufi poet Shaykh Mahmud Shabistari who wrote,

The manifestation of all things is through their opposites,
Only the Divine Truth has neither opposite nor like.

To live in the world of manifestation is, therefore, to live in a world of opposites which can be transcended only in that reality which is the *coincidentia oppositorum* and which on their own level are often in opposition and usually intolerant of each other. That is why tolerance and intolerance are not only moral issues but have a cosmic dimension. This is a point which is emphasized by traditional doctrines in the Orient where human and moral laws have not become divorced from each other and was true in the traditional West and until modern times, when the link between human morality and cosmic laws became severed. Examples of the emphasis upon this nexus can be found in classical thought, in Thomistic and other forms of Christian theology and philosophy, as well as in classical Jewish thought.

To live in this world is to live in a world of duality and also opposition, although there are also elements of harmony and complementarity that must be considered. Therefore, the question of tolerance or intolerance must be understood not simply as only a moral choice or choice of values but also as an ontological reality. According to all traditional metaphysics, which is the perspective of this essay, duality, opposition, and intolerance of opposites for each other are present in all realms of existence below the Divine Order. Moreover, this duality within manifestation, although possessing many facets such as harmony and complementarity as seen in the yin and yang in the Chinese tradition, is also seen in its aspect of irreducible opposition in many traditions, as can be seen in such realities as truth and falsehood, beauty and ugliness, or goodness and evil. It is this second type of duality from which derive intolerance and tolerance. Yin and yang or other similar dualities in other traditions result in complementarity and harmony, whereas truth and error, or goodness and evil, can never live in harmony with each other without violating the very principles of microcosmic as well as macrocosmic existence. An architect can never harmonize truth and error or falsehood on the level of his art without the building which he is constructing collapsing no more than can the individual "tolerate" evil simply as a complementary of the good without losing his or her moral vision. Such dualities can be transcended in a unity which stands above them in the ontological hierarchy but cannot be harmonized on their own level of existence. Truth remains always intolerant of falsehood and good of evil.

In every religion, intolerance is expressed toward evil and falsehood and as the Quran asserts, "If the truth comes, falsehood perishes." When the light manifests itself, the darkness disappears because here one has oppositions which are not of the same nature as yin and yang, which stands on the same ontological level. Goodness and evil do not simply have the same degree of ontological reality no matter how they appear outwardly. The good is always intolerant of evil because the good corresponds to being and evil is nothingness, parading in the garb of existence. It is in the nature of reality to be intolerant of the unreal. If this thesis be denied, one would have to surrender the very notion of the truth, which in fact much of the modern world has done in the name of relativity and sacrifice at the alter of tolerance without this step diminishing intolerance in any appreciable manner. Those who deny the truth are even more intolerant concerning those who believe that there is such a thing as the truth than most followers of one form of the Truth are of the followers of other manifestations of It. However, as long as one accepts truth and goodness, one must also accept the intolerance of truth vis-à-vis error and goodness in the face of evil. Moreover, those intolerant toward evil have in fact been praised in all societies as champions of the good.

In this context the term *intolerance*, which has become so negative and pejorative in this century of maximum hatred of human collectivities toward each other, gains a new meaning. The whole question of intolerance and tolerance becomes reflected in a new dimension when seen in the light of the true and the good, or for that matter, the beautiful and the ugly, and what lies in the nature of existence. The problem becomes, however, even more complicated when one distinguishes between absolute and relative truth and also between absolute or relative moral values which determine what is good and what is not in a particular context. Furthermore, as already mentioned, a new type of intolerance sets in among the relativizers against those who still cling to the notion of absolute truth and goodness, a phenomenon which is so prevalent in the modern West as not to need any further elaboration. In fact, the basic problem of intolerance, not seen metaphysically, but observed and experienced in the present-day world, is related precisely to this fact in addition to what concerns the very fiber of separative existence in which irreducible dualities appear. Lest we forget, most human beings do not live at that exalted center of existence which, according to the great metaphysician Nicholas Cusa, is the coincidence of opposites and which the founder of the Naqshbandiyyah Sufi order called "universal peace" (*sulh-i kull*) transcending all opposition and strife. Most of us live simply in the world of opposites and of strife unable to transcend dualities and oppositions in which one side negates the other of the two sides of opposition. Therefore, the question of intolerance and tolerance presents itself to most people as being related not to the reality that transcends all dichotomies, but as part of a world in which both seem to be real and concern man's daily life in an ever more threatening manner, thanks to the tools of destruction now available to him.

Today many people hold tolerance to be a positive virtue, which is also politically correct, whereas the term implies even now endurance of something false, painful, or even opposed to the good. One tolerates something despite its negative connotations, such as tolerating pain or this or that person whose ideas or even presence one dislikes but nevertheless tolerates. Therefore, tolerance cannot be the highest virtue but a necessary virtue which one must possess when one cannot transcend the dichotomies of opposition where such a transcendence is a possibility as between two interpretations of a truth and not of course when truth is simply opposed to error. This necessary virtue on a social level is nevertheless considered as the highest virtue by those who are secularists because it also implies relativity, the denial of absoluteness, and, if carried to extremes, ultimately the very notion of truth. To assert absoluteness in the modern world view seems to them to imply intolerance at least beyond the realms of the mathematical and natural sciences where society gives every right to scientists to be intolerant of someone who asserts that two plus two equals five or even goes beyond the boundaries of the generally accepted paradigm of knowledge now dominating the modern mentality. Rarely have people called official biologists intolerant when they lack any tolerance toward a nonevolutionary theory of biological development even if this is presented by a respected scientist.

The question of tolerance and its opposite pose in fact different sets of problems in the modern West from what one finds in traditional civilizations in which the dominating Idea or paradigm always held and continues to hold a most exalted place for the truth and the good beyond the realm of a particular form of knowledge such as modern science in the West since the seventeenth century. In the Western context, the discussion of tolerance and intolerance is most often between those who have followed the path of relativism and secularist humanism and those who still cling to the Christian and Jewish understanding of the truth. It also involves non-Western civilizations which have not for the most part as yet accepted the secularist relativization of their traditions and against which most Western relativists and secularists are even more intolerant than followers of religion in the West were intolerant toward other religions in yesteryears or as various religious communities which have confronted each other over the centuries. The question for the Western intelligentsia must therefore also include the question of tolerance or intolerance toward other religions, cultures, and ethnic groups for whom truth and goodness in an absolute sense still possess a defining role in the lives of their followers.

It must be remembered that all traditional civilizations, which means the whole of the world before the appearance of the modernist separation from the norm, held on to a truth which for them was absolute. This includes Hinduism and Buddhism considered by so many scholars as being opposed to Abrahamic absolutism. The great struggles between Buddhism and Brahmanism in India itself concerned essentially the question of the truth, and not simply social factors. Among all religions, there was one form or another of intolerance as far as views which negated their perspective upon reality were concerned, and many wars were fought over the question of truth as they are now fought over markets and economic gains or a short while ago over manmade ideologies seeking to replace religions. It is true that the crusades were carried out in the name of religions as were many other acts of a similar nature elsewhere, if not with the same persistence and ferocity. But more often than not, this kind of doctrinal intolerance was combined with practical tolerance.

A case in point is that of Islam, identified by many with intolerance today, because it seeks to cling to an immutable vision of the truth before the relativizing forces of the modern world. Muslims did fight against Christians, Shamans, and Hindus on the various borders of the Islamic world. But also Jews, Christians, and Muslims lived in remarkable peace and tolerance in Islamic Spain and Hindus and Muslims under Muslim rule during much of the domination of India by Muslim powers. Moreover, even today millions of Christians and still small numbers of Jews, as well as Zoroastrians, Buddhists, and Hindus live under Muslim rule from Morocco to Malaysia. Not only are they tolerated on the human level, but many comprise the wealthiest groups in their countries, such as the Copts in Egypt or the Chinese Buddhists in Malaysia, and they have never been "ethnically cleansed," as Muslims and Jews were in Spain after 1492 or the Tartars under Czarist Russia and present day Muslims in Bosnia, not to speak of the horrendous crimes of Nazi Germany.

In such situations in the Islamic world, the common people for the most part exercised tolerance which often included personal friendship with members of a religious community while shunning discussions of other visions of the truth which on the surface would negate their own vision of it. However, most also remembered that others were People of the Book and had received a revealed truth from God, the Truth (*al-Haqq*) and the source of all truth. Then there were philosophers and theologians who debated with Jews, Christians, and others often in a more tolerant fashion than is to be seen among the so-called tolerant modern secularists against anyone denying the premises of their world view. This fact is of course due to the common truths of a transcendental nature which exist between various traditional religions and the lack of such a basic common ground between the agnostic-secularist perspective and the religious one.

In any case, besides the theologians and philosophers, there were the Sufis who spoke so often of the Truth which embraces all religions and who sought beyond the world of forms the Formless Reality wherein is to be found that "Universal Peace" (*sulh-i kull*) transcending all confrontations, delimitations, and oppositional dualities. In contrast, in the modern world in which it is impossible to harmonize truth and error, and in which no common ground exists between those who cling to an absolute truth and the relativists, in the view of the latter new elements have entered the whole question of intolerance and tolerance: doubt and relativism. Seeing themselves of course as being tolerant, and forgetting their intolerance of the religious perspective, the relativizers glorify their own skepticism and relativism while always blaming those who cling to an absolute truth as being intolerant or fanatical, always insisting that the foundation of tolerance is doubt and relativization.

It is well known that since the Age of Enlightenment, and putting aside certain philosophers such as Lessing who sought to discover the underlying common truth of Judaism, Christianity, and Islam, the more irreligious and agnostic philosophers sought to refute any claim of absoluteness, except of reason itself. They took human nature as the basis for the creation of tolerance among human beings. Such figures as Voltaire and Rousseau became paragons of this new understanding of tolerance which would sacrifice the right of the truth, especially the Truth as such, to that of the individual. It was considered that human beings should be tolerated because they are human beings and not because of whether or not they assert the truth and live according to the good.

This century has proven how wrong was this appraisal of human nature, for in this most secularist period of human history when in the West at least religion has been to a large extent sacrificed at the altar of the secular and forced to accept relativization in order to be part of the modern discourse, not only has tolerance not increased in a profound sense, but intolerance is raising its head in an unprecedented manner, now armed with means of destroying not a few but millions of human beings. We live in a world in which in the West the relativization of nearly everything, including what has remained since the Renaissance of Christian ethics, is being carried out with great rapidity in the name of individual rights and freedoms and any opposition to this trend is immediately branded as intolerant, fanatical, and extremist. Moreover, any part of the world which refuses to participate in this process is seen as out of step with the march of history, so-called progress, and all of the other idols of eighteenth- and nineteenth-century European thought which some refuse to give up despite the observation of the unprecedented chaos of this age which it would take more than religious faith to confirm as progress.

Being in the very nature of cosmic and human reality, intolerance has continued to survive in the West itself, which claims to determine the very direction and tempo of what is called "the march of history." Needless to say, the metaphysical principles mentioned earlier in this essay continue to be operative whether one accepts or rejects them. Yet these new forms of intolerance are usually blamed upon what still remains of religion in the West and its recent partial revival in some circles and hardly ever upon the secularists and relativists themselves who keep insisting that if only everyone were to stop believing in absolute values and accept the process of relativization, then tolerance would flower all over the world and intolerance would disappear.

Therefore, it is important to examine the issue from the other side and turn especially to Islamic civilization accused today by the West of being more intolerant and fanatical than any other religion and civilization no matter how many centuries-old mosques are destroyed in India or Muslims massacred in Bosnia or Chechnya. It is especially necessary to turn to the Islamic world now because of the deliberated and orchestrated program to identify the negative attitude of intolerance, especially with Muslims to the extent of neglecting the rather remarkable record of Islamic civilization concerning minorities during most of its history, there being of course tragic exceptions. There are even those who do not want to be reminded of the facts of Islamic history even if mentioned by respectable scholars because such historical truths challenge either their own world view or their political and economic interests.

To turn to the other side of this debate, it is first of all necessary to remember once again that to be tolerant on the basis of the relativization of the truth implies also being intolerant toward those who claim the reality of absolute truth and their attachment to it. Like the thesis and antithesis of Hegelian dialectic, which Hegel probably took from Jacob Bohme and the long Hermetic tradition in the West, the very assertion of tolerance on the basis of relativism brings about the negation and intolerance toward those who refuse to participate in the prevalent process of relativization. That is why, while many people in the West talk of tolerance, they are usually very intolerant of members of other civilizations which do not accept their views even if these other civilizations pose no danger to the West. Many people speak of the Islamic world as if it had its navy in the Gulf of Mexico endangering America itself, rather than the American navy dominating the Persian Gulf and the main economic resource of all the Muslim countries in that region. A picture is drawn by the very secularist champions of tolerance that if another civilization wants to go its own way, experiment within the context of its own religion and history and with the dynamic of its own society, not accepting the prevalent secularist and relativizing models dominating the West, then it is intolerant and must be opposed. In such situations, suddenly all the decorum of tolerance falls apart and the hitherto unannounced sentiments become formulated as the motto. We are intolerant of whomever does not follow our way of doing things, but since this is not a laudable trait, we keep emphasizing that he or she is intolerant against us. We possess all the virtues, and the other, all the vices. This is where one needs to pause and think for a moment again about the metaphysical and philosophical roots of tolerance and intolerance, truth and falsehood, good and evil, alluded to briefly at the beginning of this essay.

Turning now to the Islamic world specifically, it must be asserted at the outset that Islam sees the value of human life in holding firmly to the doctrine of the absoluteness of the Divine Principle and in leading a life in accordance with the norms revealed by that Principle, norms which therefore participate in some way in the quality of absoluteness. For centuries, and despite the bigotry of a number of its scholars, the Islamic world has respected the life and property of Jews, Christians, Zoroastrians, and others living in its midst, and in doing so, it has followed the advice of the Prophet. Moreover, the Quran states explicitly that the "People of the Book" (*ahl al-kitab*), who include not only the followers of the Abrahamic religions but also those of other major religions such as Zoroastrianism and Hinduism with which Islam came into contact, have also received a divine message and that ultimately all authentic religions contain elements of the Truth within themselves. That is why Muslims are obliged according to their Sacred Law (*al-Shari'ah*) to protect the followers of other religions living in their midst even if Muslims do not agree with all their teachings. In answer to some contemporary Muslims who claim other religions to be false, one could ask why God would command Muslims to protect the rights of groups who live in error and would be condemned to hell. Traditional Muslims always saw other people in terms of their attachment not to an ethnic group or nation in the modern sense of the word, but to a religious community. That is why even today most Muslims, not transformed by modernism and Westernization, see Westerners as Christians and cannot even understand the category of secularism and the fact that many Westerners are only post-Christian and no longer attached to the Christian world view. The *faranji* for the Arabs and *farangi* for Persians (from Frankish, meaning "European") is inseparable in the mind of the people of the *bazaars* of Isfahan, Damascus, and Cairo from Christianity. Even the term *kafir* usually translated as "infidel" used for European Christians did not bear the strictly theological significance of a people cut off completely from the truth and grace as does the term *pagan* in Christianity.

Because of this basic outlook, the whole question of intolerance and tolerance is seen in a different light by traditional Muslims. Tolerance is seen as involving a person who does not accept the truth of Islam but accepts some other call from heaven as the Muslims displaying tolerance toward Christians in such lands as Syria for fourteen hundred years bears witness. The traditional Muslim's attitude has not involved a person or society which denies any divine truth and relativizes all that is absolute and desacralizes all that is sacred because for Muslims the purpose of human life is to confirm the Absolute and the Sacred without which the human being is only accidentally human. This radical difference in perspective is the cause of so many in the West having such difficulty in understanding the reaction of Muslims to the Salman Rushdie affair, judging all things from the prism of its own understanding of the Absolute and the relative, the Sacred and the profane, God's rights and human rights. And it has displayed the utmost degree of intolerance toward those who have not been willing to accept the fruits of the European philosophical and political developments of the last few centuries.

At the heart of this affair lies the basic question: What is more important, God's rights or man's rights? However, even if one speaks of tolerance and freedom of choice in the current Western sense, then every society should have the right to respond to this question by itself without either imposing its answer upon others or accepting others to impose their answers on it. Any society which claims that its answer to this question is global and that anyone who does not accept its answer is "backward" or "medieval" or some other such pejorative term based upon the myopia of progress and evolutionism, is exercising the worst kind of intolerance on a global scale. Putting aside sloganeering and emotional condemnation by taking recourse to such terms as "medieval," which paradoxically refers to the most religious chapter of Western history and is therefore also called the "Age of Faith," one must turn to the basic question about divine and human rights with logic and objectivity.

If viewed in this manner, we realize that Western societies after centuries of internal wars and social revolutions have come to the conclusion that human rights are more important than divine rights. The latter are respected only under the condition that they do not interfere with law, economics, political, and other aspects of daily human affairs. Real tolerance would mean that other societies which have not undergone the modern Western experience and have not made such a decision, societies for whom God's rights come before man's, would be respectfully tolerated as those societies must tolerate the West's decision on such a crucial matter which defines human life and what it means to be human. That of course has not happened, especially as far as the West, which speaks so much of human rights and tolerance, is concerned, while non-Western societies have little choice but to tolerate the situation because of the complete imbalance of power. It is the hiding of these basic truths which makes the situation so difficult and the discourse so tortuous today, especially in the case of the Islamic world, which is perhaps more vocal than others in announcing its abiding attachment to the Absolute and the Sacred and its choice to accept the rights of God before the rights of man, a truth which is also very much present in traditional Christianity as seen in the saying of Christ, "Seek ye first the kingdom of God and all else shall be added unto you." It is the attempt by the modern West to globalize the substitution of the "kingdom of man" for the "kingdom of God" and then label anyone who does not agree with this program as being intolerant that has taken away any claim to seriousness of much of the discourse that is now going on concerning intolerance and tolerance or human rights on a global scale.

Today we are not in a situation such as in the medieval period when the military power and economic power of civilizations were similar if not evenly matched. These days, there is no comparison in worldly power between the defenders of the priority of the rights of God and those of man not only globally but even within Western societies. The Islamic world, like what remains of other traditional civilizations, has little choice before this onslaught of alien ideas supported by overwhelming economic and military might. Those in the non-Western world who choose the favorite catchwords of this century such as democracy and human rights, whatever they might mean in a non-Western context, are endeared to the powers that be, while those who try to bring out their deeper implications as far as the Absolute and the Sacred are concerned are anathemized and not at all tolerated. We only have to wait now to see what the catchwords of the twenty-first century will be. The intolerance of the relativists against those who still hold on to the sense of the Absolute and the Sacred is a marked character of this period of human history. Intolerance continues with the same ferocity as ages gone by except that it is now camouflaged by the veil of hypocrisy according to which those who display such intolerance, evident in so many circles during the Rushdie affair, pose as champions of tolerance and identify their opponents as the only people who have a monopoly on intolerance.

These are factors which contribute to the difficulty of serious dialogue in today's world. One civilization, namely the Western, having broken from its Christian past, and possessing tremendous economic and military power, combined with unprecedented social disorder, defines itself as being open-minded, the champion of human rights and tolerance, but defines such terms in a particularly relativistic and secularistic manner, despite the presence of Christian, Jewish, and now to some extent Muslim voices within it. Moreover, although West is not the only civilization in the world, it acts as if its understanding of man, his rights and freedoms and relationships with God or lack thereof are global. It is, therefore, decidedly intolerant toward those opposed to its world view, while other civilizations now faced with the possibility of the very destruction of their particular identity are also intolerant toward the dominating power of the modern West.

The West traversed the path which led it where it is now as a result of its own inner forces and not because of the coercion of an outside force. In contrast, other civilizations, some of which, such as the Islamic, although still very much alive have not had in the recent past and do not have today the freedom and choice to decide their own futures according to the dynamics of *their* society and the principles which their people uphold. It is here that the question of tolerance and intolerance reappears. Muslims, like many others, are intolerant toward this situation of external coercion in which others, supported by extensive economic means and political pressures, want to decide for them the meaning of human life. Seeing their identity threatened not only by the external power of the West, but also by Westernized elements within their own society who are supported by the West, they have now become even more intolerant toward the modern Western world. In fact, however, they are not intolerant of the West itself, but of what the power of Westernization is doing to their society, culture, and even religion. Any society whose identity is threatened becomes intolerant of the forces which constitute that threat and the intolerance increases with the increase of the threat, for in this situation, there is not the question of complementary dualities such as the yin and yang but dualities which confront and annul each other. One cannot defend the kingdom of God and His absolute rights and at the same time, the kingdom of man and his claims to the absoluteness of his rights. One can tolerate individuals with the other view as many Muslims do not only tolerate but have close Western friends, but one cannot be tolerant toward a world view which is simply seeking to negate and obliterate one's own view of things. The West in fact displays the same intolerance, although it is not under economic or political pressure to conform to an alien perspective.

Where there is the least sense of threat to a country's identity or even economic welfare in the West, even the decorum of tolerance and human rights is cast aside as we saw in Europe during the last five years where a small decline in the economic situation caused an exponential rise of intolerance in such countries as France toward the very non-Europeans whose hard work for cheap wages helped the economic revival of the country. Who could have imagined that the country which from the eighteenth century became the vanguard of human freedom, anti-Christian rationalism, humanism, and free thinking and which also influenced the founders of America should demonstrate such intolerance toward those living for fifty years amidst its people, going to the extreme of banning Muslim girls from wearing scarfs to school. Far from condoning intolerance on the individual and social levels by certain Muslims, we wonder what the manifestation of tolerance and intolerance would be in the West, if the situation were reversed and the Islamic world were exercising as much pressure upon the West to conform to its point of view as the West is exercising upon the Islamic world.

The threat to the existence of any entity which is still alive brings with it resistance and intolerance toward whatever is threatening its existence, this being true both for the individual and for any human collectivity united as a society or civilization. Much of what is happening in the Islamic world is due to this fact and increases with the impending threat. Many Muslim societies feel threatened both from the outside and from the inside by forces closely allied to the outside without regard for the fact whether this situation is their fault, the fault of their leaders, the forces outside their boundaries, or all of them together. They are reacting in the manner of a living organism which becomes immediately intolerant toward the threatening element. The human body, for example, shows acute intolerance toward a foreign virus threatening its harmony and functioning. If it were to show tolerance, the body would become ill and possibly die. How tragic for a body which has lost its immune system and becomes over tolerant toward every foreign invasion!

Traditional Muslims always showed much greater tolerance toward others than the so-called "fundamentalist" Muslims do today, precisely because the former felt much less threatened as far as their identity and very existence were concerned than do the latter. But what I am most concerned about is that traditional Islam is still followed by the majority of Muslims who of all the different groups show the least degree of fanatical opposition to the West. It is an Islam which is very much alive and still remains very tolerant toward Christians and followers of other religions in its midst. But traditional Islam is also now being threatened. What it does not tolerate, therefore, is a world view which would deny ultimate truth altogether and which is moreover trying to impose this view upon Muslims. In such a situation the wise and the saintly cannot appeal to a transcendent truth of which Islam and this or that religion are different formal manifestations. There is in fact no common ultimate truth to be discovered in the present situation between the Islamic and the modern secularist view. The best that one can do is to have recourse to tolerance on the human level, provided each side respects the rights of the other and does not seek to impose itself by economic or cultural pressure, not to speak of political impositions, upon the other.

In the present context, therefore, where the modern West is trying to impose its view of things, which while being partial and even provincial is paraded as global and even "absolute," despite its constant change, Islam has no choice but to be intolerant toward what threatens its very existence. For Islam, the truth comes before all earthly considerations, and if forced to choose between the truth and tolerance based upon the destruction or marginalization of the truth, it would certainly choose the former and have tolerance toward the latter only on the condition that it not be imposed upon it by force. I think that many believing Jews and Christians in the West would also agree with this Islamic position, although not all dare speak about it clearly and openly rather than seeking to placate the secularizing other by bending their own teachings which, as a result, sometimes become hardly recognizable any more.

However, the problem of the Islamic world is not how to come to terms, tolerate, and even display empathy for traditional Judaism and Christianity which have so much in common with Islam. The problem is to have tolerance toward a world view which is simply the negation of Islam while at the same time seeks to impose itself upon the Islamic world. The Islamic world must learn to continue to strengthen its identity in the face of a powerful external threat always preaching to it the doctrine of human rights according to its own understanding while applying it selectively and only according to its worldly interests, and yet remain tolerant vis-à-vis this force at least on the human level. The difficult situation is complicated further by the tragedy of the lack of freedom by Muslims to charter their own course and work out a *modus vinendi* toward the modern West in conformity with their own principles and traditions. It is as if Americans and Europeans were forced from the outside to come to terms with Confucian ideas of filial piety without the freedom to react to such an alien idea creatively and freely.

As for the West and those who believe that tolerance is related to human rights defined according to a purely worldly notion of human existence and individualistic understanding of freedom, irrespective of whether man was created in the image of God or is simply an evolved ape, there is also an immense challenge but in the other direction. The challenge is how to be tolerant toward those who do not accept the Western definition of the human state, nor relativism and secularism, those who belong to other civilizations or even those within the West for whom the sense of the Absolute and the Sacred has not withered away and is not likely to wither away no matter how much one extols the glory of secularism. These beliefs will not disappear especially at a time when under the most secularist and worldly civilization ever known modern society is falling apart so rapidly from within.

The future of the world in the next few years and decades will depend obviously on how various world views and civilizations will be able to live together not simply under the banner of a relativistic and secularist view foisted by the West as global human rights, but after consideration of the different understandings of ultimate truth on the one hand, and its denial on the other. If all civilizations were still traditional, this task would have been much easier since one could not only speak of tolerance of other versions of the truth, but in the manner of a Rumi or Ramakrishna of the Truth which transcends all forms and is yet manifested in different sacred forms lying at the heart of different civilizations. One could also appeal to metaphysics and seek to understand the root of intolerance in certain types of dualities which characterize manifestation as such. But of course this is not now the case, and the challenge remains how to be tolerant of ideas, forms, and philosophies which negate one's world view at its very foundations.

Needless to say, no matter how difficult, the challenge must nevertheless be successfully answered. Interestingly enough, at this moment of history, the challenges to the Islamic world and the secularized West are in many ways reversed and opposed in nature. The Islamic world must learn to be tolerant of a world that threatens its very existence without losing its identity, and the secularized West must learn the very difficult lesson that its modernized understanding of man and the world is not necessarily universal and that it is not sufficient to boast of the virtue of tolerance while being totally intolerant toward all those who challenge the very premise of the secularist and humanist world view. Paradoxically enough, each side, the non-Western—especially the Islamic—and the Western have much to learn from each other, whether on a positive or negative manner, at this dangerous juncture of human history.

5

An Elephant, an Ocean, and the Freedom of Faith

David Cain

WHO DRAWS THE CIRCLE?

Do you remember Edwin Markham's little verse "Outwitted"?

> He drew a circle that shut me out—
> Heretic, rebel, a thing to flout.
> But love and I had the wit to win:
> We drew a circle that took him in![1]

Intolerance, toleration, and circles—an exclusive, out-shutting circle and an inclusive, in-taking circle. The exclusive circle of intolerance is so often drawn by fear, by xenophobia, and perhaps inadvertently, unsuspectingly, by language itself. "*Altérité*," "alterity," "otherness," or "that which is other" gestures toward "altarity" or an *other* otherness, which language would rape with words. In the words of Mark C. Taylor, "The word suffers crisis when a difference that is not the opposite of identity and an other that is not reducible to the same draw near."[2] The Latin *hostis* means "a foreigner, an enemy" and invites the invidious identification of the one with the other, moving to "hostile" and "hostility" rather than to "hostel" and "host." A familiar slogan proclaims, "Differences Enrich Us All"; though danger lurks in lodging positive address to difference in enrichment. What happens to differences when they do not "enrich," when they raise doubt and dis-ease, when they lower security and comfort, when they question, explicitly or implicity, one's attempts to make some sense of—to impose some order on—

existence? And if differences are not perceived as potentially posing such threats, are they perceived as—are they permitted to be—*different?* We are experts in the erosion of otherness.

Who draws the inclusive circle? "Love and I"—but many a monster has menaced in the name of "love"; and "I," alas, am unreliable, as when enrichment runs out and inconvenience or worse sets in. "Is it in the nature of religious belief to be intolerant?" This is one of the animating questions of our conference. Evidence apparently warranting an affirmative answer is everywhere at hand. Outbursts of toleration may appear to be "up to a point," with intolerance waiting in the wings. "Tolerance," from *tolerare*, "to bear, to endure"—and what does tolerance bear? Burden. What does tolerance endure? Distress, difficulty... difference. That is, the word *tolerance* readily connotes negativity. Among definitions are "to put up with" and "allowing what is not actually approved; forbearance, sufferance."[3]

Even apart from such connotation, toleration may mask indifference. I can be tolerant of what does not matter all that much to me. Søren Kierkegaard develops this suspicion, as when he refers to "our time [Denmark of the 1840s] when tolerance [*Tolerantsen*] is so broad or when indifference is honored in the name of tolerance."[4] Kierkegaard notes with approval Benjamin Franklin's suggestion that a kind of toleration is not "a fruit of reason but—of commercialism"[5] and mocks: "What a great asset toleration [is] to business—congratulations! I really believe that this is the explanation: business and shipping and railways and the whole secular amity—tolerance is an asset to all this. Long may it live!"[6]

Toleration as advantageous. Toleration as indifference. But, then, is the opposite of indifference—intense caring, zeal, passion—not intolerance? Yes. Kierkegaard is contemptuous of tolerance which is indifference, which is cowardice: "The Christian [in the Roman world] could have said: We few men, how in the world will we ever be able to convert a whole world; no, let us live quietly with our religion, a tolerated religion; Christ taken in among the other gods."

And now! Now Christianity is such a lost cause that they who insist they are the only Christians are slap-happy if they simply get permission to live for themselves, if their religion is tolerated or recognized like the other religions.[7]

> ... Christianity will actually have lost its cause—will have given up its sovereignty and be downgraded to wanting to live on equal terms with Judaism, paganism, and every other religion. Great God! Then Christ is not the Savior of the world if his followers could live to such a degree at peace with this assurance.[8]

But surely commendation of heroes of intense caring, zeal, passion is questionable—and dangerous.

EITHER/OR?

Let us not too quickly assume that we correctly see the alternatives, the all-too-evident-and-insistent alternatives: *either* zealous, intolerant heroes of Christianity *or* toleration, indifference, relativism, failure of faith. *Either das Ärgernis der Einmaligkeit*, the scandal of particularity, "Jesus Christ of Nazareth . . . for there is no other name under heaven . . . by which we must be saved"[9] *Extra ecclesium nulla salus, or* "Christ is not the Savior of the world" but, at best, one among many: *tolérance—cela ne fait rien*.

This apparently obvious alternative is false[10] An alternative to *either* faithful intolerance *or* to faithless tolerance is *faithful tolerance*; except let us tolerate "tolerance" no longer. Until a better term can be found, let us speak of "appreciation," granted the economic etymology: to appreciate, *ad*, to, and *pretium*, price, "to value; to esteem; to be conscious of the significance, desirability, or worth of . . . to recognize gratefully." "Appreciation": "sensitive awareness; discriminating perception or enjoyment, as of art."[11] "To esteem adequately or highly; to recognize as valuable or excellent; to find worth or excellence in," among other definitions in the OED is accompanied by an obsolete use which yet indicated appropriateness: "The action of praying for or invoking blessing on another."[12] So: *"faithful appreciation."*[13]

FREEDOM *OF* FAITH, FREEDOM OF *FAITH*

Faithful appreciation of otherness belongs to the freedom of faith. "The freedom of faith"—if we invest in the ambiguity of this "of" long enough, we can hear "freedom *from* faith": the freedom of faith is the freedom to be free of faith. This presupposition is decisive for these remarks. A faith which imposes itself forcefully is not faith; for force destroys freedom, and freedom is an essential condition of faith. Kierkegaard's philosophical pseudonym, Johannes Climacus, makes the point succinctly: "Without risk, no faith."[14] This view of faith holds implications for an understanding of the certainty of faith, for how one might come to embrace faith, and for the relationship between the two. We are in danger of being trampled, and no elephant is yet in sight.

The certainty of faith is not intellectual. Intellectually, what is fundamental is that faith is neither nonsense nor "blind"—be it ever so improbable.

Certainty, which is, at best, precarious and vagabond, is a function of one's lived resolve and resolve-wrestled experience. One tries to find some way in life, to celebrate the beauty and the wonder, to be at least a little honest about the atrocity, the harrowing, to hold together the contradictions and collisions of existence—outside and inside the "self"—in a way which enables one to live. To the extent that a risked faith sustains such effort, faith is indirectly validated; when experience resists faith's construal, faith is questioned, perhaps crushed. The declaration attributed to Luther at Worms, "*Hier stehe ich, ich kann nicht anders; so hilfe mir Gott!*" gets the tone right.[15] Why enter into this free and fighting risk? Because one can do no other; because one cannot say no; because one has fallen in love. Religions are love affairs, and any half-heated love affair (except "half-heated" and "love" are contradictory; love is qualitative) raises more questions than it answers.

Please note that I speak here as a Christian theologian. One stands *somewhere*. Luther stands *hier* and not there. I have referred to "religions," hoping to adumbrate an account of faith as risk in freedom which has force both within and beyond Christianity. But different accounts of faith can be given within Christianity, and to focus on "faith" is at once to shape one's reflections in ways more congenial to some religions than to others.

"Freedom of faith" may suggest freedom from faith but is primarily faith's freedom. Not least among manifestations of the freedom of faith is openness to otherness, including the otherness of others' faiths, of diverse religions: faithful appreciation.

Of course this declaration flies in the face of that caricature of faith as strait-jacket—frozen, rigid, tense, dense, and dangerous. The terrible truth is that this caraicature is too often not a caricature—and not faith.

WAYS TO AN OCEAN

Still no elephant. We would be fortunate if this absence were to continue. Meanwhile, an ocean enters by way of Henrik Ibsen's play, *Brand*. Brand—the name means "fire"—is on fire with religious zeal. After impressing villagers with his courage and strength, Brand is approached by one of the villagers with the request, "Be our priest." This exchange follows:

Brand: Ask anything of me, but not that.
I have a greater calling. I must speak to the world.
Where the mountains shut one in, a voice is powerless.
Who buries himself in a pit when the broad fields beckon?
Who ploughs the desert when fertile soil awaits him?

Man (*shakes his head*):
I understood your deeds, but not your words.

Brand: Ask no further; my time here is finished.
(*Turns to go*).

Man: Is your calling dear to you?

Brand: It is my life.

Man: If you give all, but not your life,
You give nothing.

Brand: One thing a man cannot give: his soul.
He cannot deny his calling.
He dare not block that river's course;
It forces its way towards the ocean.

Man: Yet if it lost itself in marsh or lake,
It would reach the ocean in the end, as dew.[16]

This image—reaching the ocean in investing oneself in the specificities of marsh and lake—concretely captures the potential of concreteness. Suppose that the way to the ocean of appreciateve openness to religious otherness is through faith, through trusting one's own tradition to offer resources for such openness and digging more deeply into it (precisely not backing off or "sitting loose" in an attempt to reach the ocean directly, on one's own terms, in one's own way). What if the presence of such resources were to be considered a kind of informal criterion of religious health? (Do we have "marsh or lake" or quicksand and bog?)

The decisive Christian "resource" for openness to otherness is Incarnation. Incarnation is both the freedom of the Christian God and the freedom of this God's creation and creatures. The word made flesh—"in-flesh-ment"—clears the fog of pantheistic, inevitable God relationship away. No divine hidden agenda haunts the ting-tang zing-zest of a world set free to be *real*. *This* God can be met or missed, risked or rejected, in freedom. Father William F. Lynch captures the scandal:

Against the background of enormous space time, at a completely specific and free moment in the millions of light years, within a body that occupies a few feet of the space of all our universes, [Christ] . . . seizes upon and declares importance and seriousness, his own. This is ironic, that this should happen at an infinitely small point in infinitely large space time. It is, in a completely literal way, the basic image of faith. I hope it is not blasphemous to say that it took imagination.[17]

Certainly it takes imagination to risk faith in this "image"—and perhaps a little madness, desperation, love. This is why faith imposed is faith destroyed and why no one can be faulted for saying no. The very particularity of the Christian faith sets others free to be non-Christians and non-Christians free to be other. Creatures made in the *imago dei*, in the image of a God of Incarnation, are equipped for a true *imitatio christi*. As God in Incarnation respects the integrity of creaturely otherness, so Christians are permitted, indeed, *impelled*, in ways precisely proportionate to the rigor of their faith, to intimations and, however haltingly, to imitations of Incarnation, to faithful appreciation. The more faith, the more freedom. Firmness of faith yields fullness of freedom. In faith, Christians are goaded into giving themselves away, into becoming "everything in turn to men [and women] of every sort."[18]

Incarnational investment in otherness does not mean capitulation. Becoming all things to all men and women does not translate into "When in Rome, do as the Romans do." God does not forfeit divine otherness in Incarnation—as crucifixion makes clear. Creaturely Incarnation imitation serves understanding; and understanding alone can be the basis of meaningful agreement—and of meaningful disagreement. Incarnation enables radical "dialogue."[19]

Dialogue to what end? Conversion? What of "The Great Commission"? "All authority in heaven and on earth has been given to me," says the resurrected Jesus at the close of Matthew's Gospel.[20] This need not mean that Christians should look out for and safeguard and seek to advance what they may take to be Jesus' interests when the worldly scene seems to suggest that Jesus is allowing his interests to slide. It means that Christians can trust Jesus and not the worldly scene. And what are these "interests"; what is the nature of this "authority"? "Go therefore and make disciples of all nations, baptizing them in the name of the Father and of the Son and of the Holy Spirit, teaching them to observe all that I have commanded you; and lo, I am with you always, to the close of the age."[21]

The interests and authority are incarnational. "Going" (*poreuthentes*) precedes "discipling" (the Greek reads, "*matheteusate panta ta ethne*," "disciple you all the nations") in more ways than one. Incarnational going affects the goer. Going is not the occasion but belongs to the act of "discipling." Incarnation is not a strategy but an end in itself. If the Christian God leaves open, indeed breaks open in Incarnation, creaturely response, so, presumbly, might the Christian. "But what of the salvation of the other?" A Christian is not in a position to prejudge or underestimate the grace of God, for a Christian is one who has been surprised and who lives unlikelihood. Or, in the droll observation of Wilfred Cantwell Smith, "It will not do, to have a faith that can be undermined by God's saving one's neighbour."[22] Does this mean, recalling Kierkegaard, that "then Christ is not the Savior of the world."? Not necessarily. It means that I am set free from playing savior in trying to invent ways to import Christ into otherness or vice versa.[23]

WHO SEES THE ELEPHANT?

Look! Over here! Here is an elephant, a true elephant, the elephant of religious truth. Whether or not an elephant never forgets, how can one ever forget this ecumenical elephant, the elephant of a familiar, many-versioned parable of blind persons who gropingly touch the trunk, tail, ear, foot, flank, tusk? Each person renders a description of what touch tells. The descriptions are strikingly different. A tail is not a tusk. And yet: one elephant. So, goes the parable, with different religions. Religions' descriptions are diverse, yet all are parts, little patches, limited pieces, of the one holy whole, the truth.

Who sees the elephant? The blind persons do not know they have an elephant by the tail—or toe. Who draws the circle? Who knows what the blind persons do not?[24]

John Hick sees the elephant,[25] and it is God. Hick is one of the more intrepid trespassers onto this treacherous terrain these days, calling for "a Copernican revolution in our theology of religions."[26] Jesus, the son, is not the sun, "the light of the world."[27] God is the sun: "The universe of faiths centres upon *God*, and not upon Christianity or upon any other religion. He is the sun, the originative source of light and life, whom all the religions reflect in their own different ways."[28] Hick sees the elephant—and swallows it. How? Is he not, with most of the rest of us, one of the blind persons, who precisely cannot reach out to embrace the whole of which the part he can contact *may be* a part? Johannes Climacus again: "I am only a poor existing human being who neither eternally nor divinely nor theocentrically is able to observe the eternal but must be content with existing."[29]

The Rig-Veda sometimes sees the elephant:

> They call it Indra, Mitra, Varuna, and Agni
> and also heavenly, beautiful Garutman:
> The real is one, though sages name it variously.[30]

Hermann Hesse sees some kind of elephant in that religious Esperanto, *Siddhartha*, where the elephant is fingertips, a smile, a "how." A "holy man [is holy] to his fingertips."[31] Kamala dies, looking up into Siddhartha's smile:

> It had been her intention to make a pilgrimage to Gotama, to see the face of the Illustrious One, to obtain some of his peace, and instead she had only found Siddhartha, and it was good, just as good as if she had seen the other.[32]

Siddhartha's friend, Govinda, reflects of Siddhartha, "[His] hands and feet, his eyes, his brow, his breathing, his smile, his greeting, his gait affect me differently from his thoughts."[33] Thoughts, teachings, words, elephant-part descriptions may vary but a holy "how" is one.

Suppose *how* one lives, far from unifying existence underneath diverse teachings, words, doctrines, "whats," more profoundly secures otherness?[34] That the childlike twinkle in the eye of a Buddhist can resemble freedom, peace, and joy in a Jew or Christian or Muslim or Taoist may be *seen*, *experienced*. That these citings and felt presences are analogous: yes; that they are the same is a grander claim.

Is the attempt, from one religious perspective or another, to draw an inclusive circle a temptation? Buddha an *avatar* of Vishnu, Jews and Christians "People of the Book," the "hidden Christ" of Hinduism? Back in the saving game, Christians may universalize "the Christ" and see Jesus as one manifestation thereof, one of the lights of the world.[35] Or, if there is no salvation outside of the church, perhaps a church—"invisible"—is outside the church; perhaps others are "anonymous Christians."[36] Perhaps all will have eschatological opportunity to confess, "Jesus is Lord!" Perhaps the mistake is to play God rather than to trust one's God.

Different religions may be different pieces of the great elephant puzzle of truth, but respect for otherness restrains specification of how your puzzle piece and mine fit into the whole. We rightly resist placement in one another's "systems." *If* I trust the particular, the marsh or lake of a specific religion, to direct me through itself and, hence, indirectly to the universal, the universal I reach may be an ocean of faithful appreciation of otherness. Down is up. I stand in openness, relinquishing control (or, rather, resisting the urge to try to claim control) *as if* in an inclusive circle, which I dare not draw. If I back off from the particular to aim directly at the universal, I reach an ocean of my own making, an ocean looking, on close inspection, very like an elephant. Up is down.[37]

Karl Barth, who is so easily misread on these and on other matters, asks by way of reminding:

Does it frighten us to discover how completely all that we are and do moves within the sphere of relativity? . . . *sub specie aeterni* . . . ["the great contradictions" of existence] are resolved into one comprehensive and unified view of life. This comprehensive view of life has never, however, had any concrete existence in itself, no man possesses it, for it is not what men comprehend, but that by which they are comprehended.[38]

Life is not a circus in which even one all-encompassing elephant parades before us. As Walter Lowe affirms, "the human calling is less to grasp than to be grasped."[39] or the human calling is to be called. This means the freedom to be finite rather than caught in a competitive climb toward the infinite, the eternal, the great elephant. Lowe has a dream: "The creation is free to be what it is: various, many-faceted, a festival of innocent difference."[40]

AS IF IN THE CIRCLE, WHO IS DRAWN?

The great Hasidic master, Menahem-Mendl of Kotzk, the Kotzker Rebbe, observes, "To avoid spending a lifetime tracking down truth, one pretends to have found it."[41] And perhaps it resembles an elephant. But not to pretend to find truth, to spend one's entire life searching for truth—is this not to live rudderless, anchorless, adrift in the ocean of existence, postponing commitment and commitment until one's avoidance votes no ("while the grass grows," warns Climacus, "the observer dies")?[42] Certainly not. One makes decisions. One takes risks. One risks answers. The point is *not* not to decide, commit, risk, answer. The point is *how one owns, how one holds* one's decisions, commitments, risks, answers.[43] Does one hold one's convictions defensively or openly in honesty, humility, and humor, rooted in an awareness of how one came and comes to stand where one stands? Because I can do no other does not mean that you can do no other. Your love need not threaten mine.

One of the most perceptive passages Kierkegaard penned may be placed just here:

If all the wonders of the world could be placed in your hands, everything, everything, and then add to that the willingness of the fates to humor your every whim—you might want to accept it, but on the condition that you and you alone would rule over your life, that there would be no God. Consider what you would lose, among other things, in having nothing, absolutely nothing, as the object of wonder, absolutely nothing impinging upon the shape of your life—absolutely nothing to wonder about, how wisely, how indescribably lovingly God has shaped your life.[44]

Absolutely nothing to wonder about . . .

Religions are commonly characterized as proffering different answers to essential questions of existence, sometimes as competing truth-claims, sometimes as diverse but noncompetitive poems, and as all manner of alternative in between. Assuredly, answers may be identified. But if one looks discerningly, these answers are often nuanced in indirection, in irony, in the decentering of the "answerer." In any case, the model of different religions flinging different answers at one another and at existence might benefit from meeting another model: religions as ways of wondering, of holding open the human by keeping essential questions of existence alive. Though different answers need not separate, we do *face one another* in voicing them, whereas questions bring us together. In having something to wonder about, in asking questions, we stand *side-by-side*, even in asking different questions and in asking them differently. Perhaps the challenge of the freedom of faith for faithful appreciation is to hold one's answers openly, as questions, so that one can remain alive while one lives—as if drawn in to a circle not of one's own design. We ask the question, "Who draws the circle?" A question asks us, "As if in the circle, who is drawn?"

NOTES

1. William L. Stidger, *Edwin Markham* (New York: The Abingdon Press, 1933), 137. Compare ibid., 264.

2. Mark C. Taylor, *Altarity* (Chicago: The University of Chicago Press, 1987), xxix.

3. *The Compact Edition . . . Dictionary,* revised edition, (1971), s.v. "Tolerance." II, 3343

4. Howard V. Hong and Edna H. Hong, ed. and trans., *Søren Kierkegaard's Journals and Papers* (Bloomington: Indiana University Press, 1967), 1:157 (#383). See also Johannes Climacus (Søren Kierkegaard), *Concluding Unscientific Postscript to Philosophical Fragments* (Princeton University Press, 1992), 1:567.

5. Hong and Hong, *Journals and Papers,* 4:450, (#4819).

6. Ibid.

7. Ibid., 4:480–481, (#4821).

8. Ibid., 1:243 (#599).

9. Acts 4. 10, 12, RSV.

10. Kierkegaard himself makes a distinctive move, avoiding this alternative through his treatment of "intolerance." He advocates intolerance but of a "suffering" kind: martyrdom's intolerance" (*Journals and Papers*, 4:479, #4817)—"Christianity detests the intolerance which wants to put others to death because of their faith. But to be personally willing to be put to death for one's faith—well, let us not overlook this—it, too, is intolerance, it is suffering intolerance" (ibid., 4:479 [#4817]).

11. Webster's *New Twentieth Century Dictionary,* 2nd ed., (1970), s.v. "Appreciation."

12. Ibid., 103.

13. Some distance obtains between "suffering intolerance" and "appreciation," yet the two are not irreconcilable.

14. Climacus, *Concluding Unscientific Postscript,* 204, 209.

15 See David Cain, "Motive and Mood in *The Concept of Anxiety," Liber Academiae Kierkegaardiensis,* vol. 8, *The Concept of Anxiety in Kierkegaard,* ed. Marie Mikulova Thulstrup (Kobenhavn: C. A. Reitzels Forlag, 1990), 78–83.

16. Henrik Ibsen, *Brand,* trans. Michael Meyer (London: Rubert Hart-Davis, 1960), 40–41.

17. William F. Lynch, *Images of Faith: An Explanation of the Ironic Imagination* (Notre Dame: University of Notre Dame Press, 1973), 95–96.

18. I Corinthians 9:22, NEB.

19. Of course, this is the reigning word today in the context of "global village" address to "religious pluralism."

20. 28: 18.

21. Matthew 28: 19-20.

22. Wilfred Cantwell Smith, *Religious Diversity* (New York: The Crossroad Publishing Company, 1982), 15.

23. See below, 13–14.

24. Lesslie Newbigen sees the issue keenly: "What is often not noticed is that this tale implies either a stupendous claim on the part of the teller or a confession of total agnosticism. Either it implies that the teller . . . knows the reality after which the religions of the world blindly grope. In that case we must ask him to share this knowledge with us, to allow us to test its claims. Or else it implies total agnosticism: the reality after which religions grope is unknowable, "*The Finality of Christ* (Richmond: John Knox Press, 1969), 17.

25. Or, if Hick does not *see* the elephant, he infers the existence of an elephant on the basis of blind persons' differing reports. See, e.g., John Hick, *God and the Universe of Faiths* (Oxford: Oneworld Publications Ltd, 1973), ch. 10.

26. John Hick and Brian Hebblethwaite, ed., *Christianity and Other Religions* (Philadelphia: Fortress Press, 1980), 181. The word *theology* is used so freely and often so unnecessarily if not so irresponsibly, why not speak of a "theology of religions"? Because one might choose to chasten the use of "theology" instead.

27. John 9:5.

28. John Hick and Brian Hebblethwaite, ed. *Christianity and Other Religions*, 182.

29. Climacus, *Concluding Unscientific Postscript*, 212.

30. Hick quotes this verse in *God and the Universe of Faiths*, op. cit., p. 140. See also Radhakrishnan, Sarvepalli and Moore, Charles A., Eds., *A Source Book in Indian Philosophy* (Princeton: Princeton University Press, 1957), 21 ("To Vísvedevas," Rig-veda I.164.46).

31. Hermann Hesse, *Siddhartha,* trans. Hilda Rosner (New York: New Directions Publishing Corporation, 1951), 23.

32. Ibid., 93.

33. Ibid., 120. The villager in *Brand* had said, "I understand your deeds, but not your words."

34. Climacus makes this claim: "The decision rests in the subject; the appropriation is the paradoxical inwardness that is specifically different from all other inwardness. Being a Christian is defined not by the 'what' of Christianity but by the 'how' of the Christian. This 'how' can fit only one thing, the absolute paradox [the God in time]" (*Concluding Unscientific Postscript,* 610–11).

35. See, e.g., Peter L. Berger, *A Rumor of Angels: Modern Society and the Rediscovery of the Supernatural* (Garden City, N.Y.: Doubleday & Company, Inc., 1969), 92–93. Berger writes, "I see Christ as historically manifested in Jesus but not historically given." (92).

36. This is Karl Rahner's infamous designation. See, e.g., "Christianity and the Non-Christian Religions," in Hick and Hebblethweite, eds., *Christianity*, 76–79.

37. Lynch speaks of "a specious eternity" in William F. Lynch, *Christ and Apollo: The Dimensions of the Literary Imagination* (New York: Sheed and Ward, 1960), 45. These reflections are informed by Lynch's declaration, "There are no shortcuts to beauty or to insight. We must go *through* the finite, the limited, the definite, omitting none of it lest we omit some of the potencies of being-in-the-flesh" (23).

38. Karl Barth, *The Epistle to the Romans,* trans. Edwyn C. Hoskyns (London: Oxford University Press, 1933), 465.

39. Walter Lowe, *Theology and Difference: The Wound of Reason* (Bloomington: Indiana University Press, 1993), 142. Lowe refers perceptively to Barth.

40. Ibid., 143.

41. Elie Wiesel, *Souls on Fire: Portraits and Legends of Hasidic Masters,* trans. Marion Wiesel (New York: Random House, 1972), 241.

42. Climacus, *Concluding Unscientific Postscript,* 32.

43. How one holds one's conviction can be powerfully affected by the conviction one holds. Do we have here a hint of something so bold, so dangerous, as a criterion for genuine religious convictions and, hence, for inauthentic ones? C. S. Lewis' *An Experiment in Criticism* is the development of the idea that how a book can be read may tell on literary quality. Good books can be read badly as can poor ones. But is it the case that only good books can be read well? See Lewis, *An Experiment in Criticism* (Cambridge, Mass.: Cambridge University Press, 1969), 104–119. Analogously, genuine religious convictions can be held wrongly but perhaps only genuine religious convictions can be held rightly. Rightly? Openly, freely, humbly.

44. Hong and Hong, *Journals and Papers,* 2:64 (#1254).

6

Kierkegaard and Tolerance

Edwin C. George

In his *Letters from the Earth*, Mark Twain observes, "Man is the only animal that has the True Religion—several of them."[1] He goes on to relate an interesting experiment:

> In an hour I taught a cat and a dog to be friends. I put them in a cage. In another hour I taught them to be friends with a rabbit. In the course of two days I was able to add a fox, a goose, a squirrel and some doves. Finally a monkey. They lived together in peace; even affectionately.
>
> Next, in another cage I confined an Irish Catholic from Tipperary, and as soon as he seemed tame I added a Scotch Presbyterian from Aberdeen. Next a Turk from Constantinople; a Greek Christian from Crete; an Armenian; a Methodist from the wilds of Arkansas; a Buddhist from China; a Brahman from Benares. Finally, a Salvation Army Colonel from Wapping. Then I stayed away two whole days. When I came back to note the results, the cage of Higher Animals was all right, but in the other there was but a chaos of gory odds and ends of turbans and fezzes and plaids and bones and flesh—not a specimen left alive. These Reasoning Animals had disagreed on a theological detail and carried the matter to a Higher Court.[2]

We laugh at this, and yet we recognize that it captures a sad truth about religion. Religion has become a means of divisiveness, setting man against man rather than bringing them together. It has become a primary vehicle for intolerance of every kind. Religion has shown itself to be, as Alfred North Whitehead aptly put it, the last refuge for human savagery.[3]

Christianity has not been an exception. It has by many accounts supplied the rule. But is this *necessarily* the case? Is intolerance toward other religions or secular nonbelievers an intrinsic part of being a Christian? This is a question which warrants serious consideration, and I propose to approach it in what follows by drawing upon the thought of Søren Kierkegaard.

Let's suppose, for the sake of argument, that the answer to the question is no, Christianity is not intrinsically intolerant. To the contrary, we will suppose that it provides a sound basis for religious tolerance. If this is true, as Kierkegaard believes to be the case, we are forced to find some other explanation for the source of intolerance. One logical place to look would be to the individual believers. It could be that those who profess Christianity have simply failed to realize the standards which Christianity sets for the believer. And it could be that those who profess Christianity have a complete misunderstanding of what being a Christian is all about.

Kierkegaard, for his part, was not willing to assume that those who professed Christianity were actually Christians. In his view, the vast majority of so-called Christians lived in categories totally foreign to Christianity. As he saw it, a great deal of effort was expended in coming to 'understand' Christianity, but very little in actually proving that one did understand it by 'doing' what it proposed. There was even a lot of talk in his day about 'going beyond' Christianity. Kierkegaard, of course, found such talk ironical. For him, to go beyond anything assumed that one had already made it up to the point that one had claimed to surpass. And, once again, this was an assumption that he was unwilling to make, in regards both to himself and to the age in which he lived. His primary ambition was not to go further than Christianity, but to go further in becoming a Christian. The implication of this thought for our purposes is that if individuals would concentrate on where they stood in this regard, there might be no need to speak of intolerance.

Thus, in a very general way, we could say that Kierkegaard's response to the problem of intolerance would be that those who profess Christianity should actually live it. "Truth," he says, "is that one's life must express what one says."[4] But Kierkegaard was also aware that this is a difficult course to follow—one which is made no easier if one lives in an age which obscures the difficulty or loses sight of the standard altogether. Such an age was that in which Kierkegaard lived, and it is that age to which we today are heir. His critique of the age in which he lived is, therefore, quite relevant to our own times. In particular, I believe his critique can give us insight into the nature of intolerance and enable us to envision how Christianity, as he understood it, provides a possible alternative to it.

"Let others complain that the age is wicked," says Kierkegaard (through one of his pseudonyms), "but my complaint is that it is paltry; for it lacks passion."[5] Kierkegaard was oppressed by the mediocrity which surrounded him. As he described it, the age in which he lived tended toward momentary bursts of enthusiasm, followed by periods of indolence and apathy. It was a time in which reflection and understanding had gone awry. It was an age which was easily convinced that thinking about something was just as good as doing it. Kierkegaard contrasted his reflective age with a more passionate age by relating a story of a jewel on thin ice:

> If the jewel which every one desired to possess lay far out on a frozen lake where the ice was very thin, watched over by the danger of death, while, closer in, the ice was perfectly safe, then in a passionate age the crowds would applaud the courage of the man who ventured out, they would tremble for him and with him in the danger of his decisive action, they would grieve over him if he were drowned, they would make a god of him if he secured the prize. But in an age without passion, in a reflective age, it would be otherwise. People would think each other clever in agreeing that it was unreasonable and not even worth while to venture so far out. And in this way they would transform *daring and enthusiasm* into a *feat of skill*, so as to do something, for after all "something must be done." The crowds would go out to watch from a safe place, and with the eyes of connoisseurs appraise the accomplished skater who could skate almost to the very edge (i.e. as far as the ice was still safe and the danger had not yet begun) and then turn back.[6]

Something must be done, but as we see in this parable the appearance of having done something, an outward expression of some sort, will count as good money. However, money is only an abstraction. It is merely representative of something which possesses true value. And it is a true indictment of an age that it comes to value an abstraction or representation to the exclusion of the concrete. "In the end," Kierkegaard writes, "money will be the one thing people desire."[7]

Kierkegaard saw this desire for money as symptomatic of a large-scale leveling of society. This leveling process he described as a "mathematical and abstract occupation" which reduces everything to a common denominator.[8] It was the attempt to define the individual in terms of his membership in the human race rather than in terms of his concrete relations, thus reducing him to an interchangeable, numerical representative of the anonymous 'public'. It was, in effect, the "victory of abstraction over the individual."[9]

Though this leveling characteristic of the age tended toward equality, it was, according to Kierkegaard, merely a numerical equality, an equality of sameness. "The abstract principle of levelling," he writes, "like the biting east wind, has no personal relation to any individual but has only an abstract relationship which is the same for every one."[10] There is a unity of sorts, but it is "the negative unity of the negative reciprocity of all individuals."[11] Clearly, this sort of equality is no basis upon which to build tolerance. To the contrary, it is an equality which will not tolerate difference. It is an uneasy equality motivated by an envy and resentment which constantly guards against qualitative distinction by leveling everything. In the final analysis, as an equality which emphasizes sameness, it renders tolerance, not possible, but irrelevant.

Kierkegaard complained that the qualitative differences which formerly determined relations had disappeared. He relates that "the distance separating a thing from its opposite in quality no longer regulates the inward relation of things. All inwardness is lost, and to that extent the relation no longer exists, or else forms a colourless cohesion."[12] What this meant in terms of human relationships was that the principle of association which was to unite them became something which is external to the parties involved. This 'externality' was the very essence of the clannishness which Kierkegaard so abhorred. It reduced both parties to the role of observers *of* each other rather than being related *to* one another within the relationship. In such a relationship, the distance between self and other is overcome, but this is ultimately because the difference between them is never fully recognized. It is an illusory togetherness with no real substance. In the end, both the self and the other disappear into an abstraction and no truly personal relationships ensue because neither has achieved the status of personhood.

In Kierkegaard's opinion, these tendencies just described found their fullest expression in the philosophy of Hegel. Kierkegaard was adamantly opposed to this idealistic philosophy and its pretensions to lead to absolute knowledge. In particular, Kierkegaard opposed the Hegelian notion of the mediation of opposites into a higher unity. This notion, introduced into Hegel's logic, described a necessary movement by which something generates its opposite by means of self-negation and then by means of another negation mediated the two terms into a higher synthesis. Employing this logic, Hegel felt he could describe the historical development of God and the world.

Kierkegaard objected that the necessity upon which Hegel insisted completely abrogated the role of the existing individual. The identity or mediation he described came about without any decisive action on the part of those involved. What is more, his notion of mediation did not allow for the opposites involved to be truly opposite. Self and other were merely moments in an all-inclusive movement of the world spirit. And despite the Hegelian insistence that the higher unity established an "identity-in-difference," Kierkegaard felt that the differences were never fully established and therefore the subsequent identity claimed was spurious.

In opposition to Hegel's systematic pretensions, Kierkegaard championed the category of the individual. "The individual," he says, "is the category through which, in a religious aspect, the age, all history, the human race as a whole, must pass."[13] This individual was neither the abstract epistemological subject of speculative philosophy nor the ephemeral representative of the race, or the abstract public but, rather, the single, concrete, unique individual which each person essentially is. For Kierkegaard, it was only in becoming an individual in this sense—a possibility equally accessible to each and every person—that the tendency of the age could be resisted and overcome. What is most important, it was only in becoming such individuals that a true basis for human community could come about.

Ultimately, then, in Kierkegaard's view, the only way to rescue the age was "the religious singling out of the individual before God."[14] In being singled out, the individual comes to exist alone before God. She is extricated, as it were, from the crowd or the public and for the first time is truly an individual. At the same time, by virtue of this relation to God, all other persons come into existence for her as individuals. This singling out enables one to relate to the other as truly other, and yet, according to Kierkegaard, the "other" is always viewed in Christian terms as one's neighbor. Thus, the distance between self and other is to be overcome, not by logical necessity, but by means of an act of love.

Stated otherwise, God becomes the "middle-term" between man and man.[15] This is, in effect, another sort of leveling. But, in contrast to the leveling detailed above, it is a *leveling up* which brings about the essential equality of each person as a unique individual. It is this equality which, for Kierkegaard, establishes the basis for true humanity. He writes,

> If complete equality were to be attained, worldliness would be at an end. But is it not a sort of obsession on the part of worldliness that it has got into its head the notion of wanting to enforce complete equality, and to enforce it by worldly means . . . in a worldly medium? It is only religion that can, with the help of eternity, carry human equality to the utmost limit—the godly, the essential, the non-worldly, the true, the only possible human equality. And therefore (be it said to its honour and glory) religion is the true humanity.[16]

It is upon this that Kierkegaard would base an understanding of religious tolerance. The God relation singles each person out as an individual. This relation establishes the essential equality, not *sameness*, of all humans and, at the same time, establishes each individual as a unique, irreplaceable center of value. In the God relationship, the individual simultaneously recognizes her own infinite worth and the worth of others for, says Kierkegaard, "to have individuality is to believe in the individuality of every other person."[17] However, intolerance has its roots in small-mindedness. It is only small-mindedness which sees the individuality of another as a threat or refutation of its own individuality: "Small-mindedness . . . demands of God . . . that every individual characteristic be destroyed so that it can appear that small-mindedness is right and that God is a zealous God-zealous for small-mindedness."[18] This is to behave as if God could not stand individuality whereas, in truth, God is the source and origin of all individuality.[19] Kierkegaard observes:

> Christianity has not wanted to storm forth to abolish distinctions, neither the distinction of prominence nor that of insignificance, nor has it wanted in a worldly manner to make a worldly compromise between distinctions; but it wills that differences shall hang loosely about the individual, loosely as the cloak the king casts off in order to show who he is, loosely as the ragged costume in which a supernatural being has disguised itself. When distinctions hang loosely in this way, then there steadily shines in every individual that essential other person, that which is common to all men, the eternal likeness, the equality.[20]

For Kierkegaard then, there was no doubt but that Christianity does provide a basis for tolerance. However, a difficulty still remained. The leveling tendency characteristic of the age had also had its effect upon Christianity, making it hard to determine exactly what being a Christian entailed. As we have seen, many people thought they already were Christians. According to Kierkegaard, this confusion was due, in part, to the way in which Hegelian philosophy had transformed the existential task of becoming a Christian into the intellectual task of understanding Christianity. Kierkegaard's notion of 'subjectivity is truth', though perhaps not definitive of his final position concerning Christianity, was meant to be a corrective to this misunderstanding. This notion is of concern to our present discussion because it contains a further implication for our understanding of tolerance.

His formal definition of subjectivity is truth reads as follows: "An objective uncertainty held fast in an appropriation-process of the most passionate inwardness is the truth, the highest truth attainable for an existing individual."[21]

Kierkegaard arrives at this definition by means of a critique of an objective approach to Christianity. The objective approach attempts to determine the truth of Christianity. In order to do so, it must consider Christianity primarily as a historical phenomenon. However, the greatest certainty that can be obtained with respect to anything historical is only approximate. One can never know for sure that the biblical texts are authentic or that the historical witnesses are reliable. There is always the possibility of uncovering some new evidence that places everything in question. It is thus, he concludes, "impossible in the case of historical problems to reach an objective decision so certain that no doubt can disturb it."[22] To require such certainty is not only an unrealistic craving for a superstitious security, it is entirely "incommensurate with an infinite personal interest in an eternal happiness."[23]

This infinite personal interest in an eternal happiness is what, according to Kierkegaard, Christianity presupposes. An objective approach can bring one no closer to this understanding of Christianity not only because of the uncertainty of ever arriving at any conclusive results, but also because it cancels out precisely that interest on the part of the individual which Christianity presupposes. A commitment to objectivity ultimately consigns one to always remaining on the outside, trapped in a comical, contradictory indifference regarding that which concerns, or should concern, one most. And while Christianity requires a decision on the part of the individual to relate oneself to the truth it proposes, the objective observer must continually postpone this act.

For Kierkegaard, to relate to the truth in the objective manner is to forget that one is an existing individual human being. In essence, the objective approach reduces the concrete individual to the role of an anonymous and timeless, epistemological subject, and to confuse oneself with this fictitious abstraction, according to Kierkegaard, is to be duped.

However, Christianity is concerned with the subject as an existing individual and with the subject's transformation in himself.[24] Yet, in the attempt to become an objective observer, the individual in this sense disappears entirely. Christianity requires an existential understanding, for it is concerned that the individual *exist in* the truth which it proposes. Therefore, a merely intellectual understanding of Christianity is nothing short of a misunderstanding.

To raise the question of truth subjectively, as Kierkegaard would have us do, is to concentrate on *how* we are related to the truth, that we in fact relate the truth to our own life. Kierkegaard writes: "When the question of the truth is raised subjectively, reflection is directed subjectively to the nature of the individual's relationship; if only the mode of this relationship is in the truth, the individual is in the truth even if he should happen to be thus related to what is not true."[25]

At this point, I believe we can begin to see an important implication for our understanding of tolerance. The objective indeterminateness of Christianity suggests that it is fruitless to be concerned with *proving* it to be true. Even were this possible, Kierkegaard questions whether one would thereby be related to this truth, for it is always conceivable that one could still refuse to associate oneself with this truth. The subjective approach to truth places the accent squarely on appropriation and suggests that our concern for the truth should be with *making* it true that it is true for us. In *Christian Discourses*, Kierkegaard writes: "With all this proving and proving it has been forgotten that the highest thing a man is capable of is to make an eternal truth true, to make it true that it is true . . . by doing it, by being himself the proof, by a life which also perhaps will be able to convince others."[26]

If, as Kierkegaard has suggested, Christianity is not something which can be determined objectively, then the attempt to appeal to the objective truth of Christianity in order to establish one's own superiority, or in order to forcibly compel assent, would have no convincing basis from which to proceed. Therefore, there would be no grounds for intolerance. As a subjective undertaking, becoming a Christian will necessarily remain the *free decision* of the individual, and, unlike the certainty of knowledge, a decision will always retain an element of risk.

This brings us to our final consideration. This decision to become a Christian is not to be understood as a one-time occurrence. Kierkegaard conceives of becoming a Christian as a lifelong task, to come to the point of decision and then to continuously repeat it. As a concrete human being one is always in a state of becoming, and thus one is never complete. This is especially true as regards the process of becoming a Christian. This constant striving, I suggest, is another reason why intolerance is not intrinsic to the Christian experience.

Kierkegaard's emphasis on becoming and repetition is his way of drawing attention to the strenuousness of becoming a Christian. And, quite frankly, to be overly concerned about another person's progress along the path is, for Kierkegaard, a distraction. If one is really concerned with the truth, one will eschew comparisons with others altogether. This theme runs throughout Kierkegaard's writings. In his journals he writes:

> The thing I cannot really understand in the orthodox Christian view is that in the relation of the individual to God there should be any comparison with others, so that, by the very fact of his relations to God, he becomes conscious of how others relate themselves to God, whether they are happy or not, whether they do God's commands or not etc. [27]

Kierkegaard finds that the happiness of the God relation can only be reduced by "drawing the worldly comparison that my enemies will be excluded from it."[28]

Becoming a Christian, for Kierkegaard, requires a singleness of mind and purpose. It requires the individual to be concerned first and foremost with discerning his own responsibility and fulfilling it. In *Works of Love,* we read:

For the divine authority of the Gospel speaks not to one man about another man, not to you, the reader, about me, or to me about you— no, when the gospel speaks it speaks to the single individual. It does not speak *about* us men, you and me, but it speaks *to* us men, you and me, and it speaks *about* the requirement that love shall be known by its fruits.[29]

Flannery O'Connor once wrote, "The first product of self-knowledge is humility."[30] Kierkegaard would have agreed whole-heartedly. It is, ultimately, this fruit which will not allow intolerance an entry into the life of a Christian. Humility is the fruit of a "religiosity of hidden inwardness [which] does not permit the individual to regard himself as better than any other human being; nor does it permit him to be distinguished by the God-relationship in any other way than every human being can be, much less more distinguished than others."[31]

I do not claim to have "proven" anything here. And certainly I have not undertaken to deny the intolerance which has, unfortunately, been associated with Christianity throughout the ages. It is hoped, however, that some of the things which Kierkegaard has said, and which I have related here, will prompt us to think again about the relation of Christianity to tolerance and, in particular, to reconsider whether Christianity is itself the source of the intolerance which has been committed in its name.

NOTES

1. Mark Twain, *Letters from the Earth* (New York: Harper & Row, 1962), 227.

2. Ibid., 228.

3. A. N. Whitehead, *Religion in the Making* (New York: The MacMillan Company, 1926), 36.

4. Søren Kierkegaard, *Training in Christianity*, trans. Walter Lowrie (Oxford: Oxford University Press, 1941), 229.

5. Søren Kierkegaard, *Either/Or Volume I*, trans. David and Lillian Swenson (Princeton: Princeton University Press, 1971), 27.

6. Søren Kierkegaard, *The Present Age,* trans. Alexander Dru (New York: Harper & Row, 1962), 38.

7. Ibid., 40.

8. Ibid., 51.

9. Ibid., 52.

10. Ibid., 57.

11. Ibid., 52.

12. Ibid., 43–44.

13. Søren Kierkegaard, *The Point of View for My Work as an Author*, trans. Walter Lowrie (New York: Harper & Row, 1962), 128.

14. Kierkegaard, *The Present Age*, 53.

15. Søren Kierkegaard, *Works of Love*, trans. Howard and Edna Hong (New York: Harper & Row, 1962), 212.

16. Kierkegaard, *Point of View*, 108. The translator's footnote to this passage is revealing: "A serious play on words was made possible here by the fact that in Danish the word for human equality is *Menneskelighed* (literally, human-likeness), and that worldliness is *Verdslighed* (world-likeness)—revealing what the English suffix obscures. Hence the argument: world-likeness emphasizes the differences and inequalities between man and man; the essential likeness and equality between men is apparent only before God, i.e. in religion; hence religion, since it establishes essential human equality, is humane in the highest sense, and as such is the realization of the fairest dream of the statesman who loves men and desires to affirm that 'A man's a man for a' that.' "

17. Kierkegaard, *Works of Love*, 253.

18. Ibid., 254.

19. Ibid., 253.

20. Ibid., 96.

21. Søren Kierkegaard, *Concluding Unscientific Postscript*, trans. David Swenson (Princeton: Princeton University Press, 1968), 182.

22. Ibid., 41.

23. Ibid., 26.

24. Ibid., 38.

25. Ibid., 178.

26. Søren Kierkegaard, *Christian Discourses*, trans. Walter Lowrie (Princeton: Princeton University Press, 1974), 104.

27. Alexander Dru, *The Journals of Søren Kierkegaard* (Oxford: Oxford University Press, 1938), 197, entry #639.

28. Ibid.

29. Kierkegaard, *Works of Love*, 31.

30. See Flannery O'Connor, "The Fiction Writer and His Country," in *The Living Novel: A Symposium*, ed. Granville Hicks (London: The Macmillan Company, 1957).

31. Kierkegaard, *Concluding Unscientific Postscript*, 456.

7

Faith and Intellectual Fairness

John Donovan

For the Hegelian, phronetic toleration replaces the lost Absolute. It is practical wisdom that, while retaining a substantive notion of the good, disciplines the urge toward the Aufhebung.

Is it in the nature of religious belief to be intolerant? Answers to this question are governed by one's conception of toleration as well as by one's understanding of the "nature" of religion,[1] or one's reasons for denying that religious belief has an essential nature. Given the broad range of discussion that such a combination of variables allows, I believe that the majority of them share a common presupposition. It is this. However one conceives of religious experience, and whatever notion of toleration is embraced, toleration is presented as a *constraint upon* religious experience "from without."[2] It is a constraint upon religion for the good of the other, whether that other be another religion, secular institutions nested in the same society with a religion, or an individual—a person of another faith, an agnostic, or an atheist. Less frequently, it appears as a constraint upon other institutions or individuals in a society in favor of religion's freedom of expression. In either case, toleration does not appear as a "religious virtue."

This chapter looks at a conception of toleration as a *self-regarding* virtue of religion, as a condition of the possibility of a religion's own flourishing, as a necessary condition for developing its essential possibilities. Moreover, I especially want to stress the intellectual component of such an interpretation of toleration: thus the title "Faith and Intellectual Fairness." I will argue that such a notion of toleration is best understood as a specification of the Aristotelian virtue *phronesis*. While doing this, I will show that attempts to think through the problem of religious toleration by seminal thinkers in the philosophy of religion have had the characteristic of a Kantian antinomy. I will argue that the reason for this is precisely because a concept such as *phronesis*, with its emphasis on practical truthfulness, was lacking. In short, an underplaying of the cognitive dimension of religious experience distorted phronetic toleration into antinomic toleration. The former is guided by an internal need for a respectful hearing and evaluation of claims that clash with my own, respectful at least in the sense that I recognize them as *truth* claims. To recognize them as truth claims means that I interpret their proponents to be saying something about the nature of things, and that claims they are making are right or wrong in an important practical sense. Moreover, "being wrong" about such claims means misunderstanding human agency in its search for fulfillment. The latter kind of toleration, antinomic toleration, places such claims outside the boundaries of the cognitive and interprets the existence of religious conflict as sufficient evidence that reason is simply out of its depth in such matters. Conflicting religious claims are merely "different" in a leveling sense that is unsurpassable.

I will begin my argument that—especially in the context of contemporary pluralism—toleration is best understood as a self-regarding virtue *of* religion by agreeing with Charles Taylor's description of human agency. Taylor's work is especially useful because it displays the complex set of conditions and problems at work in the West at the very time when the philosophy of religion was emerging as an academic discipline independent of confessional theology. Moreover, it was at this time that the concept of 'toleration' was being thematized. Agency in the context of modernity, Taylor tells us, should be studied through a retrieval of the "largely unarticulated understandings of the senses of inwardness, freedom, individuality, and being embedded in nature which are at home in the modern West."[3]

In part 1 of *Sources of the Self: The Making of the Modern Identity,*[4] Taylor presents a transcendental argument for the necessity of ontological frameworks—we might call them "spiritual road maps"—in articulating one's sense of self. It is just such necessity, moreover, that antinomic accounts of toleration attempt to operate without.[5] Taylor begins with a phenomenological description of a set of foundational identifications that are at the root of our spiritual and moral senses of self and then raises the question of the conditions of their possibility. At the basis of spiritual self-identity, he argues, is a set of "intuitions" that are, like the Roman god Janus, essentially two-faced. Thus it is easy to see them truly but describe them reductively by offering an account that is one-dimensional. They are, as the German word has it, *zweifach*: two layered and thus appear as both important but essentially ambiguous. Taylor unpacks these "laminated"[6] intuitions.

First, on the one side, they are "uncommonly deep, powerful, universal,"[7] and, as such, we are tempted to classify them as "instincts" in contrast to other moral and spiritual reactions that are more easily recognized as being rooted in our culture.

Second, they receive "variable shapes in culture,"[8] shapes that articulate the intuitions, giving them a dimension of intelligibility, allowing them to appear as *truth claims* that call for defense and generate debate as the subject of explicit judgments.

Third, they offer a triangulated picture of moral and spiritual goods to which we react as inchoate "selves." The first dimension's focus is on a sense of respect for or obligations to others. Normative ethics in the modern period has tended to focus on this axis and to explain moral experience through theories of *obligation*. The second dimension depicts the flourishing of fulfilled life, conceptions of the moral and spiritual good. It is especially on this level that skepticism has abounded, given a cultural pluralism that confronts us with a cacophony of conceptions of the good life. It is here that the strongest case is usually made for antinomic toleration. The third dimension's focus is on our recognitional agenda. Its concern is with notions of dignity which authors such as Hegel, in his famous lordship-bondage dialectic, have taken as foundational for the emergence of subjectivity.[9]

Having considered the distinct dimensions of such intuitions, let us turn to Taylor's description of them as generative of an inchoate self-identify. Our moral and spiritual reactions to such givens, he argues, are our most primitive activities as selves. Such reactions are "almost like instincts, comparable to our love of sweet things, or our aversion to nauseous substances, or our fear of falling; on the other hand they seem to involve claims, implicit or explicit, about the nature and status of human beings. From this second side, a moral reaction is an assent to, an affirmation of, a given ontology of the human."[10]

What distinguishes the set of intuitions which Taylor is attempting to display as the basis of selfhood from instinctual responses such as the fear of falling and stomach sickness? It is the phenomena *call* and *strong evaluation* that are part of them, and neither of which seem to be accounted for in antinomic views of toleration. Let us consider an example. Taylor offers the following: We experience life as calling forth a response of respect. For Taylor, such a call is part of the first profile of such intuitions discussed above, the "universalistic, almost instinctual" side. It is also true to experience that various cultures set the parameters of such respect through what Geertz has called "thick descriptions." This is the second profile, the culturally specific but also truth-claiming dimension of such intuitions. For most today, respect for the dignity of life has become "coterminous with the human race and for believers in animal rights, it may go wider."[11]

For example, if we observe those fighting for animal rights, both the truth-claim dimension of their position, and the sense that "what they see" in animal life is intrinsically connected to an authentic awareness of self-identity seems unmistakable. Life—in this example animal life—is experienced as *calling* for, demanding a response of reverence on our part. Those who miss this seem to be "getting it wrong," not "seeing what is there" rather than "creating an alternate set of values" which animal rights advocates must "tolerate." Those who do not "see," moreover, are making an important mistake on the level of praxis, regarding the truth about how we should live with other species on this planet.

This example allows us to focus on the *strongly evaluative* dimension of moral or spiritual ontologies of the human. It draws our attention to a reaction that such intuitions provoke. This reaction is the practical intellectual impatience that demands action; it is the disquietude of those who "see what should be done" *because* they "see what is there." It is unmistakable in the lives of those who believe themselves to be responding to great causes, to what Taylor calls "hypergoods."[12]

By way of contrast, a theory that simply interprets our animal rights advocates to be saying, "I feel this way; do so as well!" with the implied imperative that all, as leveled expressions of valuation, should be tolerated is simply a bad theory. Moreover, this example also gives us a clue as to why we should regard toleration as a self-regarding virtue for religion. It shows that there are concerns that call forth responses from and are constitutive of the deepest levels of our identity, but which traditional religious frameworks either do not articulate or whose articulations we judge to be wrong.

The *strongly evaluative* dimension of ontologies of the human confronts us with the practical truthfulness of their claims. Toleration among them must deal their cognitive claims. Their being strongly evaluative is registered by us as a distinction between how we in fact feel or desire—for instance, given our animal rights example, the desire for a hamburger—and the call of "what is desirable." Our experience seems to run counter to Mill's claim that the desirable is identical with what is in fact desired. Moreover, intuitions outside of the class of those making such strongly evaluative claims cannot be described in this way. To say that I experience rotten meat as nauseating, but that I *should not*, seems nonsensical. Taylor tells us that a "good test for whether an evaluation is 'strong' . . . is whether it can be the basis for attitudes of admiration and contempt."[13] His point is that intuitions significant for self-identity are experienced as claims which may conflict with or constrain our factual desires. Moreover, the experience of such conflict indicates an inchoate awareness—needing to be brought out in explicit judgments—that one can, by "following one's immediate wishes and desires, take a wrong turn and fail to lead a full life."[14] Our responses either lack or contain a kind of practical truthfulness.

It is this second dimension of the class of that we have been describing—their quality of embodying moral ontologies that constitutes and shapes them as inchoate truth claims. Moral ontologies make our seeing praxis-laden, displaying what things are, and what they are for, and who we are in our dealings with them. It is here—in this dimension of experience—that we uncover the root of the problem of toleration. We can present it by making three points:

First, ontologies of the human are unavoidable frameworks, but frameworks that our increasing awareness of the claims of cultural pluralism tempts us to ignore. Since we are socially conditioned by being brought up in different, often conflicting ontologies of the human, it is difficult to conceive of how we might adjudicate disputes on this level. There is a procedural bias, if Taylor is correct, that pushes us to simply accept, even celebrate, difference as difference: "The temptation is great to rest content with the fact that we have such reactions, and to consider the ontology which gives rational articulation to them to be so much froth, nonsense from a bygone age."[15]

Ontologies of the human, as articulations of "deep powerful and universal" human reactions, really are unsurpassable frameworks; however, theories that attempt to avoid them cannot be well informed. That is, they will operate off of a set of substantive presuppositions that officially they cannot acknowledge. Taylor's long study has as one of its central goals to show this specifically. Naturalistic, especially utilitarian, conceptions of agency seem to be his special target, but he also offers a sustained critique of the deconstructive celebration of difference.

Second, such frameworks are strongly evaluative. It is the nature of a moral ontology that it be a *truth claim*. He argues that "it is a form of self-delusion to think that we do not speak from a moral orientation which we take to be right. This is a condition of being a functioning self, not a metaphysical view we can put on or off."[16]

Taylor offers the *conflict* that accompanies such intuitions as phenomenological evidence of their truth orientation. Our reactions to them, while basic to our identity, are experiences as being accompanied by *conflict* as a kind of spiritual or moral static. It is a static notably absent from other universal reactions more properly classified as instinctual such as our nausea at certain smells. With the former,

> We don't acknowledge that there is something there to articulate, as we do in the moral case. Is this distinction illegitimate? A metaphysical invention? It seems to turn on this: in either case our response is to an object with a certain property. But in one case the property marks the objects as one *meriting* this reaction; in the other the connection

between the two is just a brute fact. Thus, we argue and reason over what and who is just a brute fact. Thus, we argue and reason over what and who is a fit object of moral respect, while this doesn't even seem possible for a reaction like nausea.[17]

The conflict, the spiritual and moral static that attends some of our intuitions, is generated by the fact that (a) we *see* the same things as our opponents; and (b) we *both see* such things *as important*; but (c) we read them as addressing us—as telling us that they are and what they are for—in contrary or contradictory ways.

Third, the modern West experiences frameworks themselves as problematic. There is a further phenomenon, one that specifies as distinctively Modern and Western the experience of conflict which I have described as a kind of static accompanying our basic spiritual and moral reactions: "Frameworks today are problematic . . . .What is common to them all is the sense that no framework is shared by everyone, can be taken for granted as *the* framework tout court, can sink to the phenomenological status of unquestioned fact."[18] There seems to be a gain and a loss here. The gain is an awareness of the angular nation of our spiritual road maps, a gain which is the root of my claim that we should see toleration as a self-regarding virtue. The loss is that we do not experience a specific road map as englobing the truths which are in fact constitutive of our identity. The implications here are first, that we cannot dispense with such ontologies, for they are constitutive of our self-identity, second, that we cannot and will not simply and playfully celebrate the differences among such ontologies. It is play in the sense of "playing with" because part of having a moral ontology is perceiving it as making truth-claims. For example, in the *Closing of the American Mind*, Bloom accuses Woodie Allen of "playing with his Jewishness"[19] in just this sense.

Third, we *cannot* see one ontology as having, in Taylor's words, "the phenomenological status of unequestioned fact." This implies that we tend to experience ourselves as being on *both* sides (or a number of sides) of the great spiritual and moral issues of the day. Our experience looks somewhat like this: we register the truthfulness to the claims about an individual's dignity *qua individual* which classical liberals clothe in the language of rights; we also see truth in the vision of communitarians such as MacIntyre. We cannot interpret our experience of the plurivocal call of moral ontologies as one that levels difference a simple cacophony of voices with their conflicting insistential calls, nor can we, as some passages of the encyclical *Veritatis Splendor* suggest, seem to experience a wholeness of truth in one vision that must be respectfully but insistently offered to those who do not quite "have it in focus" yet. Our experience of the pluralism of ontologies is an experience *both* of the attractiveness of their angular *intelligibility*, of their unique ability to show "what things are and what they are for," *and* of their essential incompleteness. There seems to be more to practical truthfulness than any one of them displays. Given this, and given the indispensable role that such ontologies play in constituting our self-identity, what is called for is an interrogation that takes truth claims of one's own ontology seriously, yet *for its own sake, in order to account for aspects of one's own identity,* remains open to truthfulness found in others, and is able to suggest a plausible, if tentative principle of evaluation of the practical truth claims found in each. This, I submit, is a heuristic sketch of *problem* of toleration. I will now show how Taylor's account attempts to fulfill these conditions by offering a conception of toleration as a form of moral reasoning that specifies Aristotle's notion of 'phronesis' to the modern Western context.

Taylor's discussion of moral reasoning begins by distinguishing the substantive accounts that characterized premodern philosophy from the proceduralist accounts that typify modern deontological and utilitarian conceptions. Proceduralist accounts locate the excellence of practical reasoning in correct method. Proceduralist justification "can't be defined by the particular outcome, but by the way in which the outcome is arrived at."[20] Proceduralist accounts, characterized by Taylor as "bad models of moral reasoning," look to resolve practical disputes by searching for criteria that are both *neutral* (able to be established "even outside the perspectives in dispute") and yet *decisive* (practically motivating: sufficient to cause me to "change my mind" regarding the proper way to act.) In Taylor's words:

> As long as the wrong, external model of practical reasoning holds sway, the very notion of giving a reason smacks of offering some external considerations, not anchored in our moral intuitions, which can somehow show that certain moral practices and allegiances are correct. An external consideration in this sense is one which could convince someone who was quite unmoved by a certain vision of the good that he ought to adopt it, or at least act according to its prescriptions.[21]

Substantive accounts, on the contrary, see the evaluation of practical reasoning as a function of the conception of the good life that emerges from it. "To be rational was to have the correct vision, or in the case of Aristotle's *phronesis*, an accurate power of moral discrimination."[22] That is, one "reasons morally" by thinking within the call of a good. (Taylor, as we have seen, has argued that our fundamental intuitions are experiences both as calls of the good, and as invitations to think.) The reason that I am calling such a practical reason an exercise in toleration is that our situation, as we have seen, is that we must reason within the context of the call of conflicting goods. Given this context, it will be insufficient simply to employ Aristotle's conception of practical wisdom in maximizing and ordering goods. Rather, *phronesis* must be considered as suggesting a model of substantive moral reasoning, whose conditions can be met in the context of contemporary pluralism.

Aristotle's own account of such substantive practical thinking has the following characteristics:

1. He characterizes *phronesis* as a state of grasping the truth about what is good or bad for humans. To do this, "we should first study the sort of people we call practically wise."[23] This implies that we already "see" and in an inchoate way "understand" what we are trying to study: the nature of the good life in general.
2. Practical reasoning, though it depends upon such an inchoate vision of the good life, is a move from vagueness to clarity. Its deliberation identifies the sorts of actions and states that living well consists in.
3. As deliberative, its scope is limited to *praxis*: no one deliberates about what cannot be otherwise, or what cannot be achieved by her action. Also, it is not *simply* deliberative in the sense that the end at which it aims is simply taken for granted. This would be mere cleverness.
4. While distinct from the moral virtues, it is inseparably present with them. The Humean distinction between reason and desire is not operative here, as it is not in Taylor's notion of an "intuition." Vices are a habitually bad attunement, a sort of spiritual atmosphere that prevents the kind of understanding of the good at which phronesis aims. Thus, if we see what is right, but our doing of what is wrong becomes habitual, we will no longer "see" it as wrong.
5. Phronesis as practical wisdom is a grasping of the general in the particular. It is a seeing of *this* situation as the kind that leads toward or away from happiness. It is not a special "moral sense," but an exercise of practical intelligence. It is an understanding that recognizes opportunities to move toward or away from one's goal. Taylor's "intuitions" should be read in this way.

Taylor adapts the following version of Aristotelian moral discrimination to a context in which we experience the competing calls and conflicting strong evaluations of various moral ontologies:

Practical reasoning . . . is reasoning in transitions. It aims to establish, not that some position is correct absolutely, but rather that some position is superior to some other. It is concerned, covertly or openly, implicitly or explicitly, with comparative propositions. We show one of these comparative claims to be well founded when we can show that the move from A to B constitutes a gain epistemically. . . .The argument fixes on the nature of the transition from A to B. The nerve of the rational proof consists in showing that this transition is an error-reducing one. The argument turns on rival interpretation of possible transitions from A to B, or B to A."[24]

Taylor's account is substantive. Practical reasoning is a showing that the good that a person has already recognized is more practically comprehensible (can be attained by intelligent action) from another perspective. It is "reasoning in transitions." To be reasonable in this sense requires the best sense of what we call "toleration." To be reasonable from this point of view is to recognize the other's experience of and participation in worthwhile goods, and to address her as such. Substantive views of moral reason, as we saw above, think within the call of goods. What is new here is the conception that there must now be a kind of agnostic substantiveness. We see ourselves in the context of more than one ontology in a way that Aristotle did not, and our moral reasoning is an attempt to overcome the distraction, the dispersal of our selves into higher, integrative viewpoints. Moreover, to engage in this type of reasoning is to at least implicitly acknowledge that there may be perspectives, ontologies of the human, that we would have to admit are more powerful articulations of our own notion of the good than our present perspective. To be reasonable is to be "open to transitions." This is what I am terming *"phronetic toleration"* as a self-regarding virtue. But how do we become practically reasonable in such a fashion, given our situatedness in one framework, one ontology of the human?

Aristotle's answer is that "we should first study the sort of people we call practically wise." He meant for the most part his fellow citizens. Taylor modifies this to the claim that the "form of practical reasoning has its source in biographical narrative."[25] If practical reasoning is reasoning about transitions from worse to better ways of seeing and moving toward important goods, then specific arguments persuade by defending concrete conceptions of human development toward them. Such claims are always open to challenge, and the word "genealogy is the name for this kind of probing. . . . Genealogy goes to the heart of the logic of practical reasoning. A hypergood can only be defended through a certain reading of its genesis."

Genealogy will be a study of how one ontology came to better account for people's experience of the good life than its rivals. The most obvious examples would be Nietzsche's account of the triumph of slave morality or Foucault's deconstructions. As both of these examples suggest, critical inquiry into the claims of a particular ontology to offer a more powerfully practical account of the good life may unmask the claims as failures or frauds. But there is no a priori necessity that genealogical reflection must move in the direction of a hermeneutic of suspicion. Taylor's claim is that genealogical arguments may show that (1) some human goods have in fact been lost by transitions to higher ones; and (2) that viewpoints that have succeeded in overcoming others are themselves always in principle open to the critique of more powerful ontologies. Moreover, given our experience that no framework is catholic, our practical intelligence's drive toward the good demands such genealogical reflection which may unmask our present conceptions. This is a further specification of phronetic toleration.

I would now like to apply these thoughts to the relationship between religion and this conception of toleration as a self-regarding virtue. It is commonplace to claim that (1) religion (Judaism, Christianity, Islam) serves as an over-arching spiritual road map, interpreting our fundamental intuitions of the good life, giving us—up until modernity—our sense of spiritual identity in the West, and (2) that, through a series of developments vaguely collected under the term *secularization*, religion's role as the China of the spiritual life, the "center kingdom," has gradually eroded so that now it is an ontology among ontologies. Perhaps it is not so much that religion has waned as that other frameworks have waxed. Toleration, as a set of *constraints upon* religion, as a limit to what Locke called "enthusiasm," is understandably necessary as one of the bridges that lead, for better or worse, to our plurivocal experience. But *given* our experience, described just above, of the many-voiced call of truthfulness, of our experience of the *irreplaceableness* of elements of our identity that come from conflicting spiritual road maps, toleration must come to mean an internal discipline, a practical thinking about transitions to higher, more integrative viewpoints, and thinking that demands an intellectual openness to the force of the call of truth in other ontologies. It must be religion's own openness to what Taylor called "biographical narrative as the source of the form of practical reasoning."[26] It should respond in the spirit of admiration, awe, and thankfulness that significant disclosures evoke, in order to understand its *own* self-identity as an attunement toward the good. Toleration as self-regarding is the ability to respond critically to the ersatz, the not-well formed, the parochial, in one's own ontology because of openness to the other.

But is this all simply rhetorical excess? Is it in the nature of religion to display this kind of toleration? Our ending here leads us back to the beginning, to the first question that I raised. Let us one last time follow Taylor's suggestion, and think of the kind of practical reasoning that I have called "phronetic toleration" as a "reasoning in transitions" informed by biographical narratives. Let us also, as Aristotle admonishes, judge a thing's nature— in this case the nature of contemporary religious experience—by its best manifestations, not its everyday ordinariness.

Three figures come to mind as embodiments of this kind of toleration: John Henry Newman, Thomas Merton, and Mahatma Gandhi. Each, to use Gandhi's formulation, "experimented with truth." That is, each explored the great ontologies of the human with a critical tolerance and attempted to live out the truth which they found, whatever its source. The theologian John Dunne—reflecting on Malraux's question "How many centuries is it since a great religion shook the world?"—has argued that something new regarding religion *is* coming into the world, and it is precisely such "experimenting with truth" that is grounded in a tolerant openness to the claims of other ontologies of the human.[27]

Allow me to close, in good phronetic style, with an example, a showing of the universal, toleration as a self-regarding virtue—in a particular, a particular, however, that discloses the religious experience of the three figures mentioned, and also, if Dunne is right, about the "something new regarding religion that is coming into the world." Merton recounted his experience at a Conference on Democratic Institutions held in Santa Barbara, California, in which he was introduced to revolutionary student leaders from France. He tells us: "I introduced myself as a monk. One of the . . . student leaders immediately said: 'We are monks too.' This seemed to me an interesting and important statement . . . a sort of undertone of suggestion that perhaps he was saying: 'We are the true monks. You are not true monks.'" In the same lecture, his last, a lecture on Marxism delivered to monks, Merton acknowledged:

> We have to face with sorrow the bitter truth that the life of many monks and many dedicated women, and many other dedicated people, is a life of total alienation in the sense that it is a legal surrender of things that perhaps they should not have surrendered, and a failure to fulfill potentialities that the monastery should have allowed them to fulfill.[28]

Merton here is seeing the truth in claim of the young revolutionary's claim to be "real" monks, and acknowledging the reified conventionalism that he experiences in his own life-form. Here we are far from religious apologetics. This is an instance of toleration as a self-regarding virtue, an Aristotelian kind of instance, in which the best of a phenomenon shows itself.

NOTES

1. I will not argue for a specific conception of religion in this chapter. However, I do believe that there are three constitutive dimensions of religion in which the

problem of toleration arises, and in terms of which it should be concretely thought through: dogma, cult, and personal piety.

2. I do not mean to suggest—given the historical conditions (e.g., the Thirty Year War) that obtained with the discussion of toleration began in earnest during the early modern period, and that still obtain today (e.g., the situation in Bosnia)—that notions such as Lockean umpire rationality legislating political toleration "from without" are not necessary. Rather, I am claiming that there is a richer notion of toleration that is a condition of healthy religious experience itself, and that the historical conditions that obtained when the philosophy of religion originated have obscured this from the view of classical authors such as Hume and Kant, thus predisposing them to reductive accounts of religion *because* of their concern for toleration.

3. Charles Taylor, *Sources of the Self: The Making of the Modern Identity* (Cambridge: Harvard University Press, 1989), ix.

4. Ibid.

5. An antinomy is a Kantian term for a kind of irrational rationality. Kant takes it as evidence that reason is out of its depth. We can formally define an antinomy as the drawing of a contradictory set of conclusions from the same premises or givens. The first articulate exploration of what I am calling "antinomic" toleration is found in Hegel's *Phenomenology of Spirit*. In chapter 6, Hegel focues on "Enlightenment's struggle with Superstition." He shows that works such as Hume's *Dialogues on Natural Religion*, which attempt to empty the truth dimension out of religious ontologies of the human, both 1) covertly presuppose contrary ontologies which they operate on *as if* they were truthful, and 2) allow a contrary set of conclusions to be drawn by their opponents, conclusions which will also appear as "truthful." An interesting example of this is Fritz Jacobi's usage of Hume's phenomenalism *as the basis for* a defense of a fideistic account of religious truth in *David Hume über das Glauben* (New York: Garland Publishing, 1983). Students of Hume's *Dialogues* might think of this as Demea's revenge.

6. An apt metaphor used by Robert Sokolowsky to describe the kind of identification at the basis of moral agency. Cf. *Moral Action* (Bloomington: Indiana University Press, 1985), 61–63.

7. Taylor, 7.

8. Ibid, 5.

9. Let us offer an example of such triangulated "seeing," the response to which Taylor takes as constitutive of "who we are." Suppose we "see" a person as "worthy of respect" as a "child of god." This is one dimension of Taylor's laminated intuition. It presents us with a "universal profile," the principle of personality as calling for respect, and an *articulation,* a inchoate moral ontology that (1) renders such a call intelligible and (2) as a truth-claim (people who don't "see" this are "getting it wrong) needs defense and calls forth counterclaims. But this is not all we "see" in the concrete phenomena. We might see in this individual someone who, while

commanding our respect as human, seems to be quite ignorant of what we take to constitute a fulfilled life (the second axis). Nevertheless, we might further see her as brave, as worthy of a special kind of admiration. We might see her, to use Hegel's phenomenology, as a person in bondage whose revolt shows an awareness that there is more to being a self that survival concerns.

10. Taylor, 5.

11. Ibid., 4.

12. Ibid., 63.

13. Ibid., 523. See also note 4.

14. Ibid., 14.

15. Ibid., 5.

16. Ibid., 8.

17. Ibid., 6.

18. Ibid., 17.

19. Alan Bloom, *The Closing of the American Mind* (New York: Simon & Schuster, Inc., 1987), 144–46.

20. Taylor, 86.

21. Ibid., 73.

22. Ibid., 86.

23. Aristotle, *Nicomachean Ethics* 1140a.25.

24. Taylor, 72.

25. Ibid.

26. Ibid.

27. John Dunne, *The Way of All the Earth* (South Bend, Indiana University of Notre Dame Press, 1978). cf chapter 1, "Experimenting with Truth."

28. This quotation is from Merton's last lecture, given at the 1968 Bangkok Conference on Monastic Renewal. His audience was largely Buddhist Monks, and his topic was the truthfulness to be found in Marxism. This is an excellent example of the kind of toleration that I have tried to describe. We have here three ontologies, the Christian, the Marxist, and Buddhism. Merton does not level them, but he tries to learn about his own experience through an interrogation of the truthfulness of the others. In Donne's categories, this is an exercise in "crossing over and coming back." I would term it "phronetic toleration." Cf. John Donovan, "Marxism and the Monastic Perspective," in *Liberation Theology and Sociopolitical Transformation* (Burnaby, BC: Simon Fraser University Press, 1992).

8

Beyond Toleration

William O'Meara

The history of Christian theology has had a range of attitudes, beginning with a negative image of other religions and growing toward a stance of political toleration of other religions, including an openness toward learning from the moral and spiritual heritages of various religions. However, the question facing many religious people today is whether Christian theology can transcend its Ptolemaic way of evaluating other religious traditions always in reference to its own emphasis upon Christian doctrines and grow toward a new stage even beyond toleration and dialogue. The question is whether Christian theology can undergo a Copernican revolution and begin to evaluate both its own moral and religious doctrines as well as those of other traditions in the light of a new emphasis upon the Deity that transcends all our various concepts of God in the West and in the East.[1]

STAGES IN THE RELATIONSHIP OF CHRISTIANITY TO OTHER RELIGIONS

We may select Catholic Christianity to examine various stages in one Christian tradition's attitudes toward other religions. Richard McBrien finds four historical stages in the development of Catholic Christianity's teaching about other religions. The first stage was primarily negative, taking for granted that other religions could not lead to salvation. There was only one mediator between God and humankind, Jesus the Christ, and all other Christs were false.[2] Although, at first, the Christian community of Jerusalem, led by the brother of Jesus, James, was as much Jewish as it was Christian, the gospels and epistles of the later part of the first century were more and more anti-Jewish. The culmination of this development in the first century occurred in the gospel of John, which expressed a high Christology in which Jesus even explicitly claims oneness with God, saying, "Before Abraham came to be, I am."[3] In this first stage, then, the normative Christian theology proclaimed the absolute uniqueness and necessity of salvation through Christ because Jesus Christ was the only begotten Son of God.

The second stage developed in medieval times when the church, for example, declared in the General Council of Florence of 1442 that "[the Holy Roman church] . . . firmly believes, professes and preaches that 'no one remaining outside the Catholic Church, not only pagans, but Jews, heretics or schismatics, can become partakers of eternal life . . . unless before the end of their life they are received into it."[4] However, a theologian such as Thomas Aquinas in the thirteenth century could write in response to one Christian ruler about treating the Jews tolerantly under her rule.[5] And even in 787, the Second General Council of Nicea did not wish to force Jews to convert but to allow them to do so voluntarily if they sincerely desired to do so. "Otherwise," McBrien writes, "the Council declared that "they should be allowed to 'be Hebrews openly, according to their own religion' " (canon 8)."[6] Furthermore, Pope Gregory VII wrote to the Muslim ruler of Mauritania in 1076, affirming that Muslims and Christians "believe and confess one God, although in different ways, and praise and worship Him daily as the creator of all ages and ruler of this world."[7] Nevertheless, the ending period of medieval times is infamous for the persecution of heretics under the Spanish Inquisition and the expulsion of the Jews from Spain under Ferdinand and Isabella. This period may be the greatest period of intolerance in Christianity despite the positive statements of the Second Council of Nicea toward Jews and of Pope Gregory VII toward Muslims. These latter statements and the explorations of the medieval theologians about state toleration of Jews show the potential for harmonious living for Christians, Jews, and Muslims in this second stage of Christian teaching about other religions. A third stage of development occurred in the nineteenth century under the influence of liberalism and its open acceptance of all religions as equally good if they are in accord with the insights of reason. Liberalism is classically expressed in the rational principles of the French Revolution. All peoples should be freed from the bonds and shackles that restrict their equality, their liberty, and their fraternity. Any religious belief which would impose inequality, loss of freedom, and enmity amongst peoples may not be endorsed by the political state. Every person must be free to accept religion or to reject it so long as their beliefs do not give rise to actions destructive of equality, liberty, and fraternity.[8] A number of official papal pronouncements in the nineteenth century explicitly condemn religious indifferentism, the view easily compatible with liberalism and a consequent acceptance of all religions as equally good or as equally bad.[9] Nevertheless, despite the church's attitude that error has no rights, Pope Pius IX proclaimed in 1854 that people who through invincible ignorance hold religious doctrines in error from the true Christian faith are "in ignorance of the truth through no fault of their own and so 'are not subject to any guilt in this matter before the eyes of the Lord.' "[10]

Vatican Council II in the 1960s reveals a more profound change in toleration than any previous stage of the church's attitude toward other religions. In this fourth stage of development, the council is very positive in stressing what unites Christians with other believers in religious and ethical beliefs and practices, respecting by name not only Hinduism, Buddhism, Islam, and Judaism, but also religions of precivilized peoples. The council finds precious religious values in these religions, treasures of ascetical and contemplative life, and rituals and symbols both expressive of the goodness intrinsic to human life and responsive to the revelation and inspiration of God even in non-Christian religions. The council resolves to adopt an entirely new approach toward non-Christian religions, respecting whatever truth and holiness can be found in them and even doctrinal beliefs which are different than those of Christianity because even such beliefs may contain some truth. The council does not see such truth and holiness found in non-Christian religions as deriving from unaided human effort but as coming from the generous gifts of God to all of humanity. Because civil society has the moral duty to respect the moral right of all persons to be free from coercion in matters of religious belief, the council opposes all forms of discrimination, including religious discrimination. But more than just tolerating the multiplicity of religions in civil society and the freedom of individuals to believe according to the dictates of their conscience, the council recommends all forms of dialogue, motivated by justice and love, seeking moral and spiritual enrichment.[11]

FOUR INTERPRETATIONS OF PRESENT-DAY DIALOGUE AMONGST RELIGIONS

This recommendation for a dialogue based on justice and love is interpreted by one contemporary Catholic theologian, Richard McBrien, as follows: We should encourage all religions, including Christianity, to engage in self-criticism and purification, bringing out their best understanding of the truth and holiness in their own religions. The religions can seek to understand other religions and to understand themselves from the viewpoint of the other religions. For example, Christians can explore a Christian theology of Islam as well as learn from an Islamic theology of Christianity.[12] Nevertheless,

"Christianity in dialogue will not shrink from emphasizing its own uniqueness, but dialogue will make it increasingly open to the religious richness and salvific value of the other great traditions."[13]

This emphasis upon the uniqueness of Christianity is not simply that it has a unique cultural tradition and various sets of religious rituals but primarily that it proclaims faith in Jesus Christ, the only begotten Son of God, as the Way, the Truth, and the Life just as the early Christians of the late first century so proclaimed. Vatican Council II remains within the Ptolemaic way of evaluating all other religions in relationship to the saving truths of Christianity. The love and truth that peoples of other religions have attained with the help of God's gracious gift of revelation are, the council declares, "looked upon by the Church as a preparation for the gospel."[14] As Pope Paul VI wrote in the encyclical letter *Ecclesiam Suam* in 1964, "there is one true religion, the Christian religion, and . . . we hope that all who seek God and adore Him, will come to acknowledge this."[15]

A second Catholic theologian, Karl Rahner, has developed the notion of seeing non-Christians who live according to their conscience in the search for truth, love, and justice, whether they are atheists or people from other religions, as anonymous Christians. They are Christian in spirit even though they do not know it. Since Christian faith in God's love is supposed to enable Christians to live conscientiously in the pursuit of truth, love, and justice, anyone who lives thusly, even without explicit faith in the Christian God, is living in and through God's love. This attitude of Rahner is a generous appreciation of the conscientious pursuit of truth, love, and justice in all religions. However, this attitude remains within a Ptolemaic way of evaluating other religions in relation to Christianity. If Christians were to be evaluated as anonymous Muslims by a Muslim theologian or as anonymous Buddhists by a Buddhist theologian, how would Christians feel then? They would realize that they are not the only ones who have had a profound experience of God's saving love and truth in their own religion. They might then become open to a Copernican revolution in theology, evaluating their own religious tradition as one valid but limited way of approaching the Deity beyond all the religious insights of all the various world religions

A third Catholic theologian, Hans Kung, attempted to achieve a generous interpretation of all religions in the spirit of the new pronouncements of Vatican Council II. He affirms that every person's religion of birth may be viewed as the ordinary way of human salvation and that membership in the Catholic church may be viewed as the extraordinary way. It is the political right and moral duty of every person "to seek God within that religion in which the hidden God has already found" that person.[16] Nevertheless, Kung does support the missionary activity of the Christian church in its attempt to bring non-Christians to convert to Jesus Christ as the definitive manifestation of God's saving truth and love. Still judging in a Ptolemaic way all other religions by their relationship to Christianity, Kung writes that "the individual people in the world religions are called upon by the Church of Christ to make the decision of faith in Christ only at that point in time when . . . [the] Gospel *itself* is preached to them."[17]

In addition to these three Catholic attempts to reconsider the relationship of Christianity and other religions, there is the liberal Protestant approach of Wolfhart Pannenberg, who offers an expanded interpretation of Jesus' descent into hell. The symbolic meaning of this descent in Christian theology is that Christ then made salvation available to those who, having lived and died before Christ, could not therefore have come to salvation through knowledge of and conversion unto Christianity. In a similar manner, Pannenberg argues, even those who have lived after Christ and who have not had a true opportunity to accept Christ as their savior during their lifetime may also have an opportunity to accept Christ after death.[18] Like the three Catholic theologians, Pannenberg is sensitive to the conscientious search of non-Christians for truth and love and their deep commitment to their religious truths and values, but he also remains within a Ptolemaic way of evaluating non-Christian religions. They are adequate until a person has a true opportunity to confront Christ either in the gospel or even in the world to come.

A COPERNICAN REVOLUTION IN THEOLOGY

The Copernican revolution in astronomy enabled people to see the earth and the planets as revolving around the sun instead of the older Ptolemaic way of seeing the planets and the sun as revolving around the earth. The question that Christian theology can now face is whether it can undergo a similar transformation in the way it views itself and other world religions. Instead of the traditional way of evaluating other religions always in relation to Christianity, a way which is inherent in all four stages of development in Catholic theology, for example, can Christian theology "shift from the dogma that Christianity is at the centre to the realisation that it is *God* who is at the centre" and that all religions revolve around this transcendent Deity whose truth and love are greater than any religion's insights into truth and love?[19]

The possibility of bringing about such a Copernican revolution in theology depends, first of all, upon a deeper acknowledgement of the Socratic commitment to the examined way of life at the heart of all the disciplines in the university. At first, in the pursuit of truth in all our various disciples, whether philosophy, theology, psychology, sociology, economics, physics, biology, or chemistry, we may have thought that we were making steady progress from ignorance toward truth, based upon methods and assumptions which were true without question. However, at some point in our intellectual career, we realized that there were fundamental paradigm shifts in the history of our disciplines and that we even personally had undergone some significant transformations of our own fundamental assumptions. For example, the analytic philosopher realizes that Wittgenstein himself underwent profound transformation of his basic intellectual assumptions from his early works to his later works. For example, again, the theologian begins to relate theology to evolution of the human species and begins to reevaluate sacred scriptures in light of historical-critical scholarship, thereby reconsidering an interpretation of the Book of Genesis that had stood for centuries in Christianity. Again, the theologian is raised as a child to believe in the classic understanding of redemption, the death of Christ on the cross, as a payment to God's justice for the ransom of sinners. However, then the theologian grows personally beyond the adolescent stage of moral thinking about God and humanity in terms of justice and grows toward a living love relationship with God. Then the theologian discovers that Scripture scholars have gone beyond St. Anselm's Roman-law-influenced interpretation of redemption in *Cur Deus Homo, Why God Became Human*, and have grasped a God of love acting to liberate and redeem humanity, and that it really is contradictory for the old Anselmian theory to hold that God's love pays back God's justice by having Jesus lovingly pay the debt that sin requires in justice, the death of a God-human, the death of a perfect man. If Christian theology can change its understanding of the Book of Genesis and its understanding of redemption, may it not be possible for theology to change even further its understanding of the relationship of other world religions to Christianity?

Another precedent in Christian thought for the possibility of such change has developed within philosophy of religion. John Hick, one of the leading Christian philosophers of religion, has argued well that neither theism nor atheism can be proven. On the one side, religious experience that so profoundly transforms and inspires many people suggests God as the source of this experience. Yet, on the other side, the terrible reality of suffering suggests a universe without a God who cares. Again, on the one side, the order of the physical universe and the order of morality suggest a Divine Intelligence as the cause of world and moral order. Yet, on the other side, the fact of chance in the evolution both of the physical and of the biological orders of the universe and the fact that God is not a useful hypothesis for any scientific explanation suggest that the universe is simply a natural phenomenon. There are evidences on both sides of the question. Can we weight these evidences on some scale? It would seem subjective to do so. Some people would weight some claim to divine revelation and the efficacy of prayer more significantly, but other people might weight the apparently pointless suffering of those in desperation and great pain more significantly. Consequently, Hick concludes:

It seems, then, that the universe maintains its inscrutable ambiguity. In some aspects it invites whilst in others it repels a religious response. It permits both a religious and a naturalistic faith, but haunted in each case by a contrary possibility that can never be exorcised. Any realistic defence of the rationality of religious conviction, must therefore start from this situation of systematic ambiguity.[20]

In my experience of teaching philosophy of religion with a reasonable examination both of theism and of naturalism, I have found that a convincing case cannot be made either way for the students. Some students conclude theistically, but others conclude naturalistically, and still others are agnostic. They have all heard the same lectures, considered the same arguments, but choose to resolve the question differently. In light of the ambiguity of philo-sophical argumentation about God and the ultimate nature of the universe, should not the famous Socratic statement of ignorance become even more important to our acceptance of our various theologies of the various world religions? Socrates affirmed that the only thing he knew was that he did not know. Should we not say that same statement about our knowledge of God? Is there not a penumbra of darkness surrounding all our claims to knowledge of God? Is it not possible, therefore, that Christian theology could undergo a Copernican revolution and cease evaluating other religions by the Christian concept of God and Christ?

John Hick proposes that we reflect upon the creative, interpretive qual-ity of our knowledge and faith, whether natural knowledge, moral knowledge, or religious faith and knowledge. As for natural knowledge, we cannot prove that our experience discloses an external world. Descartes' famous methodic doubt questioned whether he could tell the difference between a dream world and a real world and whether he could overcome the doubt that an evil spirit was tricking him into falsity in everything that he claimed to know. Many philosophers have found these doubts a labyrinth from which there is no escape. "As the history of modern western epistemology has established, there is no theoretical proof that we perceive a real world, or even that there is a real environing world to be perceived."[21] Nevertheless, the human inter-pretation of our perceptual and emotional experience is that we do live in a natural world and that we can pragmatically interact with things and events in this world in order to survive and even flourish. All our perceptual expe-rience has the character of experiencing-as. For example, we do not simply experience what is on the table as a pie tin. We experience it as a container for a pie. We interpret the thing as meaningful within our causal interaction with it. Such interpretations are not fixated. For example, we can creatively interpret the pie tin as a frisbee. In general, the interpretation that we do live in a natural world with which we causally interact works, but we cannot prove it conclusively.[22]

So also for our knowledge of other persons. One significant question in twentieth-century philosophy has been our knowledge of other persons. Just as Descartes raised the issue of how we know the external physical world, a similar issue derived from his method about how we know that other persons or minds exist. While we cannot prove that the external world exists, neither can we prove that other persons exist. Nevertheless, the fundamental interpretation of ourselves as living in interaction with other persons works and works very well. We are born without any concept of ourself or others as persons, but we gradually learn to interpret our experience of our own body as the center of a consciousness that lives in relation to other bodies that are also centers of consciousness. This fundamental experience of others *as* persons "is so basic that someone who did not perceive in this way would probably have to be controlled in a mental hospital; for this way of experiencing-as is the basis of the moral and therefore of social life."[23] In general, the interpretation that we live in a natural world with other persons and that we have moral responsibilities to them works and enriches our lives pragmatically, but we cannot prove this fundamental interpretation conclusively.

We can develop an example that shows the ambiguity of experience as capable of being interpreted on a natural level and on a moral level. Suppose someone is hit by a car and lies unconscious by the side of the road. An individual drives by, simply interpreting this event as having natural significance. An object was impacted by another moving object at a certain velocity and a specific angle resulting in an impetus to the first object off to the side of the road. This interpretation remains on the level of natural significance. To interpret this person as needing help and to interpret myself as morally responsible to help in some manner is to experience this event as having moral significance. Now it might be possible to train an individual by rewards and punishments to conform to a set of social rules in responding to such situations, but such conditioning would not conclusively prove to such an individual that one should adopt the inner attitude of morality.[24] The inner attitude of morality requires, Hick affirms,

> mutuality, or the acceptance of the other as another person, someone else of the same nature as oneself. The fundamental moral claim is accordingly to treat others as having the same value as myself. This is in effect a transcription of the Golden Rule found in the Hindu, Buddhist, Confucian, Taoist, Zoroastrian, Jain and Christian scriptures and in the Jewish *Talmud* and the Muslim *Hadith* . . . , and is likewise a translation of Kant's concepts of a rational person as an end and of right

action as action which our rationality, acknowledging a universal impartiality transcending individual desires and aversions, can see to be required.[25]

Just as there is a creativity involved in our perceptual experience of natural objects *as* having potential meanings for our interaction, so also is there a creativity involved in our moral experience of other persons *as* having potential meanings for our interaction. But this freedom in how we interpret our experience of other persons in moral ways is much greater than our freedom in interpreting our perceptual experiences. Morally, we might limit our sense of mutuality to our own family or ethnic group or nation. Preliterate tribal societies and even slave-owning societies until the nineteenth century typically did not interpret people outside of their tribe or outside of their racial grouping as entitled to the same moral considerations as people of their own group. Even today, our "perception of the human person as an end in him- or herself, as a neighbor to be valued as we value ourselves, is an ideal seldom achieved."[26] It cannot be conclusively proven that we ought to value all humanity as an end in itself. We have a significant degree of freedom and creativity in our consciousness of our moral responsibility to others, and it is reasonable to say that moral conversion to a more inclusive sense of mutuality for all persons is what we are called to by the better possibilities of human nature.

Just as there is some creativity in our perceptual experience and a greater degree of creativity in our moral experience, there is an even greater degree of creativity in our experience of the ultimate meaning of our natural and moral experience. On the one hand, we have seen that it is reasonable to interpret our natural and moral worlds as religiously significant. The theist sees the natural world and moral responsibility as deriving from the God who creates matter, energy, and life and who inspires moral responsibility and moral conversion to a life lived in the spirit of the golden rule, even loving all humanity as God loves all humanity. On the other hand, we have also seen that it is reasonable to interpret our natural and moral worlds naturalistically. The atheist holds that it is reasonable to interpret the natural world without God as an explanatory hypothesis. The atheist also holds that it is reasonable to interpret our moral responsibility to all human beings as ends in themselves as revealing the better possibilities of our nature. Even if God does not inspire morality or does not punish evil-doers, still moral values are ends worth seeking for their own sake. Their future realization can deeply motivate human beings even though they do not believe in an almighty personal being who is Perfect Truth and Perfect Love. Our cognitive freedom, our creativity, in interpreting the ultimate significance of our natural and moral worlds is very great. If we understand "religious experience very broadly, as the whole experience of persons in as far as they are religious, then the element of free responsive choice within this would seem to lie at the heart of faith."[27] Faith in this broad sense is defined in Wilfred Cantwell Smith's well-known account as: "an orientation of the personality, to oneself, to one's neighbor, to the universe; a total response; a way of seeing whatever one sees and of handling whatever one handles; a capacity to live at a more than mundane level; to see, to feel, to act in terms of, a transcendent dimension."[28]

While there are, of course, theistic interpretations of faith in Western religions and pantheistic interpretations of faith in Eastern religions, it is important to recognize that there have been atheistic, nonrealist interpretations of faith by such thinkers as Ludwig Feuerbach, John Dewey, John Herman Randall, Jr., Julian Huxley, R. B. Braithwaite, and many others. Such nonrealist interpretations of the transcendent dimension of human experience grasped in faith seem, Hick affirms: "to offer everything that is of indubitable value in religion—the quest for inner peace and purity of heart, the development of love and compassion, the outgrowing of the natural ego with its obsessive cupidity and corrosive anxieties—without the encumbrance of a system of supernatural beliefs which has lost its plausibility for many modern minds."[29]

Consequently, we cannot charge the atheist with ignoring the transcendent faith dimension of human life. The atheist can interpret a religious dimension to the universe and morality but still do so naturalistically. We cannot resolve the argument between the theist and the atheist with conclusive proof. Socratically, we need to acknowledge our own ignorance at the very heart of our interpretations of the ultimate significance of the natural and moral worlds.

CHRISTIANITY AND OTHER RELIGIONS

If we have some creativity in our perceptual interpretations of natural objects and the world, more creativity in our moral interpretations of relationships with other persons, and even greater creativity in our religious interpretations of our natural and moral worlds, whether these interpretations be theistic, pantheistic, or atheistic, is it not reasonable to suspect that there is a profound degree of cognitive freedom in our interpretations of God in the various world religions?

There does appear to be an opening in the theologies of many of the world's religions for recognizing a significant distinction between God as existing within the Divine Reality itself and God as existing for human worship and conceptualization. Hindu theologians recognize a difference between Brahman without attributes, which cannot be grasped in human concepts, and

Brahman with attributes, worshipped and conceptualized as the personal creator and governor of the universe. Buddhist theologians have a similar distinction. Shinran, the founder of the Pure Land tradition in Japan of Mahayana Buddhism, followed another great Buddhist theologian in holding a distinction between dharmakaya-as-suchness, the Buddha essence as such, and dharmakaya-as-compassion, the personal Buddha of infinite compassion. The Taoist scripture also affirms a distinction between the Tao that can be expressed in human conceptualization and the eternal Tao. Furthermore, in the Western religions of Judaism, Christianity, and Islam, there is a similar distinction between God in God's own infinite being and God in manifestation to human awareness and conceptualization. Hick relects upon the reason for the distinction between deity in itself and deity for humans:

> In one form or another such a distinction is required by the thought that God, Brahman, the Dharmaykaya, is unlimited and herefore may not be equated without remainder with anything that can be humanly experienced and defined. Unlimitedness, or infinity, is a negative concept, the denial of limitation. That this denial must be made of the ultimate is a basic assumption of all the great traditions. It is a natural and reasonable assumption: for an ultimate that is limited in some mode would be limited by something other than itself; and this would entail its nonultimacy. And with the assumption of the unlimitedness of God, Brahman, the Dharmakaya, goes the equally natural and reasonble assumption that the Ultimate, in its unlimitedness, exceeds all positive characterisations in human thought and language.[30]

Relying upon this distinction between the Deity in itself and the Deity as humanly conceptualized-and-experienced, Hick proposes (1) that the great world faiths represent different conceptualizations and real experiences of Deity as related to humans and (2) that they can all serve the primary function of religious experience and faith of bringing about human transformation from self-centeredness to centeredness upon Deity and the universal community of humankind and nature.[31]

For the first point, Hick develops a theory of religious knowledge somewhat similar to Kant's theory of knowledge. Kant held that the human mind contributes categories, ways of interpreting all sensible experience into perceptual experience so that there is a difference between the world as it is in itself, the noumenal world, and the world as it really, that is, empirically, appears to us, the phenomenal world. For example, Kant affirms that all perceptual experience of the world is structured by the category of cause-effect relationship such that when any event happens, the human mind must conceptualize that event as an effect flowing necessary out of some immediately preceding state of events as a cause. What exactly that cause would be would take careful experimentation to discover, but that there must be a cause of any event is a fundamental contribution of the mind to any perception of events in the empirical world. In a manner similar to Kant's theory, Hick distinguishes between Deity as it is in itself, noumenal Deity, and Deity as it is for humans, phenomenal Deity. Although Kant believed that the categories for interpreting perceptual experience were universal and necessary structures of the human mind, Hick affirms that the categories of religious experience are not universal and necessary structures of our minds but are on the contrary culture-relative. Theists, pantheists, and atheists can all live reasonable lives without using the fundamental interpretative religious categories of the other ways of living. Furthermore, even when one lives within a religious tradition, one's way of conceptualizing and experiencing Deity can undergo personal and cultural change because of both personal and cultural transformation.[32]

The two fundamental categories for interpreting real experience of Deity are first, the concept of Deity "as personal, which presides over the various theistic forms of religious experience; and second, the concept of the Absolute [Deity] . . . as non-personal, which presides over its various non-theistic forms."[33] These two ways of *conceptualizing-and-experiencing* Deity, as personal and nonpersonal, may be compared to the ways of *conceptualizing-and-experiencing* light, as waves and as particles. Light is not experienced in itself but only as it appears to us. If we hypothesize and seek experimental results in one way, we will succeed in finding light to appear objectively to behave like a shower of discrete particles. However, if we hypothesize and seek experimental results in another way, we will succeed in finding light to appear objectively to behave as a succession of continuous waves. Similarly, Deity is not known and experienced in itself but only as it appears to us. If we hypothesize within some cultural traditions and seek experiential results in one way, the mode of the I-Thou encounter, human beings can successful attain *conceptualization-and-experience* of Deity as personal, namely, "as the God of Israel, or as the Holy Trinity, or as Shiva, or as Allah, or as Vishnu."[34] However, if we hypothesize within other cultural traditions and seek experiential results in another way, in the mode of nonpersonal awareness, human beings can successfully attain *conceptualization-and-experience* of Deity as nonpersonal, namely, "as Brahman, or as Nirvana, or as Being, or as Sunyata."[35]

One objection to Hick's proposal that various religions of West and East both have valid ways of *conceptualizing-and-experiencing* Deity for humans will come from Christian believers who emphasize that Christ is the only begotten Son of God who claimed explicitly to be one with God and that all other concepts of Deity are inadequate. While this is a most serious difficulty, Hick proposes that the objection itself is not now recognized by many major Christian Scripture scholars as based in authentic statements attributable to the historical Jesus. Many Scripture scholars understand the gospels as faith proclamations of the Risen Christ, and they find many evidences of gradual development of various Christologies in the gospels and epistles in the early church. Consequently, there is a possibility in Christian theology for reinterpreting the relationship between Deity and Jesus since the historical Jesus himself may not have had the definitive understanding of himself at which the early church and, indeed, the early councils of the church in the fourth and fifth centuries finally arrived. It is highly unlikely that Jesus understood himself in terms of the Greek philosophical concepts of substance and person which were used in the counciliar pronouncements and creeds.[36] In this post-Kantian and post-Hegelian world of thought which recognizes the interpretive creativity of human thought and the profound influences of history and culture upon various stages of thought, a Socratic re-examination of Christology and of the relationship of Christianity to other religions is most appropriate.

For the second point, Hick argues that the primary function of religious experience and belief in Deity is not to give humanity information about Deity in itself, but to give significance to human life. Just as interpretive awareness of the external world guides our natural interactions with things and events and just as interpretive awareness of our moral existence with other human persons guides our social interactions, so also interpretive awareness of Deity guides our interactions with Deity and also with all of humanity and nature, giving ultimate significance and worth to our lives. Consequently, the ultimate criterion of true religious belief is not a question about abstract statements about God and humanity, but a question of human transformation toward saintliness, including both spiritual and politico-economic liberation. However, even with such a criterion, it is most difficult to evaluate the transforming effects of the various religious beliefs and experiences. There have been many good and many bad practices in all the major religious traditions, but all have helped to produce outstanding, saintly figures who have called humanity by their living example to transform themselves from self-centeredness to centeredness upon Deity and the universal community of humankind and nature.[37] Christianity cannot claim a monopoly upon such exemplars of human transformation. Consequently, a Socratic re-examination of the relationship of Christianity to other religions is most appropriate. Christianity may be able to grow beyond its Ptolemaic way of evaluating other religions always in relationship to its own experiences of and beliefs in God and grow toward a Copernican way of evaluating itself and all other religions by the transcendent Deity which is infinitely greater than all our religious experiences and doctrines.

NOTES

1. John Hick, *God and the Universe of Faiths* (London: The MacMillan Company, 1973), 120–32.

2. Richard McBrien, *Catholicism* (San Francisco: Harper & Row, 1981), 273.

3. John 8:58.

4. McBrien, *Catholicism*, 275.

5. Thomas Aquinas, *Aquinas: Selected Political Writings*, ed. A. P. D'Entreves and trans. J. G. Dawson (Oxford: Basil Blackwell, 1978).

6. McBrien, *Catholicism*, 274.

7. Ibid.

8. Charles Herbermann, et al., eds. *Catholic Encyclopedia* (New York: Robert Appleton Company, 1910), vol. 9, s.v. "Liberalism," by Hermann Gruber.

9. McBrien, *Catholicism*, 275.

10. Ibid.

11. Ibid., 276–77.

12. Ibid., 272–73.

13. Ibid., 273.

14. *Dogmatic Constitution on the Church,* ch. 2, para. 16; quoted in Hick, *God and the Universe,* 126.

15. McBrien, *Catholicism*, 277.

16. J. Neuner, *Christian Revelation and World Religions* (London: Durns & Oates, 1967), 52; quoted in Hick, *God and the Universe,* 128.

17. Neuner, *Christian Revelation,* 56.

18. Wolfhart Pannenberg, *Jesus—God and Man*, trans. Lewis L. Wilkins and Duane A. Priebe (Philadelphia: Westminster Press, 1967), 272.

19. Hick, *God and the Universe,* 131.

20. John Hick, *An Interpretation of Religion* (New Haven: Yale University Press, 1989), 124.

21. Ibid., 135.

22. Ibid., 140–41.

23. Ibid., 147.

24. Ibid., 148–49.

25. Ibid., 149.

26. Ibid., 150.

27. Ibid.

28. Ibid.

29. Ibid., 205.

30. Ibid., 237–38.

31. Ibid., 239–40.

32. Ibid., 240–44.

33. Ibid., 245.

34. Ibid.

35. Ibid.

36. Hick, *God and the Universe*, 145–79.

37. Hick, *An Interpretion of Religion*, 301–14.

III

Politics

9

Disagreement: Appreciating the Dark Side of Tolerance

Edward Langerak

The dark side of tolerating diversity is that—as the Latin root *tolerate* connotes—it involves the *enduring* of something disagreeable, perhaps even abhorrent. If utopia involves agreement on everything that really matters, it has no place for tolerating anything. There is some debate about the extent to which the sort of disagreement relevant to toleration involves matters of morality. Some seem to claim that we *cannot* tolerate actions that we regard as morally wrong,[1] whereas others suggest that toleration applies *only* to matters of which we morally disapprove.[2] Perhaps both sides are right, depending on the culture; it has been remarked that the genius of American politics is to treat matters of principle as if they were merely conflicts of interest while the genius of French politics is to treat even conflicts of interests as if they were matters of principle.[3] However, I agree with those who argue that we probably cannot draw a line between what we dislike and what we disapprove[4] and that, in any case, the issue of toleration can arise whenever there is disagreement about any matters regarded as important, be they mores or morals. The point to notice is that everyone in this debate agrees that toleration is to be sharply distinguished both from indifference toward diversity and from broadminded celebration of it.

However, we sometimes think of tolerant persons as those who are very accepting of differences and tolerant societies as those that encourage diversity. Here tolerance connotes the sort of affirming that renders the notion of begrudging endurance unnecessary, even offensive. In fact, a recent book suggests that liberalisms' broadminded attitude is actually a threat to toleration.[5]

As the authors put it paradoxically: "The more tolerant we become the less tolerant . . . we become." That is, as liberalism cultivates a more open and approving attitude, it pushes us beyond merely enduring diversity. They suggest we use "tolerance" to refer to an accepting attitude and "toleration" to refer to enduring the disagreeable. If we take this suggestion, we might say that tolerance undermines toleration and that the genius of political liberalism is its ability to do precisely that. My thesis is that, although we do need a conceptual framework that allows us to respect many of the views we regard as wrong, it also must allow us to judge that these respectable views are disagreeable and even that sometimes actions based on them should not be tolerated.

I

First I want to note that ambivalence about the disagreement involved in toleration extends to the history of its justification. I take the following to be part of the consensus history of toleration in Europe: Even before the Reformation there were conflicts between religious outlooks—such as Christianity and Islam—which, unlike the localized religious of Greece and Rome, believed in a revealed but universal doctrine of eternal salvation. In obedience to the only God and out of compassion for the unsaved, they sought to expand their control everywhere they could. Although commercial and even moral motivations sometimes elicited a practical *modus vivendi*, heresy was seldom tolerated whenever religious passions dominated. Obedience to God, concern for the general good, and even care for the heretic prevented a stable policy of peaceful coexistence. As long as this conflict was between different territories and races, societies could still flourish, at least away from borders and between crusades. But with the Reformation, one of these religious turned this sort of conflict in on itself. Hence the religious wars, with the atrocities on both sides that made life uncertain at best and, at worst, nasty, brutish, and short. Terror and exhaustion, if not prudence, motivated Europe to heed calls such as Locke's *Letter concerning Toleration*, which stressed the irrationality of coercing beliefs that must be voluntary,[6] as well as the rationality of accommodating certain types of religious differences.[7] Locke was not one to celebrate diversity; he merely argued the irrationality of not enduring it. Even then he is notorious for not extending such begrudging toleration to "Papists" and atheists, on the grounds that they threatened to harm the state (the former because they pledged allegiance to a foreign prince and the latter because they were incapable of making any pledges at all.[8] Anglican and Puritan practices could be tolerated because, although one or the other of them was terribly wrong, they could be endured without undermining civil order.

So the early justifications for toleration allowed and, in fact, insisted on its disapproving dark side. Later justifications of toleration could also be comfortable with it, even when the justification appealed to moral or theological principle rather than to prudence or rationality. Respecting another's rights to autonomy, whether motivated by moral commitment or by religious awe toward those created in the image of God,[9] is quite consistent with disliking, disapproving, and even abhorring the tolerated behavior. But with Mill's *On Liberty*, a new element was added. Of course, Mill did defend toleration of diversity on the prudential ground of its leading to truth[10] and on the moral ground of a utilitarian right to liberty.[11] But, in addition, he supported measures that would nurture diversity and not merely endure it. Mill himself may have had a personal taste for the eccentric,[12] but he also argued that everyone should see human diversity as the means for human progress.[13] Thus he listed public opinion, and not just legal coercion, as undesirable constraints on natural human growth.[14] Indeed, he was fond of comparing the use of such traditional constraints to the Chinese practice of foot binding.[15] Not only did normal adults have the moral right to freedom, but encouraging them to pursue diverse visions of the good life was both necessary and sufficient for the ongoing improvement of society.[16] Therefore, as long as people were not allowed to harm each other, society should encourage and not merely allow diversity. It is clear that Mill's liberalism advocates a pluralism whose broadminded acceptance of diversity makes toleration (in the sense of enduring the disagreeable) as unnecessary as it is undesirable.

II

The above history of justification for toleration is, I hope, relatively uncontroversial.[17] It helps us understand some of what is behind the tension in political liberalism between tolerating differences and affirming them. It also reminds us that people would rather be celebrated than put up with, and that liberals find it nicer to accept something than endure it. What Betrand Russell once said about friends also applies to strangers: "A sense of duty is useful in work, but offensive in personal relations. People wish to be liked, not to be endured with patient resignation."[18] However, this point reminds us why some worry that the "affirmation" side of liberalism flirts with relativism. The most stiff-necked dogmatist can tolerate disagreeable things, but can one accept (almost) everything and still have convictions of one's own, commitments that provide guidance, structure, and meaning for one's life?

The ambivalence in liberal attitudes toward toleration was underscored for me last year when I served on a "Cultural Diversity Task-force" for the local public schools. Our mandate was to develop a plan "to ensure that all students will have an appreciation for cultural diversity and global interdependence." A "strategic planning retreat," which had earlier written the mandate, provided us with ten basic beliefs, including the belief that "diversity enriches society." It became clear that much of the positive attitude toward diversity derived from the "inclusive education" approach that the State of Minnesota is pushing in all its school districts. Students should be affirmed rather than discounted because of differences in age, wellness, ability, social and economic class, sex, physical and psychological characteristics, color, race, religion, and so on. Although most of these sorts of differences can be found even in a homogeneous society (so they can hardly be construed as cultural diversity), many of them do involve differences that should be celebrated rather than endured, and not only because of political correctness. Thus those at the strategic retreat agreed on something like Mill's "diversity enriches society" thesis, and it is not surprising that this attitude was generalized by some educators to almost all differences, including genuinely cultural differences. Indeed, the pedagogy that the teachers on our task force seemed most comfortable with stressed the importance of being nonjudgmental when encountering customs that conflict with one's own.

Sometimes "nonjudgmental" simply translated into the wise policy of being very careful about making judgments and very selective about expressing them. Other times it seemed to reduce to the claim that we cannot really understand other cultures, a claim similar to the sort of "moral isolationism" that Midgley has argued is incoherent.[19] Most often those stressing a nonjudgmental attitude wanted students to avoid negative evaluations and felt that the best way to teach this was to nurture an open and affirming attitude toward cultural differences. (Thus they agreed that "nonjudgmental" really means "positive-judgmental.") Of course, these teachers knew that some behavior must be judged wrong; however they thought that such behavior is not about cultural differences but about the sort of mutual respect required for education, safety, and citizenship. Such teachers find support from Nick Fotion and Gerard Elfstrom in their very helpful book *Toleration*, which emphasizes "the repugnant nature of tolerating"[20] and note that people "naturally wish for others to hold them in esteem rather than be objects of reined-in contempt."[21] Fotion and Elfstrom believe that "substantive reasons exist for believing that liberal doctrine readily allows societies to be cleansed of toleration."[22]

Such a cleansing might appeal to those interested in cross-cultural understanding. In terms of Robert Hanvey's "An Attainable Global Perspective" (copies of which the task force received and read), educators typically want students to go beyond the level 1 awareness of the exotic sort of differences noted by tourists and readers of *National Geographic,* and beyond the level 2 awareness that relates these differences to the cultural traits noticed by those caught in cultural conflicts. They want students to acquire the level 3 cognitive skills of understanding the outlooks of others in a way that makes them believable, and the level 4 empathy skills that enable one to see oneself in the others' situations. Having supervised an international college program in Asia, I certainly agree that these higher level skills are important in a globally interdependent world. I also realize that one tempting pedagogy for nurturing them is to cultivate a reluctance to make disapproving judgments and to affirm whatever differences one finds.

But it should not be surprising that many parents oppose such a pedagogy. One does not have to be a fundamentalist to worry that this is a way to teach empathy by implying that one religion, morality, or practice is as good as any other. If students think that they have no grounds for believing that others are wrong, they will eventually infer that they also have no grounds for thinking anyone is right.[23] When such relativism gets too closely associated with liberal tolerance and public school pedagogy, one can expect trouble.

One might try to cope with parental worries by asserting that "the child's right to an education must be seen as more fundamental than the parents' right to transmit their view of the world."[24] Perhaps then the school board could patiently explain to the parents how "those cultural groups that see children merely as means of perpetuating their culture and not as ends in themselves must be seen as morally flawed."[25] But, whatever one thinks of this hardline Kantianism, its frank rejection of communitarian values in favor of individualism can hardly serve as an argument for being nonjudgmental.

If one were somehow to cultivate the refusal to make negative cross-cultural evaluations, it could result in even more trouble. For one thing, it could provide rhetorical support for the violation of human rights by encouraging repressive regimes to classify toleration itself as little more than a Western hangup. As thirty-four Arab and Asian governments argued in the "Bangkok Declaration" at the Vienna Conference on Human Rights,[26] the notion of human rights can itself be seen as relative to the cultural, religious, and historical diversity of nations, and therefore it should not be used "as an instrument of political pressures." One cultural difference has to do with the metaphysics of individuals and groups. If individuals are not the basic unit in society—if they are primarily parts of a group—then role expectations may be a more important value than individual rights. Moreover, the locus of diversity would be between *groups* rather than *individuals,* and, in order to maintain group diversity, there may have to be definite limits on freedoms available to individuals within the groups. Indonesia, for example, has long toyed with the idea of banning Hollywood movies in order to maintain a distinctive cultural identity. One can sympathize with its foreign minister, who proclaimed at the Vienna Conference that "no country or group of countries should arrogate unto itself the role of judge, jury, and executioner over other countries" on such "critical and sensitive" issues. However, Indonesia also contains groups which practice an especially mutilating form of female circumcision[27] and which cultivate female role responsibilities that, to Westerners, seem especially repressive. United States Secretary of State Warren Christopher, arguing at the conference for a new emphasis on women's rights, claimed, "We respect the religious, social and cultural characteristics that make each country unique, but we cannot let cultural relativism become the last refuge of repression." The question is how one can respect certain types of cultural diversity while, far from accepting them, being quite selective about tolerating them.

A related problem with a pedagogy that prefers tolerance as acceptance over toleration as endurance is that it has trouble with what has been called the paradox of toleration:[28] if I find that, in spite of my best efforts, I cannot approve of something, why should I tolerate it? If I am genuinely convinced that something is truly wrong, why should I not try to persuade the majority to ban it? I believe the best answer is that sometimes my obligation to respect autonomy overrides my disapproval of another's behavior. But the pedagogical implication of this answer requires that we cultivate not the disposition to approve but the disposition (selectively) to endure what one disapproves. Then we can nurture strong convictions about right and wrong—even local loyalties and parochial solidarities—and still avoid dogmatic intolerance by teaching the appropriate role of tolerating (at least some of) the disagreeable. Therefore I conclude that we should teach toleration precisely because we should teach how to disagree.

III

So far I have suggested there is wisdom in keeping the disagreeable in the verb *tolerate* and the adjective *tolerant*. Since these associate with both of the nouns *tolerance* and *toleration*, I do not endorse the proposal (Fotion and Elfstrom) that tolerance means "acceptance" and toleration means "enduring." Rather, I think confusion is best avoided if all of these terms retain the root meaning of enduring something disagreeable. Moreover, we should notice that generally it is behavior, rather than persons or beliefs, that is tolerated. Presumably, the alternatives to enduring persons or (the mere holding of) beliefs are such drastic measures as death, banishment, or brainwashing, which generally are not realistic options in a pluralistic society. Hence I would like to see the terms *tolerance* and *toleration* used interchangeably and defined as "I disagree with your position on this matter that I care about but I will not attempt to coerce your behavior." Intolerance[29] of course, does try to coerce behavior—either directly, through personal interference, or, indirectly, by trying to make the behavior illegal or proscribed in some way.

It is important to notice that tolerance is quite compatible with trying to change the other person's mind by rational argument. Indeed, if one were to speak of tolerating beliefs (as opposed to the behavior of communicating them), presumably one would mean something like "not try to change the other person's opinion by any means other than rational argument."[30] Sometimes, especially in a pluralistic society, one can disagree with another's position and go beyond tolerance to cooperation. A cooperative stance says, "I may disagree with your decision but I will help you carry it out." Sometimes cooperation with what is disagreeable is motivated by timidity, moral cowardice, lack of integrity, or overeagerness to please. But sometimes it can derive from principled compromise (Benjamin) and from moral conviction as when, for example, a physician respects a patient's autonomy enough to abide by the patient's decisions even when they do not seem medically indicated. Notice that an uncooperative stance is not yet intolerance. A nurse can refuse to assist during an abortion without trying to prevent others from carrying it out. Of course, there can be borderline cases, as when a public resignation is intended to create pressure to change a policy. But, in general, tolerance is not sufficient for cooperation. (Nor is tolerance necessary for cooperation, since we can cooperate on matters about which we agree or toward which we are indifferent.)

Tolerance is not the same as resigning oneself to the disagreeable out of a sense of helplessness. To be tolerant implies that one believes (perhaps falsely) that one could interfere in some way with the disagreeable behavior. Of course, one could decide that coercion would come at too high a price, which decision could elicit a begrudging tolerance.

Tolerance is very different from refusal to blame and from forgiveness toward the blameworthy. We can be intolerant of the behavior of parents, who on religious grounds refuse necessary medical treatment for their children and, at the same time, refuse either to blame them or to forgive them if we do. And we can blame and refuse to forgive pornographers while tolerating (within limits) their behavior. Similarly, sympathy and empathy cut across tolerance and intolerance.

IV

Having surveyed the conceptual geography of tolerance, and having restricted it to disagreeable behavior that we endure, we need another notion to capture what is undeniably an important part of pluralism and of political liberalism, namely the willingness to admit that views we disagree with can still be entirely respectable. Although intelligent people may vary somewhat on their (largely implicit) standards for what makes positions respectable, there is likely to be a fair amount of overlap on such common-sense criteria as consistency, clarity, comprehensiveness, plausibility, and practicality. These criteria allow us to endorse a position's adequacy without endorsing its truth.[31] What makes a position respectable includes not just the propositional content of the belief but also the way in which the believer arrived at and defends the belief. The content of one's horoscope may be fairly intelligent, but most of us would regard as irrational believing it solely on the say-so of a fortune teller (unless, of course, the latter has proved much more reliable than most soothsayers). Similarly, one might find implausible the content of another's religious belief about karma and reincarnation but admit that the other's believing it is quite reasonable. So what I call the "attitude of respect" applies more to believings than to beliefs or to believers.[32] You can disrespect a particular position without disrespecting the person who holds it, though if you could not respect a fairly high percentage of a person's positions it probably would have implications for your attitude toward that person's character. Similarly, I could hold you in high regard and still think that you hold a few (perhaps charmingly) irrational views.

I suggest we characterize an attitude of respect as "I (may) disagree with your position but I believe that it is reasonable." As Rawls[33] has lately argued, the term *reasonable* has some moral as well as intellectual bite. Perhaps in some narrow sense a purely selfish decision could be *rational*, but a *reasonable* decision, while not necessarily altruistic, is sensitive to the interests of others; it has as much to do with Kant's practical reason as his theoretical reason. Rawls seems to build a commitment to equality right into the notion of reasonable,[34] but I think that an intrinsic concern for others can be expressed in undemocratic ways. Hence some forms of theocracy or monarchy can be perfectly respectable positions. By the same token, respectable positions can evaluate each other as respectable but harmful to the public good. Thus, I claim that you can grant that a decision is respectable, and therefore reasonable, without accepting it, approving it, or even liking it. Indeed, you can be intolerant of it, as illustrated by the previous example of physicians who get a court order to override what they may regard as a respectable decision by parents, who on religious grounds refuse to allow a lifesaving medical treatment for their young child. Noticing that respect and intolerance can be combined is socially important in a pluralistic society where even friends sometimes have to let political force decide a dispute between themselves. However, you can tolerate and even cooperate with a position you do not respect, as when you work with knaves or fools to defeat a common opponent. Noticing that disrespect and tolerance and cooperation can be combined may also be important in a pluralistic society where even enemies sometimes have to join forces to win a political dispute.[35]

The attitude of respect requires one to be open-minded enough to understand and even appreciate the reasonableness of diverse and contradictory views. But it does require Mill's broadminded delight in and affirmation of diversity. I submit that this latter feature of respect is a distinct advantage in a pluralistic society. We now know that our differences will remain deep and wide, that resolutions are more often the result of compromising than of convincing, and that sometimes sheer political power must be exercised. Instead of hoping for increasing consensus about the good, we are now trying to figure out how "incompatible yet reasonable comprehensive doctrines"[36] can coexist in one quarrelsome but nonviolent political union. What reasonable citizens owe each other's views is not broad-minded agreement, affirmation, approval, or admiration but openminded[37] respect and, when appropriate, tolerance and cooperation. Even when tolerance seems inappropriate, as it does to some of the factions in the abortion conflict (who try to prevent violation of what each side regards as basic rights, by directly or indirectly interfering with each other's activities), opponents can grant that some of the opposing views are reasonable. Such recognition could at least raise the level of the debate, enhance civility, and perhaps even motivate the search for common ground.

Assuming that people should follow their conscience when it is reasonable, respect should be interpreted as what has been called "moral non-dogmatism."[38] This is the view that if I believe your position is reasonable, then I should agree that you ought to try to do what you think is right. ("Try to" is necessary in the definition because, as noted earlier, I may also decide I ought not tolerate your reasonable but wrong behavior.) Moral nondogmatism has been rejected by some[39] because is seems to contradict the central moral criterion of universalizability. When we make a moral judgment, we universalize it because we agree that anyone who is in a relevantly similar situation is permitted or obliged to do what we think we are permitted or obliged to do. This is what distinguishes morality from mere matters of taste, one can plausibly argue. But if respect is interpreted as moral nondogmatism, then when I respectfully disagree with your position I seem to say both that if I were in your position I would not do what you think is right and that you ought to try to do what you think is right. So if I respect your decision and I also universalize my moral judgment about what I should not do, I seem to say both that you should and that you should not try to do what you think is right.

I believe that the above argument is unsound for the same reason that universalizability does not entail specific universal obligations. People are often in relevantly different situations, so universalizability does not entail that they have the same specific obligations. And your having a different but reasonable position from mine will often put us in relevantly different situations. Of course, if having any sort of different beliefs would put us in relevantly different situations, universalizability would be trivialized. Saddam Hussein would have different obligations toward the Kurds just because he believes they do not have moral rights. But respect applies only to reasonable believings, so it implies only that different reasonable believings can put us in relevantly different moral situations. Therefore, I think that the nondogmatic interpretation of respect is consistent with universalizability and that using it can be socially important in a divided but nonviolent pluralistic state. It can enable us to honor the consciences of those with whom we disagree, even when we feel obliged to oppose them.

Sometimes respect, like tolerance, is associated with uncertainty, skepticism, relativism, or even nihilism. However, it should be clear that one can respect or tolerate a position and simultaneously believe that one knows the objective truth that the position is wrong. Of course living in a pluralism of respectable yet conflicting doctrines is likely to elicit the humility of admitting that one might be wrong. And a powerful argument for tolerance is that it can be an instrument for correcting the human tendency to make mistakes.[40] But we can admit that we might be wrong and still believe that we are right. We can also admit that we have a lot to learn from discussion with those who hold conflicting views and still believe that our own view is closest to the truth. We can even believe we do not have anything to learn from another position and still regard it as worthy or respectful discussion. I grant that those who reject the notions of objective truth or knowledge can give pragmatic justifications for respect and tolerance, but I think it is important in a pluralistic society to see that those who believe they know right from wrong also can respect and tolerate some positions and behaviors they believe are wrong.

V

I noted earlier that Fotion and Elfstrom say that in liberal doctrine there are good reasons for encouraging the replacement of tolerating diversity with the approval of it. I should also note that they recognize reasons for keeping "the prickly and uncomfortable concept of toleration in the liberal pantheon."[41] In particular, they say, there will always be groups such as the Nazis, the Ku Klux Klan, and pornographers who are "genuinely despicable and worthless"[42] but who ought to be tolerated anyway. Moreover, precisely because of its dark side, tolerating them implies no compromise of one's convictions—one is enduring, not affirming, such groups.

However, I hope I have shown that it is a better idea to recognize the various combinations of respect, tolerance, and cooperation (and their opposites)[43] and to appreciate, if not celebrate, the disagreeable side of tolerance. This conceptual framework recognizes the important fact that in a pluralistic society there will be a diversity of respectable yet conflicting outlooks and that sometimes one must combine respect and intolerance. For example, even when the factions in the abortion dispute restrict themselves to "public reasons" (which liberals insist on as the way to keep church and state separate) when arguing their case, there will be respectable positions on opposite sides and, at some point, political power may have to decide which activities will not be tolerated.[44] Meanwhile, keeping the social fabric in usable shape depends on the factions being able to take a political stand without pushing all of their opponents into the same boat with Nazis and the Ku Klux Klan. By keeping it clear that it is behaviors, not people, that are intolerable, and that even respectable positions can sometimes yield behavior that the majority has good reason not to tolerate, we can perhaps make sense of Warren Christopher's reply to Indonesia: we respect your religious and cultural traditions, but we will not allow even a respectable tradition to become the refuge of repression.

The last point underscores how much remains unsettled, even if my conceptual framework is acepted. What are the legitimate reasons for intolerance? Can "harm to others" be explicated by "public reasons," or does it require a thicker theory of the good? Are the reasons different in different contexts, such as interpersonal, professional, community, national, and international contexts? Appreciating the disagreeable in tolerance is only the first step in answering such questions.[45]

NOTES

1. Mary Midgley, *Can't We Make Moral Judgements?* (New York: St. Martin's Press, 1991), 70.

2. Peter Nicholson, "Toleration as a Moral Ideal," in *Aspects of Toleration,* ed. John Horton and Susan Mendus (London: Methuen, 1985); and D. D. Raphael, "The Intolerable," in *Justifying Toleration,* ed. Susan Mendus (Cambridge: Cambridge University Press, 1988), 139.

3. Robert Paul Wolff, Barrington Moore, Jr., and Herbert Marcuse, *A Critique of Pure Tolerance* (Boston: Beacon Press, 1969), 21.

4. Mary Warnock, "The Limits of Toleration," in *On Toleration,* ed. Susan Mendus and David Edwards (Oxford: Clarendon Press, 1987), 127.

5. Nick Fotion and Gerard Elfstrom, *Toleration* (Tuscaloosa: University of Alabama Press, 1992), 124.

6. John Locke, *A Letter concerning Toleration*, trans. William Popple (Indianapolis: Hackett Publishing Company, 1983), 27.

7. Ibid., 44.

8. Ibid., 50–51.

9. I have defended such a theological grounding of respect for autonomy in Edward Langerak, *Christian Faith, Health, and Medical Practice* (Grand Rapids, Mich.: Eerdmans Publishing Company, 1983), 57–66.

10. John Stuart Mill, *On Liberty*, ed. Elizabeth Rapaport (Indianapolis: Hackett Publishing Company, 1978), 50.

11. Ibid., 11.

12. Ibid., 64.

13. Ibid., 54–71.

14. Ibid., 9.

15. Ibid., 66.

16. Mill thought that encouraging diversity was *necessary* for progress because only by exposure to diversity could one escape the confines of tradition. See ibid., 54. He thought that it was *sufficient* because he believed in the pefectability of humans— that they would, in the long run, choose the better options. See ibid., 60, 61, and 67. Some commentators (See David Edwards, "Toleration and Mill's Liberty of Thought and Discussion," in *Justifying Toleration*, ed. Susan Mendus [Cambridge: Cambridge University Press, 1988], 94; and Christopher Megone, "Truth, the Autonomous Individual, and Toleration," in *Toleration: Philosophy and Practice,* ed. John Horton and Peter Nicholson [Aldershot, England: Avebury, 1992], 140). Note the tension in Mill between his celebration of diversity and his belief that, as society is challenged by diversity, it will move toward the truth and thereby toward conformity of belief. See Mill, *On Liberty*, 42. I suspect Mill thought that conformity on matters of truth was compatible with diversity in lifestyles and that the latter would always be necessary to nurture the best in human nature.

17. Susan Mendus, *Toleration and the Limits of Liberalism* (Atlantic Highlands, N.J.: Humanities Press, 1989), 22–68; John Rawls, *Political Liberalism* (New York: Columbia University Press, 1993), xxi–xxv; and Fotion, *Toleration*, 75–80.

18. Bertrand Russell, *The Conquest of Happiness* (Garden City, N.Y.: Garden City Publishing Company 1930), 157.

19. Mary Midgley, *Heart and Mind* (New York: St. Martin's Press, 1981), 160.

20. Fotion and Elfstrom, *Toleration*, 129.

21. Ibid., 130.

22. Ibid. As I note later, they do recognize a remaining role for toleration.

23. Peter Gardner, "Propositional Attitudes and Multicultural Education, or Believing Others Are Mistaken," in *Toleration: Philosophy and Practice*, ed. John Horton and Peter Nicholson (Aldershot, England: Avebury, 1992), 72, 76.

24. N. Kach and I. DeFaveri, "What Every Teacher Should Know About Multiculturalism," in *Contemporary Educational Issues: The Canadian Mosaic*, ed. L. L. Stewin and S. J. H. McCann (Toronto: Copp Clark Pitman, 1987), 135.

25. Ibid., 175. As quoted by Dwight Boyd in *The Challenge of Pluralism*, ed. F. Clark Power and Daniel Lapsley (Notre Dame: University of Notre Dame Press, 1992), 155–156.

26. *Star Tribune* (Minnesota), 15 June 1993.

27. Susan Sherwin, *No Longer Patient* (Philadelphia: Temple University Press, 1992), 61.

28. Mendus, *Toleration and the Limits of Liberalism,* 18; and Raphael, "Intolerable," 149.

29. The term *intoleration* is hardly ever used, which is another reason for using *tolerance* and *toleration* interchangeably.

30. Carl R. Kordig, "Concepts of Toleration," *Journal of Value Inquiry* 16 (1982): 63.

31. Nicholas Rescher, "Philosophical Disagreement," *Review of Metaphysics* 32 (1982): 243.

32. Jackson agrees that what reasonable people believe depends on social context, so she defines the term *reasonable* in terms of a "credentials test" that applies to the believer rather than to the belief. The believer must be well informed, reflective, clear headed, and of apparent good will (30). Since such a believer can still have unreasonable believings, I think that it is better to apply 'reasonable' to believings or to positions. See Rawls, *Political Liberalism,* 48. Rawls defines "reasonable" primarily as a virtue of believers, though he also lists three elements of reasonable doctrines (59). Making the (counterfactual?) assumption that reasonable persons affirm only reasonable doctrines, he notes that a reasonable if it can be affirmed in a reasonable way (60n). I think it is clearer to apply 'reasonable' to believings, but all I note here is that my notion of respectable overlaps Rawl's notion of reasonable.

33. Rawls, *Political Liberalism,* 48–54.

34. Ibid., 50.

35. We can easily cooperate with a belief that was arrived at foolishly but has acceptable content, such as when we cooperate with those who believe the message in a fortune cookie. And we can give pragmatic or pedagogical reasons for sometimes cooperating with the foolish decisions of co-workers or children, at least when the foolishness is not dangerous. But I think one can also give moral reasons for sometimes cooperating with, say, a foolish order from a superior. My students who are

nurses have given me a number of examples in which cooperation involved little risk to third parties, whereas uncooperation would have caused significant harm. Of course, when significant risk to patients is involved, the appropriate attitude is probably uncooperation or even tolerance.

36. Rawls, *Political Liberalism*, xvi.

37. See Gardner, "Propositional Attitudes," 69. By "openminded" I do not mean Gardner's notion of entertaining a belief without believing or disbelieving it. One can be openminded toward a position one regards as wrong by trying carefully to understand it as possibly respectable.

38. Brenda Cohen, "An Ethical Paradox," *Mind* 86 (April, 1967):150.

39. Ibid., 159.

40. Cf. Karl Popper, "Toleration and Intellectual Responsibility," in *Aspects of Toleration*, ed. John Horton and Susan Mendus (London, Meuthen, 1985).

41. Fotion and Elfstrom, *Toleration*, 131.

42. Ibid.

43. In two of my publications ("Values Education and Learning to Disagree," in *Values in Teaching and Professional Ethics*, ed. Carlton T. Mitchell [Mercer University Press, 1989], 135–48, and *Christian Faith, Health, and Medical Practice*, co-authored with Hessel Bouma, Douglas Diekema, Theodore Rottman, and Allen Verhey, [Grand Rapids: Eerdmans Publishing Co., 1989.]), both of which overlap with some of my discussion here concerning respect, tolerance, and cooperation, I argue that six (rather than eight) combinations are possible and plausible. I rejected as incoherent any combination involving intolerance and cooperation. I have become convinced that my rejection depends on debatable views concerning the identity and description of events and actions. A few years ago, Minneapolis Police Chief Tony Bouza regularly had his officers arrest his wife, Erica, when she joined war protestors blocking the driveways of the Honeywell Corporation. He also cooperatively gave her a ride from home to the protest site. I have always interpreted his stance as a combination of respect, intolerance, and uncooperation, much like that of a judge who admires the view of a conscientious objector, but, as a judge, sends her to prison anyway. (Erica Bouza spent several weeks in the county workhouse.) However, others have insisted to me that they can give a description of such activities which combine intolerance and cooperation in a coherent way. Incidentally, that marriages such as that of the Bouzas can both survive and even thrive has always struck me as confirming the wisdom of sometimes combining respect and intolerance.

44. This point is underscored in Ronald Dworkin's recent analysis of the abortion dispute, *Life's Dominion: an argument about abortion, euthanasia, and individual freedom*. New York, Knopf, 1993.

45. I thank Steve Evans, Rick Fairbanks, and Charles Taliaferro for giving helpful comments on an ealier draft of this chapter.

10

Toleration and the Idea of Progress

Gordon Graham

The modern liberal world, if we may speak of such a thing, believes in toleration, which is to say that it regards moral, religious, and political toleration as a virtue. It also believes, by and large, that the emergence of toleration as a historically widespread phenomenon is a commendable achievement. At the same time, the robust belief in moral progress typical of the nineteenth century has fallen into decline. Indeed, part of the modern ideal of toleration is widely held to be a willingness to abandon the idea that some cultures are better than others because they are more developed or represent a higher stage of civilization.

It is not difficult to see that there are the makings of a contradiction here. If the emergence of toleration is a welcome development in human history, this must represent a measure of moral progress. Therefore, it would seem, those societies in which it has emerged have, to this degree at least, progressed beyond those in which it has not, and for that reason are to be preferred. Yet this, it seems, is the sort of judgement which the modern ideal of toleration forbids us make. How is this contradiction to be resolved?

I

We can begin the exploration of the conflict by examining first the relationship between toleration and moral relativism. Implicit in much moral argument, it seems to me, is the assumption that moral relativism supports toleration. This is because relativism holds that unconditional truth cannot be ascribed to any one moral or political view, and if no one belief or set of beliefs is superior to any other in terms of truth, all must be accorded equal respect. Conversely, an objectivist meta-ethic implies the endorsement of just one set of proscriptions and prescriptions as true, and these are for that reason regarded as absolutely forbidden or required. This in turn legitimizes the suppression of other erroneous views. Thus a belief in toleration requires us to subscribe to relativism, and conversely, the rejection of relativism licenses the suppression of moral variation on the general ground that error has no rights.

But is this common assumption correct? Is an objectivist in ethics committed to moral absolutism? By moral absolutism I mean the belief that there are some action types which ought never to be performed, irrespective of context or consequence. Just what these actions are will vary, of course, according to specific moral codes. Some, like Kant, may hold that it is always and everywhere wrong to lie, a view that is unlikely to attract very widespread support nowadays, but equally absolutist is the view that it is always and everywhere wrong to sexually abuse children for fun, a view more likely to resonate with the modern moral consciousness. A consequentialist will hold, by contrast, that we can always imagine circumstances in which the consequences of not performing such an act are so horrific that any consistent ethic must license its performance. Consequentialism is thus highly flexible and commends itself to many in large part just because of the unattractive inflexibility of absolutism. But whatever is to be said about the respective merits of each side of this comparison, it is not hard to see that the arguments to be adduced here are different from the arguments that rage between objectivist and relativist.

The best known form of consequentialism is utilitarianism, and the utilitarian ethic is as objectivist as any ethic can be. Since it holds that the rightness or wrongness of an action is a function of the happiness it produces or fails to produce, and since consequences for happiness are in principle empirically determinable, whether an action is right or wrong is, for utilitarianism, a question of empirical truth and falsehood. Critics of utilitarianism, of course, have raised difficulties about the notion of happiness it employs, but in fact the same point can be made about the alternative variety of utilitarianism which operates with preference satisfaction; what the relevant preferences are and whether they are satisfied or not are both empirically determinable questions. If so, however, it follows that objectivism cannot be taken to imply absolutism, since utilitarianism is an ethic that combines both objectivism and the rejection of absolutism.

There are, it is true, complications here. A question arises as to whether the judgement that an action is right or wrong is to be based on estimated likely consequences or on a retrospective assessment of actual consequences. This is a very important issue, but, depending on what we say about the estimation of probabilities, it is not one which need affect the general point about separating absolutism and objectivism. Whether we are talking about actual or likely consequences, the determination of right and wrong in utilitarianism can still be construed as an empirical question.

A further and more troubling question arises over whether the utilitarian ethic is empirical (or for that matter consequentialist), all the way down so to speak. What about the fundamental principle that says that the best action is that which maximizes happiness; is this one which admits of truth or falsity? To many people it will seem not, but even if we answer this question in the negative, the main point I am making is again unaffected. It is not the fact, if it is one, that at bottom utilitarianism rests upon a subjective or relativistic principle that makes it nonabsolutist, but the fact that its basic principle characterizes a *class* of actions and not an action *type*. We can even say, if we like, that utilitarianism is absolutist with respect to this one fundamental principle (meaning by absolutism here that it admits of no qualification), but unlike Kantian deontology, it still allows for the potential moral rightness of any specific course of action. In short, whether we hold that utilitarianism is an objectivist ethic through and through or not, the contrast with absolutism as I have characterized it still holds. Thus the common association between objectivism and absolutism still fails; there is in fact no necessary or even conceptual link between them.

Equally superficial is the association between relativism and toleration. Even radical subjectivism, as Nietzsche's writings demonstrate, need not issue in toleration. Nietzsche believes objectivism in ethics to be an illusion, but this leads him not to the conclusion that all moral views are worthy of equal respect, but that in matters of the moral will might is right (though not of course *objectively* right). If there is no truth, what other mark of discrimination, or superiority can there be but the brute assertion of a heroic will? Thus Nietzsche supposes, with Thrasymachus in *The Republic*, that in matters of value justice cannot be more than the assertion of the will of the stronger. Against this background it seems implausible to expect either the Nietzschean Übermensch or the Thrasymachean ruler to be models of toleration. It is true that in places Nietzsche seems to suggest that the true Übermensch will be so supremely confident in his own will that he can afford to tolerate the wills and beliefs of lesser beings. Indeed, at least on occasion, tolerance might be thought to be the very mark of his strength of will. But it is evident that this is not a logical requirement. There is nothing inconsistent in an expression of dominant will through the supression of others, and the fact that this is a more natural reading of superiority may explain the ease with which connections have been forged between Nietzsche's philosophy and the creeds of Nazism.

In similar fashion the acceptance of cultural relativism may be accompanied by intolerance. Mussolini (or Gentile) believed that war, not truth or reason, was the adjudicator between cultures. This is not a view that is familiar among or likely to commend itself to modern cultural relativists, but it is consistent nonetheless. Respect in the sense of toleration is only one attitude among many that may accompany the perception of cultural incommensurability, and truth is not the only criterion by which cultures may be judged. Those who hold that there is no truth in these matters may still regard some cultures as admirable and others as contemptible, and to be defended or suppressed for these reasons. Whether we take a subjectivist or relativist reading of the terms *admirable* and *contemptible* here is of no significance. Slav culture may appear contemptible only to those of an Aryan culture, but that is still the way they see it.

This is a point worth stressing. I may hold that my moral views are no better grounded in reason or the nature of things than yours, and yet seek to suppress all opposition and deviance. I may simply hate your way of life or conduct and take an entirely subjective pleasure in securing its destruction. More important still, if there is no moral truth and the choice between cultures is no more rationally based than the choice between flavors of ice cream, we seem to have *lost* some support for toleration rather than gained any. Far from objectivism implying an accompanying intolerance, it can provide us with grounds for caution about the views we deride or dismiss. They may, after all, embody something of the truth we are seeking. Being true of objectivism, this is obviously true of moral objectivism also, but it is perhaps easier to make the point in other spheres. Take for instance mathematics. The practice of mathematics encourages criticism and dispute at the higher levels. The interpretation of mathematics, like the interpretation of morality, admits of disagreement between realists and intuitionists, but whichever side we take, it is clear that we must give some account of the possibility of criticism, dispute, and resolution since these are facts about the practice we are seeking to understand. A thoroughgoing realist about mathematics can consistently hold that there is a transcendent truth in these matters but that proof and refutation of the sort identified by intuitionism are the sole methods of arriving at it. Realism can also hold that dispute and disagreement must, in the interests of truth, be tolerated, even that they must be encouraged. Similarly, those, like Popper, who take a falsificationist view of natural science may think that progress toward the truth depends upon conjecture and refutation. Thus commitment to the practice of scientific investigation, if it does not depend on tolerating any and every view, nonetheless depends on the toleration of many views that are held to be erroneous.

So too with morality. We may hold, as Mill did, that tolerating the public expression of what we believe to be error is an ineliminable part of the public process of arriving at what we hold to be the truth. And it is worth observing here that this sort of endorsement of toleration is more than the recognition that error has rights. Whether error has rights or not—if the possibility of error is a necessary accompaniment to the possibility of truth—then the pursuit of truth has, so to speak, a self-interested motive in tolerating expressions of error.

II

Contrary to first appearances, then, a belief in toleration is not specially well supported by relativism and may find better support in an objectivist view of value. Why then is there this common association? The answer lies, I think, in a motivating fear, the fear that a belief in the truth of one moral view will be understood to license the suppression of those opposed to it. This fear is not, I have argued, rooted in the logic of relativism since relativists may as readily and enthusiastically suppress opposing views as anyone else. But there is another mistake in the background here also, and this is the idea that toleration requires us to acknowledge the validity of views which are tolerated. That this is a mistake is something which is rather easy to show. If beliefs and values we acknowledge not to be our own are regarded as in no sense bad or inferior, it is hard to see what we are called upon to tolerate. If someone else's style of dress differs from mine, but is acknowledged by me to be no less good than mine, what is there for me to tolerate? In cases where I recognize wholeheartedly that tastes differ and that one is no better than another, I cannot think of myself as required to exercise toleration, any more than I am required to tolerate the fact that grass is green. Since there is nothing wrong with it being green, there can be no requirement for me to tolerate this fact.

What this shows is that relativism, precisely by eroding the basis on which the conduct of others might be judged bad, removes the moral space in which tolerance is required to operate, and this provides us with yet another reason to break the familiar connection between relativism and toleration. However, this conclusion does not by itself allow us to forge any special connection between toleration and objectivism, still less with the idea of moral progress. To do this we have to look a little further into the nature of toleration.

Toleration implies the need for a measure of forbearance. To be tolerant, in the standard case, is to have objections to something, but to forbear with respect to a certain range of actions. Such forbearance is only properly intelligible if there is some reason militating against it, and if, at the same time, that reason is overridden by a stronger claim. Toleration on my part of the conduct of others, therefore, requires both a ground for thinking that their conduct really is objectionable, and a further ground which, despite the objectionableness, overridingly requires forbearance.

In illustration of this consider a simple, and not obviously moral, case. Suppose I give my children some money to spend. If they are young children the chances are, on occasion at least, that they will choose to spend in it ways that are wasteful and with which, I can see from the vantage point of experience, they are almost certain to be dissatisfied in the end. There is thus real reason to prevent them from exercising their choice, reason moreover which is rooted not merely in my valuations, but in their own. Nevertheless, the purpose of giving them money over which *they* exercise control is to accord them a measure of autonomy, and from this point of view there is good reason to forbear from interference.

What this simple example reveals is a general moral structure. Tolerance is only required when the conduct of others brings into play two competing values, and where one is overridden, but not canceled, by the other. However, there are two further features of this structure that need to be recorded, which I shall call the "overriding value" and the "primary value." The first of these further features is the need for some explanation of the primacy of the primary value, since clearly not all circumstances generate the same order of values. Consider the example of children again. Faced with a competition between the prevention of waste and the according of autonomy in the circumstances described, we lend primacy to the according of autonomy. This is a value that also may be called into play when children are left to sort out some dispute among themselves. But if and when such a dispute might result in serious injury to one of the children, the order of values changes and we are required not to forbear, but to intervene.

The second feature is this. The primary value overrides but does not cancel the secondary value. That is to say, the secondary value still has some call upon action. So, to pursue the same example once more, autonomy requires forbearance with respect to preventing the children from spending their money as they choose, but it is still permissible and may be required of us that we point out to them the wastefulness of the choices they propose to make.

If we apply these observations to cases of toleration of the sort that interest us here, the following conclusions emerge. Faced with the religious practices of others that I have reason to think objectionable, for example, the virtue of toleration may require me to forbear from prevention or punishment, without requiring me to forbear from denunciation. Thus, in those Islamic countries where the Christian Mass is forbidden by law on the grounds that it involves the consumption of alcohol, Muslims who believed in toleration would have reason to oppose such laws, but not to suspend their belief, or its public expression, that the Mass is wrong because it involves conduct condemned by the Prophet. However, to declare something a religious practice is not sufficient ground for such forbearance. A religion might require child sacrifice, and in this case the value attaching to the protection of innocent life is primary and outweighs the value of religious freedom.

Of course, the cogency of these examples relies upon evaluative judgements that may be disputed. What are we to say to the Muslim who regards the enforcement of Islamic law as more important than religious freedom, or the child sacrificer who regards religious observance as more important than the protection of life, even, like Abraham, the protection of life specially entrusted to his care? It is in providing an answer to these important questions, I shall argue, that we have reason to invoke the idea of moral progress.

III

Let us return here for a moment to the parallel with mathematics. When children begin mathematics, they begin with rote learning—of the multipication tables for instance. There is neither scope nor point at this stage of their mathematical education to encourage anything that might be called "critical understanding." Nevertheless, even at this stage, the ultimate end in view is to bring students not merely to know the right answer, but to arrive at it for themselves. Rote learning of the $2 + 2 = 4$ variety is a necessary preliminary, but an education in mathematics which remained at this level would properly be regarded as stunted. As such an education proceeds, different students may stop at different stages, but all can be seen to be on a single continuum, one which begins with unquestioning instruction in the rules and ends with self-generated critical inquiry into those rules themselves.

It is the existence of such a continuum which allows us to speak of progress, and not merely change, because the ultimate end, though not actively present, is implicit in the earlier stages and makes them intelligible.

We can see too that the relationship between teacher and student changes at points along the continuum; at the earliest stage it is a highly unequal one in which intervention, direction, and correction are all appropriate; at the highest stage it is a relationship of equality in which minds are involved in mutual exchange and none enjoys a privileged position over the others.

The value of these observations on mathematical education lie in the light they throw on the structure of progress. This progress is to be found both in the development of the individual mathematician and in the subject itself over time. And something similar, it seems to me, can be said about morality. Though there are important differences, moral education can also be construed as a development from instruction in basic patterns of behavior to a critical grasp of the principles underlying such patterns and sensibility to the nuances of human conduct and relationships. Moreover, just as mathematics has progressed from rudimentary beginnings which permitted relatively little in the way of creativity or innovation for the mathematical imagination of the individual, so morality can be construed as developing in ways that permit an increasing degree of sophistication in moral endeavor.

In part, this advance is marked by an appreciation of the complexity of moral issues, and in part by a refinement of the very idea of the moral itself. The history of morality is one in which additional values continuously come into play, relationships between them are perceived to admit of dimensions hitherto unrecognized, and the morality becomes more clearly distinguished from religion, politics, and the law.

The sort of progressive development has revealed that in morality there is no *simple* right and wrong, and it is the realization that this is so which has fed cultural relativism and modern subjectivism. But both of them make the further inference that because there is no simple right and wrong, there is no right and wrong at all. This is erroneous, however, for we may as well infer from the advanced state of higher mathematics, in which there is considerable disagreement and uncertainty, that the very idea of reaching an answer has no meaning and, consequently, that the pursuit of mathematical inquiry has lost its purpose.

Among the moral values which the passage of time has brought into play are those of human equality and individual autonomy, values which need to be given scope and importance in morality no less than in mathematics. The point in morality, as in mathematics, is to bring about a world in which people can arrive at the right answers for themselves. In the case of mathematics, this is a truism, in the case of morality a rather more contentious claim. Yet it seems to me that its application to morality throws an interesting light on disputes between objectivism and subjectivism, since it combines both objectivist and subjectivist elements in a way which gives a more satisfactory understanding than either would do taken on its own.

The need to give scope to human equality and individual autonomy, however, can be seen to go hand in hand with a belief in the value of toleration. If toleration is, as I have suggested, moral and political forbearance without moral nihilism, it is best made sense of, not by the relativism with which it is commonly associated, but through appeal to the real value of human equality and individual autonomy. And it is the increasing perception of the importance of these values by which the history of morality is marked that has led to the modern belief in the value of toleration. If this is true, the paradox with which we began can be dispelled as a mistake of an ahistorical modern mind. Moral objectivism, a belief in progress and a belief in toleration can not only be made consistent with each other, but can be shown to be mutually supporting.

The argument for this conclusion, of course, relies heavily on two elements, the existence of a convincing parallel between education and morality and a progressivist interpretation of the history of both. As far as morality is concerned, Whig interpretations of its history are not nowadays very much in favor among philosophers. More importantly, the appeal to a progressivist account of history might reasonably be thought to presuppose a great deal of what it is intended to show. If there is objective moral progress over time, and the modern period is marked by a belief in toleration, then indeed the belief in toleration will find support from the idea of objective moral progress. But such claims about the past are, to say the least, highly contentious and likely to be more contentious than any of the claims that they might be invoked to support.

This line of criticism is natural and reasonable. However, it raises issues too large to be dealt with adequately here. In conclusion, therefore, I shall have to rest content with a few remarks in defence of the line of thought I have been exploring. First, my appeal to the history of morality plays no part in the argument which aims to show that there is no logical connection between relativism and toleration. But if there is not, believers in the value of toleration have reason to look more closely at any suggestion that it might better be defended by appeal to objective moral values. Second, if toleration is indeed best thought of as implying forbearance without nihilism, it is plausible to think that the values of equality, freedom, and individuality are among those most easily accommodated within the structure of toleration. Third, it seems to me a matter of historical record that these values have emerged over time to occupy the place they do in the modern mind, and that it is at least plausible to construe their emergence as a progressive development. In the present century, we have too readily come to dismiss as fanciful an idea that struck the century before us as obvious, and in doing so, I think, there is the danger of an uncritical acceptance contemporary beliefs. But fourth, if the history of morality, in part at any rate, is indeed a story of progressive development, this is a matter for history as much as a philosophy to show, which makes its defense a much larger task than could be undertaken here. All I have intended to do is to start inquiry into a line of thought which is too easily dismissed and which may have greater interest and substance that those which are commonly thought to have displaced it.

11

The Justification of Toleration*

Richard H. Dees

Religious pluralism is perhaps the least controversial aspect of the tremendous diversity that has come to characterize the United States. No one is particularly upset by the proliferation of religious sects and subsects: no one writes worried reports that wonder how all of these groups can be accommodated; relatively few feel oppressed solely on account of their religion; and the First Amendment seems to offer security to every religion.[1] Practically speaking, such pluralism requires toleration. Without tolerance, diversity can—and often does—lead to civil war. Undoubtedly, a pluralism that *celebrates* diversity requires more than tolerance; it requires people to value different cultures and beliefs for their own sake. Groups that *merely* tolerate each other exist in a cold war. But toleration is a necessary first step.

Even though religious toleration is widely accepted, a philosophical justification for it is not so easy to find. Indeed, I argue, none of the traditional arguments for toleration—from John Locke to John Stuart Mill to John Rawls—succeeds against its opponents. To make the case for toleration, I think, we must embrace a more pragmatic justification that places the practices of toleration within the larger context of the justification of liberalism.

LOCKE'S ARGUMENTS

In his 1689 *Letter concerning Toleration*, Locke presents the arguments for toleration with which we are still familiar. These arguments are significant not only because we still use variants of them and because they were used to

134

justify the religious clauses of the First Amendment,[2] but also because they set the tone for the kinds of arguments that liberals after Locke have used to expand the scope of toleration and to support their conceptions of rights.

Basically, Locke contends that the church and state must be separated, because they occupy different spheres of life and that, therefore, they have no business meddling in each other's affairs. The case against state intervention in religious matters, he argues, can be made on three grounds: first, saving souls is not the business of the state; second, its efforts to do so must fail, because it cannot force people to truly embrace a religion; and third, the state cannot, in any case, guarantee the salvation of its subject. Each of these arguments is enormously appealing. Unfortunately, they all fail.

Coercing Belief

The most important argument Locke offers—and the one that modern audiences find the most compelling—is his claim that a state religion is pointless, because the state cannot force people to profess a religion sincerely:

> The Care of Souls cannot belong to the Civil Magistrate, because his Power consists only in outward force; but true and saving Religion consists in the inward perswasion of the Mind, without which nothing can be acceptable to God. And such is the nature of the Understanding, that it cannot be compell'd to the belief of any thing by outward force.[3]

People can only be saved if they truly believe the true religion. As Locke puts it, "I cannot be saved by a Religion that I distrust, and by a Worship that I abhor" (38). Therefore, the state could only save souls if it could force people into a sincere profession of faith. But, while the state can force people into outward actions that simulate sincere belief, Locke argues, it cannot coerce genuine faith. It can only create hypocrites, not converts.

This argument is too good to be true: if it worked, as Jeremy Waldron points out, it would show that intolerance is not simply wrong, but *irrational*. If it worked, we would not have to worry about the "messy business" of showing people that intolerance is immoral; we only have to show them that coercion will never achieve their end. Coercing belief, we could point out, is simply never effective, so attempting it is futile.[4]

Unfortunately, Locke's argument, as attractive as it is, fails miserably. It is based on a premise that is clearly false: we can, in fact, compel people to believe things. Brainwashing, after all, is not the stuff of science fiction. It is often difficult, and it requires an extraordinary degree of psychological manipulation, but sometimes it works. And when we brainwash someone, the beliefs she comes to have are as sincere as anyone could want. The new convert feels that her beliefs are genuine, and she acts in ways that confirm that impression: she will spontaneously defend her beliefs, often with vigor, and she will hold onto her new beliefs long after she has left the environment in which they were produced. Indeed, if the brainwashing has been success-ful, we must "deprogram" her if we want to rid her of her new convictions. There is, then, no reason to think that she does not have an "inward perswasion of the Mind."

Brainwashing large segments of a population is, of course, extraordinar-ily difficult. But the obstacles here are technological, not conceptual. Besides, even Goebbel's crude propaganda campaign, we should remember, was largely successful—if only for a short time. With better tools, more sophistication, and the right plan, someone else might succeed where he failed. Insofar as Ameri-cans find these suggestions unsettling, they show how much we accept the values of free choice and how much we are indeed Locke's children.

Yet even if such psychological manipulations did always fail, a state religion might still be useful for one of at least three reasons. First, since many people simply do not consider religious issues with sufficient care, they may be persuaded to embrace the true religion if they thought about it care-fully. If so, then force may be an effective way to get people to consider the arguments for the true religion, as Jonas Proast argues.[5] Second, even if the use of force could never convert anyone, it might still keep dissenters from corrupting *others*. By suppressing other sects, the state can keep them from proselytizing, and so it can save the timid and the less-committed believers who might otherwise be tempted to stray.[6] Third and most important, others may be persuaded if we provide them with external rewards for embracing it. Just as we might offer a child fifty cents to play a game of chess and another fifty cents if she wins in the hope that she will learn to appreciate the intel-lectual activity of the game for its own sake,[7] the state may provide incentives to follow the true religion in order to lead people to accept it for themselves. Indeed, the process I have just described is the basic mechanism for *social-ization*. By socializing the children of the nation—especially the children of dissenters—a state religion may be able to influence the next generation, even when it fails on the present.

If we are successful in any of these efforts, then the new converts will accept the true religion, and we have saved a soul. With a constant, steady pressure, the state may be able to convert almost everyone and thereby save many souls. A state religion, then, may be highly effective.

The Religious Function of the State

Locke's other two arguments concern the right by which a government can act to promote religion. First, he asserts that God has not given the state any special religious function, "[b]ecause the Care of Souls is not committed to the Civil Magistrate any more than to other men"[8] and that no one would ever consent to give the government such a right, "because no man can so far abandon the care of his own Salvation, as blindly to leave it to the choice of any other."[9] Second, the state has no right to impose a religion on its people, Locke argues, because it cannot guarantee the salvation of its subjects: "For there being but one Truth, one way to Heaven; what Hopes is there that more Men would be led into it, if they had no Rule but the Religion of the Court, and were put under a necessity to quit the Light of their own Reason?"[10]

More people will be saved, Locke argues, if we allow each individual to follow his own conscience and choose his own path than if we force them all into one religion.[11]

The latter argument has an empirical ring to it that we would expect from Locke. He seems to be reporting the results of a scientific study that showed that more souls were saved in a study group in which people were allowed to choose their religion than in the control group in which they were not. But, of course, such an experiment is impossible. The real argument here is that since the state cannot guarantee that it has chosen the correct religion, it cannot guarantee salvation, even to those who sincerely profess the official religion. But in a matter as important as eternal salvation, Locke suggests, we cannot simply place our souls in the care of others in the *hope* that they are right; we must actively seek the true path to salvation. Everyone, he thinks, must follow the "light of their own Reason," and they cannot rationally delegate that search to anyone else. So, essentially, the second argument is a special case of the first: the individual should not blindly follow the lead of the state, because he cannot expect it to be in any better position to find salvation than he is himself.

Locke's claims in both these arguments, then, rest on his assertion that people should not, as a general policy, entrust the care of their souls to the government. While we post-Lockeans may think such an assumption is eminently reasonable, our attitude is not borne out by our practice: we feel reasonably comfortable deferring to scientifically advised governmental panels in technical matters with long-term consequences for the economy and for the planet. But issues of religion are even more abstruse, and the consequences are even more serious, so we should not in principle find the idea of entrusting these decisions to a religiously advised authority objectionable.[12] Such a course of action is not, at any rate, conspicuously irrational.

Arguments for a State Religion

Indeed, Locke's opponents can produce at least three arguments for the rationality of a state-imposed religion. First, the best hope for salvation, they could argue, lies within a state religion that has been sanctioned by the authorities who are in a better position than ordinary people to judge the relative merits of specific doctrines. The decision, they could say, is not unlike that of transporting a large number of people a great distance: it is safer to put them all on an airplane than it is to let them drive their own cars, even though everyone will die if the plane crashes and even though each individual might feel more comfortable driving him- or herself. Likewise, the "safest" means for spiritual travel may be to keep everyone together, and the authorities may be in a better position to make that judgment, even if that judgment is fallible. Indeed, to leave such an important decision to unqualified individuals, Locke's critics would argue, would be morally irresponsible.

Locke might respond that religious authority is more suspect than scientific authority—a claim that most Americans would quickly accept. And in fact, in his replies to Proast, Locke adopts a variation of this argument: unless the state can *know* which religion is the true one, he claims, it has no right to impose a religion on its subjects. But, he argues, we can only have opinions, not genuine knowledge, about matters of religion, and so the state must stay out of religion.[13] But a mere lack of certainty is not enough to support Locke's conclusion. If the state must be certain that a harm will occur before it can act, it would be paralyzed; it would be unable to prevent most murders, thefts, and assaults, because it could not *know* that these crimes would occur. But if the state can rely on best available opinion, then Locke can no longer exclude religion from its scope without embracing a thoroughgoing religious skepticism that would make all religious beliefs irrational.[14]

Second, Locke's opponents could argue that toleration is unacceptable, because it guarantees that heretics will be left to damnation, an act hardly suitable to the active charity that Christianity demands.[15] The state, they think, is morally obligated to save all those it can—by coercion if necessary. To abandon these activities, they think, would undermine the core of their faith. In addition, they view salvation as a kind of *public* good—one that can be best achieved by a cooperative venture. We can better insure salvation for each in an atmosphere in which everyone can actively support the spiritual needs of everyone else. Members of different religions can supply limited support at best, and so toleration destroys the support system that is necessary to save souls. Thus, Locke's contention that toleration is the best means to save souls seems false.

Finally, they can reject these arguments for toleration on Locke's own grounds. Even if Locke is correct to think that the goals of the state must be entirely secular, his opponents could still argue that toleration is not even the best means for achieving those goals. First, peace and security will often be achieved in the long run by enforcing a single religion than by allowing hostile religions to live in constant tension.[16] More important, toleration can undermine what Locke's opponents think is another important function of the state: developing a sense of community. A tolerant state can never be a true community, Locke's opponents argue, because its members will always be divided by their religious values and ideals. Those differences will always keep them from feeling the deep bond of solidarity that a good society should foster.[17] Those who feel that America has lost its moral center because they think government no longer supports Christianity share a version of this claim. They, like Locke's opponents, conclude that toleration undermines even the secular functions of the state.

CONTEMPORARY ARGUMENTS

Unfortunately, the modern versions of Locke's arguments do not fare any better. We want to say that state has no business dictating religious views, but that position already assumes the separation of church and state that is under consideration. We want to say that the government does not have a good grasp on religious truth, but such a position assumes that the government could not become the best repository of religious truth that we have. Mostly, we post-Lockeans want to scream that a government cannot coerce belief, but with the advent of modern propaganda, we are all too aware that the government can very effectively manipulate belief. So we cannot accept anything like the arguments Locke gives.

We must, then, find another basis for our commitment to religious toleration. As a first pass, we might argue that the demands of the freedom that we value so highly require religious toleration. Insofar as we value freedom, we must allow people to have the freedom to make mistakes about religion and the freedom to pursue their lives as they see fit. But this argument does not help much: religious freedom is *constitutive* of the freedoms we think are essential. So this analysis only moves the question back one step: why should we value *these* particular freedoms, and why should we value them as much as we do? Even if we value freedom highly, religious toleration is not morally required unless we think freedom is more important than salvation. The opponents of toleration will assert that freedom in this world, however sweet, cannot possibly be more important than eternal salvation. Against such a contention, two lines of argument suggest themselves: a consequentialist argument and a deontological argument.

Mill and the Liberty of the Individual

The classic consequentialist argument for toleration is found in John Stuart Mill's "On Liberty," in which Mill argues that toleration is the best means for securing both truth and happiness.[18] First, Mill argues, we must tolerate different views, because a diversity of views promotes truth, even when most of those views are false. By forcing us to defend the truth cogently, false opinions help us to understand it better.[19] In addition, since humans are fallible creatures, we should also tolerate other opinions, because they might turn out to be true.[20] Rectifying mistakes, Mill argues, requires an open discussion that allows received opinions to be challenged without penalty.

Second, Mill contends, toleration will lead to greater happiness. The "cultivation of individuality," he says, "brings human beings themselves nearer to the best thing they can be."[21] Because utility is "grounded in the permanent interest of man as a progressive being,"[22] anything that helps fulfill human potential promotes happiness. Therefore, individuality promotes happiness. We must allow people to live their lives as they see fit and to express their own opinions as an expression of their own sense of self.[23] To do so, however, we must tolerate their "experiments in living" as long as they do not harm others.[24] By allowing people to develop their own lives in their own ways, they become more valuable both to themselves and to others.[25]

Mill's arguments, like Locke's, are enticing, but they too fail to provide the kind of justification we want. Free discussion often leads to truth, but it does not always do so. Frequently, the rough-and-tumble of the "marketplace of ideas" favors the eloquent and the forceful over the truthful. As Herbert Marcuse points out, a completely free discussion leads—at best—to an official neutrality that encourages confusion and invites complacency. The usual effect, he claims, is to preserve orthodoxy, not to discover truth. At worst, a completely free discussion gives an equal voice to groups who are more interested in aggression and violence than in freedom and truth and who can use their freedom to effectively silence others.[26] Of course, we need some openness or no one will be able to challenge accepted beliefs and improve our knowledge. But the interests of truth may be served better by carefully constructed restrictions than by complete toleration.

Mill's second argument—the argument from individuality—faces two different kinds of problems. First, even Mill admits that individuality can be constrained when it harms others.[27] So, depending on how we define what constitutes a "harm," repressing certain lifestyles—or religions—may be justified. If, for example, the existence of religious dissenters threatens the psychological stability of adherents of the true religion, then the very existence of those sects may "harm" the pious. Or if the existence of dissenters shows that the pious have been insufficiently zealous in preaching the word of God, then their presence may "harm" the chances of the pious to attain salvation. We may find these "harms" unreal, but, unfortunately, defining "harm" in a way which would exclude these cases, yet which would include the many intentional and unintentional psychological harms that can severely damage a person's life is extraordinarily difficult. To hear someone ridicule full-immersion baptisms may cause someone as much stress as a sexually sugges-tive remark. What these examples demonstrate, more than anything else, is that what constitutes a "harm" is defined in part by our conception of a good life, as John Horton points out.[28] Thus, to assume that "real harms" do not include harm to someone's chance for salvation begs the question against Mill's opponents. So, at best, Mill's argument here seems unpromising.

Second, to accept Mill's argument, we must accept the value of indi-viduality as paramount.[29] Yet, however much we post-romantics are seduced by the image of the "individual," it is hardly an uncontested good. As a personal ideal, individuality is rejected by many traditional religions as a manifestation of pride, so they will want to suppress it for the sake of salva-tion. Even if that individuality does make people happier, they would argue, it is not as important as other goods—such as eternal salvation. So, promoting individuality as a personal ideal assumes that the goals of salvation are sub-ordinate to individuality and thus begs the question against the opponents of toleration.

Mill can still argue that the value of individual freedom lies not in its adoption as a personal ideal, but in its value to society as a whole. Allowing each person to find her own personal ideals for herself—whether that ideal includes developing herself or not—best promotes happiness, he can claim. Yet to create a society in which people have the opportunity to discover their own ideals requires us to constrain the activities of groups that dissuade or prevent their members from exploring other ideals. The members of these groups and their philosophical defenders, the communitarian critics of liberal tolerance, see Mill's conception of individuality as a threat to the strong communities they hope to build.[30] Such communities require a depth of com-mon sentiments based on shared beliefs and shared values that do not allow the individuality that Mill encourages. To sustain his argument, then, Mill must assume that individuality and the values it promotes are more important than the values that are central to a religion or to a community. In doing so, however, he once again begs an important question against his opponents.

The problem that Mill's arguments face will almost certainly arise in any traditional consequentialist justification. If we want to justify toleration because it leads to a certain good that is not toleration itself, two problems will always result. First, we must insure that toleration really is the best means to achieving that good. Second, pursuing that good must not already preclude the goods that the opponents of toleration espouse. The only hope, then, is to show that some universally accepted goal—such as happiness—requires toleration. Such an argument may be possible, but if we define hap-piness in a manner that does not beg any questions, then I suspect it will no longer *require* toleration. People seem perfectly capable of being happy in societies that are not particularly tolerant; indeed, they are often made more unhappy by the confusion and bustle of societies that are completely open. So the traditional consequentialist justifications do not offer much hope.

Toleration as a Condition for Respect

Deontological views of toleration justify it as necessary to show respect for other people as moral agents, as ends in themselves. To respect someone as an end in herself, we must respect the ends that she chooses for herself. To do so, we should seek to promote her ends. As Kant puts it, "The ends of any person, who is an end in himself must as far as possible also be my end."[31] Similarly, the early Rawls argues that liberty of conscience is one of the fundamental bases of self-respect, which must be guaranteed to everyone.[32] At minimum, we should not interfere with those ends, unless we would violate a moral duty by doing so.[33]

The chief problem with these arguments centers on what it means to "respect" someone as an end in herself. To respect someone, Kantians argue, is to respect her autonomy, and so interference is justified only if a person acts in a way that jeopardizes the autonomy of others—say, by killing them or by stealing from them.[34] But opponents of toleration argue that we do not truly show respect for someone if we allow her to damn herself by her actions. We show the most profound respect for her, they argue, if we care for her soul rather than for her transient desires and decisions. To assume that we respect her only if we treat her as a rational and self-governing agent whose decisions, however wrong, must be valued assumes that the true core of her identity lies in her capacity to make decisions rather than in her potential for salvation.[35] To respect her true core, they think, we must save her soul, by whatever means are available; if we must ignore the decisions she makes for herself to do so, then so be it. To assume that respect entails tolerance, as Kantians do, assumes the liberal view of the person that is at issue.[36]

Another Kantian tack is to argue that toleration is presupposed by the very idea of argumentation and communication.[37] To argue at all, these neo-Kantians maintain, we must make claims of truth that require us to offer reasons to our opponents. In so doing, we must recognize that our opponents have the right to present counterarguments, and so we implicitly respect the right of each participant to have opinions and to give reasons. We thus embrace a form of toleration.

However, this Habermasian transcendental argument, if it worked, would only show that each must tolerate someone as long as she sincerely "argues." But opponents of toleration may see no reason not to use arguments merely for strategic purposes; they may use them more often as a tool for converting others than a means of discovering new truths. Even if they are willing to offer some form of toleration as long as the argument lasts, they can still suppress their opponents as soon as the talking stops. Thus, they can engage in arguments without being committed to the kind of open discussion that requires genuine toleration. They can still think that salvation is more important than respecting others in the sense that the Kantians intend.

Kantians and neo-Kantians could try to bolster their argument by adding an epistemic spin to it. Because we do not know what constitutes the good, they could argue, we can best show our respect for a person and her arguments by allowing her to exercise her autonomy, rather than by imposing some particular notion of the good on her. However, this argument rests on precarious grounds. If we have *no* intersubjective ideas about what is good, then we have no reason to think that respecting a person's autonomy is a good. But if we *can* make some reasonable judgments about the good, then salvation has a strong claim as a value of some importance—one that is perhaps much more important than autonomy. If we then deny a role for the value of salvation in the public realm, we are simply assuming that such religious values have no place in politics—but, once again, we have essentially assumed what we were trying to prove.

The problems with the Kantian approaches are perfectly general. They all start by assuming the value of freedom and autonomy as such or of free communication. But these assumptions already presuppose a liberal perspective that precludes the values—like salvation and community—that the opponents of toleration think are more important than that kind of freedom. If they are right, then they can argue that some freedom may be taken away for the sake of the higher value of salvation. Yet, *anyone* who believes that religious values are paramount—indeed, anyone who takes the claims of religion seriously—must maintain that salvation is more important than freedom. They may think freedom is highly valuable, but only if and when it does not conflict with salvation.[38] So any attempt to convince them is bound to fail.

TOLERATION AND THE JUSTIFICATION OF LIBERALISM

However, perhaps, the whole approach we have been using is mistaken. Perhaps searching for an argument supporting toleration that should convince the opponents of toleration is futile. If so, then perhaps we should start over and try to think about Locke's arguments in a different way. Suppose that Locke is not trying to present a general argument for toleration, but a pragmatic solution suited to the specific historical circumstances in which he found himself.[39]

A New Look at Locke

The Britain of 1689 was a politically charged, religiously polarized society. Within Locke's memory, Episcopalians and Presbyterians had fought a long and bloody civil war and beheaded a king over religious principles. Yet the result of the English Revolution was not the commonwealth of the saints that the Puritans sought, but a rather ordinary military dictatorship directed by Oliver Cromwell. The Restoration of the Stuarts was supposed to settle all these questions, but the Exclusion Crisis of 1679 through 1683, prompted by Whig attempts to keep Charles II's Catholic brother (who would become James II in 1685) out of the line of succession, threatened to lead to another civil war. Thus, the threat of renewed warfare in the 1680s was very real—as Locke was well aware.[40] Yet neither side in that potential conflict could have had confidence in victory: both sides knew that the last war was long and costly and that its outcome was ambivalent. Prudence seemed to dictate a compromise.

So Locke proposes one. Imagine a political landscape, he suggests, in which we regard the institution of the state and the institution of the church as completely separate. In this new politics, he says, we must appeal to reasons that are completely secular to justify actions by the state. If we accept this new political arrangement, Locke argues, no religious group will be threatened by the state, and religious dissent will no longer constitute political rebellion. Members of every church can then become loyal members of the state.[41] Diverse religious groups will then be able to live together, and civil war can be averted. Accepting Locke's proposal is, then, less a matter of rational persuasion than an exercise in imagination.[42] His arguments in the *Letter* then should be read in a new spirit: his first point is not that we *cannot* force beliefs upon people, but that we *should not*; the second is not that a state *cannot* guarantee salvation, but that it *should not* try.

Read in this way, Locke's claims are not tight philosophical arguments, but adept moves within a new vision of politics—a politics with toleration at its core. Thus, when Locke says that a church is "a voluntary Society of Men" and that "nobody is born a member of any Church,"[43] he is not making two conspicuously false factual claims; instead, he is suggesting that we *should* view the church as a voluntary society in which people unite to worship God as they think best. Seen in this way, however, we must take on a larger task if we are to justify toleration: we must justify a whole vision of politics in which toleration plays a key role. We must, in a word, justify a liberal view of politics.

Part of that justification comes from a close look at the options available at the time. The alternative to his proposals, Locke says, is grim:

> If this [the separation of church and state] be not done, there can be no
> end put to the Controversies that will always be arising, between those
> that have, or at least pretend to have, on the one side, a Concernment
> for the Interest of Mens Souls, and on the other side, a Care of the
> Commonwealth.[44]

Essentially, Locke argues that in the context of late seventeenth-century Britain, a state religion will be a constant source of controversy. But he is actually worried about more serious consequences: "No Peace and Security, no not so much as Common Friendship, can ever be established, or preserved amongst Men, so long as this Opinion prevails, That *Dominion is founded in Grace*, and that Religion is to propagated by force of Arms."[45] Religious controversies in these contexts, he thinks, will inevitably lead to civil war. Thus, Locke rests his argument for a liberal separation of church and state on the possibility of avoiding civil strife.

If Locke is right, then his opponents must argue that even the costs of civil war do not outweigh the benefits of saving souls. Salvation, they must argue, is a prize of immeasurable worth, and killing a few people to achieve it for others is not too high a price—just as we think that the emancipation of the slaves was worth the bloodshed of the American Civil War. Today, of course, to even claim that we should promote religion by force is to undermine the view: we find it repugnant to kill people over metaphysical differences. But our attitude only shows once again how much we already accept Locke's view and not that his opponents are inherently irrational.

However, we post-Lockeans can put the point better. War, we should insist, is itself an evil: it produces pain and suffering, and it instills dispositions that lead to acts of cruelty that corrupt even the souls of the pious. So a civil war is likely to lose more souls than it saves, even if the forces of the true religion win. And if the other side wins, even more souls will be lost since they will impose their religion on the true believers. To risk a civil war, then, is to risk everything, so the defenders of a state religion can sanction a civil war only if they know that they have a good chance of winning. In these circumstances—but only in these circumstances—toleration is a prudent compromise. From the point of view of the pious, it will hardly be ideal, but it may be the most practicable means to maintain the true religion. Both sides, then, can accept toleration as a *pragmatic* solution to their problems. And insofar as the disagreements about religion can still ignite American society, that pragmatic compromise still works for us.

The Context of Toleration

Toleration would not have made sense in 1689, even as a pragmatic proposal, unless a number of other social changes had already taken place. In a hierachically structured world, the idea that each individual could decide for himself whether to join one religion rather than another would be ludicrous. So, before liberal tolerance could become a live option, hierarchy as a model of politics had to be undermined. In the seventeenth century, a number of changes facilitated its fall. First, the rise of modern science helped destroy the Aristotelianism that had been associated with the old hierarchies. Second, the rise of Protestantism itself was a potent force against authority. The Reformation taught each individual that he has a personal, unmediated relationship with God and that he must read and interpret the Scriptures for himself. He did not need to rely on the intervention or the interpretation of priests and bishops to find God. Third, that new religious outlook facilitated the rise of a market economy, as many believed that their financial success was a sign of their spiritual election. This change made the "middle station of life" an acceptable and even virtuous place. These economic changes encouraged the greater use of explicitly contractual arrangements in daily life, and the contract became a natural model for politics. Together, these changes gave dignity to the individual and to his ability to choose a life for himself.[46]

In that context, Locke's arguments, with their implicit appeal to the right and the ability of each person to decide his own religious fate, acquire political force. They project a new voice into politics, a voice of hope that resonates and amplifies the emerging individualism of the market society and the increasing breakdown of feudal hierarchies. Only in such an environment does toleration make sense, and thus only in these circumstances is it justified.

Of course, the social changes of the seventeenth century defined the timber and the texture of that voice. If the ideology of natural hierarchy had been destroyed in a different way—if, say, its fall had occurred in a society that emphasized the supreme importance of communities—then the pragmatic proposal would have taken a different form, perhaps, by emphasizing group, rather than individual, rights. In such different circumstances, a different solution would have been justified. But in the context in which Locke actually found himself, a proposal like his was warranted.

Beyond Pure Pragmatism

A purely pragmatic acceptance of toleration, however, is surely inadequate. If toleration is accepted *merely* as a *modus vivendi*, it will be abandoned as soon as one side or the other feels it is to its advantage. Nevertheless, if toleration is accepted as a *modus vivendi*, in time, it may be embraced for its own sake. Before they can sustain even a minimal form of toleration, people must create practices and institutions that support toleration as a value.[47] So, for example, they will need to educate their children to understand that they can at least live with people who hold different religious beliefs. In the process, they create a new social dynamic, one in which religious divisions may lose their political significance and in which an atmosphere of even greater toleration can flourish. Thus, an attitude of religious toleration may naturally lead us to extend toleration to political beliefs, ethnic values, and sexual orientation.[48]

However, to accept toleration as a value does not imply that we must tolerate everything. Toleration, like all virtues, has its limits. After all, what looks like bravery in some contexts will be foolhardy in others. Broadly speaking, toleration is always limited when harm comes to others. Of course, as I have already argued, we cannot define "harm" in a value-neutral manner, so the limits of toleration will be determined by the needs of a particular context. The demands of toleration must be balanced against other values in the society that help us define what constitutes a "harm."[49]

Once we create an atmosphere in which toleration is a value, however, we have already created the social conditions for a new form of individuality. The society can then support a flamboyant individuality which goes beyond that which the Puritans could understand, much less approve, but which Americans now idolize and romanticize. At that point, the individual herself becomes the object of toleration, and then—but only then—do Mill's arguments acquire political power. Only then can people understand and appreciate how much they can learn about themselves and others by interacting with those who are different. People with differing views, they learn, can help them to see the flaws in their own views, and thereby help them to strengthen their own position and explore new possibilities for themselves. They can then value diversity not only because it may help them to discover the truth, but also because it may help them express themselves better as individuals. Toleration encourages "experiments in living," which can test alternative lifestyles and which may help people learn to live richer individual lives. Viewed in this light, people see diversity as a way of improving their lives, and they can begin to appreciate and celebrate diversity for its own sake.[50] By accepting toleration, however provisionally, people put themselves in a position in which they can begin to appreciate the unique value of toleration, a value far beyond anything that Locke could have imagined in 1689.

Toleration and individuality thus interact dynamically to create a new normative landscape, one in which the ideal of autonomy becomes central and in which the politics of individual rights becomes salient. When that happens, all the pieces have come together to create a recognizably liberal society. Liberalism is thus justified partially by the same factors that justify toleration and individuality. Yet toleration and individuality are themselves justified as pragmatic responses to particular social changes, some of which were created by the practices of separation (like that between the church and state) that define liberalism.[51] Once these liberal practices become established, they justify further expansions of the ideals of autonomy and toleration to include ever-greater areas of our lives, which then further support liberal institutions. In that way, liberalism, toleration, and autonomy mutually reinforce each other to form a powerful view of politics and social life.

Liberalism is, thus, a product of the complex interaction between contingent values and social practices that arose from the political experience of Western Europe. And it is justified in the United States—and elsewhere—only insofar as it succeeds in presenting a political vision that is compelling to us, given our experiences.[52]

CONTEXTUAL JUSTIFICATIONS

One reaction to the enlightened pragmatic account I have given is to reject it either as inadequate or as irrelevant. It is inadequate, we might think, because it seems to suffer the same problems as the consequentialist arguments. And it is irrelevant, because it only *explains* the rise of toleration and liberalism; it does not *justify* them.

THE PLACE FOR TOLERATION

The pragmatic account I have sketched works only insofar as the parties seek peace rather than religious salvation, so it promotes goals that may not be shared by the opponents of toleration. Thus it seems to suffer all the problems that we found in consequentialist arguments, because toleration will only promote those goals in rather unusual circumstances. It does not, then, provide a general argument for toleration; it is limited to those cultures which have developed a fairly robust sense of individuality and which have a deep conflict that cannot be resolved by any other means without considerable costs.

The thrust of the pragmatic approach, however, is to accept these limitations. Toleration cannot survive as a value in a society whose members would rather kill each other than tolerate differences. We may be able to get both sides to see the advantages of adopting a policy of toleration, but until they arrive at a point at which those advantages seem important—either through social changes or through sheer exhaustion—a policy of toleration is pointless. In our world, a world in which many cultures have accepted and flourished in an atmosphere of toleration, getting cultural combatants to see the potential advantage of toleration should not be as hard as it was in Locke's day. However, those advantages are not obvious, and most of them cannot be understood—much less appreciated—until people have accepted toleration at least as a *modus vivendi*.

The Role of Contexts

The second objection is more serious. Even if the story I have told is correct, some might say, it does not constitute a justification either of liberalism or of toleration. A justification, they contend, requires a context-independent rational argument, not a historical narrative. Yet such ahistorical arguments for toleration, I have suggested, are unpromising. Besides, the story I have told is not merely history: it shows how certain *arguments* make sense in a particular cultural milieu. Justification always takes place against a background of assumptions in the culture, of values implicit in its practices, and of the peculiarities of particular situations. Only within the complexities of a context can the arguments of Locke and Mill become compelling, and only then can the practices they support be justified. To show that a practice is justified, I am suggesting, is to demonstrate that it is the best response to the situation given those background assumptions and values.

In one sense, my point is perfectly banal: arguments can be accepted only in situations in which they can be understood and appreciated. Acontextual justifications are *politically* irrelevant: if no one sees them as possible arguments, they do not present a live option to the people involved. But, in another sense, my point is more radical: it rejects the view that what people think about a practice only tells us something about whether they can adopt it, but nothing about whether it is justified. On my view, these acontextual justifications are *philosophically*, as well as politically, irrelevant. Moral philosophy, I believe, is a *practical* discipline; it is supposed to help people live their lives. If so, it must be relevant to the lives that people actually live. We cannot, then, think that people are morally amiss if they do not take into account possibilities that are technologically or conceptually unavailable to them. If someone wants to insist that toleration was justified before the conceptual resources were available that made it both possible and attractive in a given culture, then they are expecting the impossible. Their claim is simply beside the point.[53]

The more interesting problem, I think, is to determine when a practice such as toleration becomes a genuine option, one which we can blame people for accepting or rejecting.[54] Consider, for example, whether toleration was a genuine option before 1689. Certainly, others had proposed it before Locke.[55] So, unlike computers, toleration was something that the parties had the conceptual resources to contemplate. In addition, they had the basic knowledge of how to institute such a plan, since the Dutch example could have served as a guide. The only question, then, is whether the British could have seen it as *valuable*. Here the question becomes muddy: in 1642, both the Puritans and the Anglicans understood the value of life and the risks of war, but neither could see them as things that took precedence over salvation—or rather, they *could* have seen them as such, but to do so would have betrayed their whole moral outlook. Only after the Civil War do those considerations become compelling. Maybe, if the risks had become vivid to them, they could have adopted a plan of toleration earlier, but that possibility seems unlikely. However, the answers to just these questions of detail are crucial to our judgments about whether, say, Charles II's refusal to grant toleration in 1660 was justified or not. If I am right, questions of justification will always depend on just such details. For that reason alone, the acontextual project in political philosophy that underlies the traditional interpretations of Locke, Mill, and Kant is doomed.

At one level, of course, Kantians and traditional consequentialists can agree that contexts are important, but both underestimate its significance. Kantians rarely talk about it; they tend to focus on human capacities in general, rather than on the capacities people have at a particular moment. Consequentialists are more attuned to context, because they know that the context will determine the best means to a given end. But, context must play an even deeper role in moral thought: it must shape our thinking not only about the best means to a given end, but also about the *end itself*. The goals of British society were changing in Locke's lifetime from collective salvation to individual choice, and Locke's arguments served both to reflect and to solidify this new perspective. These two goals were not simply two different means for achieving some higher goal such as happiness—unless we define "happiness" so broadly that it covers anything people pursue and thereby ceases to serve as a meaningful guide. In addition, we cannot dismiss these historical changes as irrelevant to what is "really" moral without stripping the concerns of real people from moral and political thought. Only if the goals themselves are defined within the contexts in which people live can morality serve as an effective guide.[56]

CONCLUSION

We have now come full circle. I began this essay by giving reasons why we should reject the arguments of Locke's *Letter concerning Toleration*. Now, I hope, I have shown why we should accept them. The arguments Locke gives are good arguments for us, because we—even more than Locke himself— accept the separations that support them. In fact, we accept a separation not only between church and state, but also between ethnic groups and the state, between the market and the state, between the church and the market, and between the market and ethnic groups. In our liberal world, the same kinds of arguments for toleration of churches now apply to these other domains as well. In our new context, we can give new arguments for toleration which Locke himself would find shocking, but which seem perfectly reasonable to us. In a world of toleration, we can appreciate the value of individual autonomy both for its own sake and for the help it can give us in learning more about both the natural and the moral worlds. Thus, our society has evolved in ways that reinforce the ideal of toleration.

Unfortunately, however much we accept toleration as an ideal, we are still reluctant to practice it. We, like the Puritans and the Anglicans of Locke's day, are frightened of those who differ with us about fundamental values, and we think that our society must surely fall apart unless we can agree about these basic issues. However, if the experience of Britain is any indication, we have at least some reason—however small—for hope.[57]

NOTES

*Previously published as "The Justification of Tolerance" in *Values and Public Life: An Interdisciplinary Study*, ed. Gerald Magill and Marie D. Hoff (Lanham, MD: University Press of America, 1995), 29–56.

1. There are, of course, some problematic cases, like the native American church, which the Supreme Court ruled could not use peyote in its ceremonies. But compared to the difficulties surrounding cultural and ethnic diversity, these problems are relatively rare.

2. For an account of Locke's influence on the American debates, see David A. J. Richards, *Toleration and the Constitution* (New York: Oxford University Press, 1986), 103–62.

3. John Locke, *A Letter concerning Toleration*, ed. James Tully (Indianapolis: Hackett Publishing, 1983), 27.

4. Jeremy Waldron, "John Locke: Toleration and the Rationality of Persecution," in *John Locke, "A Letter concerning Toleration" in Focus*, ed. John Horton and Susan Mendus (London: Routledge, 1991), 98–124. The quotation is on 120.

5. Jonas Proast, *The Argument of the Letter concerning Toleration, Briefly Consider'd and Answer'd* (Oxford, 1690; reprint, New York: Garland Press, 1984), 4–8. Proast was Locke's most important contemporary critic, and he and Locke engaged in a pamphlet war that extended over ten years, three replies by Proast, three additional letters by Locke, and literally hundreds of pages (most of which are in Locke's ponderous *Third Letter for Toleration*).

6. See J. W. Gough, "Introduction: Locke's Theory of Toleration," in John Locke, *Epistola de Tolerantia*, ed. Raymond Klibansky and J. W. Gough (Oxford: Clarendon Press, 1968), 33.

7. Alasdair MacIntyre, *After Virtue*, 2d ed. (Notre Dame, Ind: University of Notre Dame Press, 1984), 188.

8. Locke, *A Letter concerning Toleration*, 26. Oddly, Locke offers very little biblical evidence for this assertion, even though many of his opponents offer biblical proof for their claim that God gives rulers power by divine right and, therefore, that they *do* have a special function to care for the souls of their subjects. However, in the first of his *Two Treatises on Government*, published in the same year as the *Letter*, he presents an excruciatingly detailed textual argument against Robert Filmer's version of divine right. See Locke, *Two Treatises on Government*, ed. Peter Laslett (Cambridge: Cambridge University Press, 1960).

9. Ibid.

10. Ibid., 27.

11. In the seventeenth century, it could only be *his* path; women had virtually no legal rights at all. However, Locke himself is surprisingly progressive in this regard. See, for example, Locke, *Two Treatises*, 300–01. See also Melissa Butler, "Early Liberal Roots of Feminism," *American Political Science Review* 72 (March 1978): 135–50.

12. Similarly, Proast argues that since people know that by themselves they will "be so much swayed by Prejudice and Passion," then they should leave the choice of religion to others, and the state seems to be the best agent. See Proast, *The Argument of the Letter*, 22–23.

13. Locke, *A Third Letter for Toleration*, ed. Jonas Proast, in *The Works of John Locke*, 10th ed. (London, 1801), 6:141–546, especially 143–50, 421. See also *A Second Letter concerning Toleration* (1690), in *Works*, 6:111. I was directed to these passages by Peter Nicholson, "John Locke's Later Letters on Toleration," in John Locke, *A Letter concerning Toleration, in Focus*, ed. John Horton and Susan Mendus (London: Routledge, 1991), 176–80.

14. For a similar point, see Proast, *Third Letter concerning Toleration* (Oxford, 1691; reprint, New York: Garland Press, 1984), 47.

15. Proast, in fact, argues that it is the duty of all Christians to care for each other's souls as an act of charity. See Proast, *The Argument of the Letter*, 19–20 and Locke, *Third Letter*, 32.

16. Even a liberal such as Montesquieu argues that toleration is only the best solution to religious diversity once a new religion has become established within a state; otherwise, he says, dissenters should be suppressed for the sake of unity. See Charles de Secondat, Baron de Montesquieu, *The Spirit of the Laws*, trans. Anne Cohler, Basia Miller, and Harold Stone (Cambridge: Cambridge University Press, 1989), 487–88.

17. Contemporary communitarian criticisms of liberalism offer a variation of this argument. See, for example, Michael Sandel, *Liberalism and the Limits of Justice* (Cambridge: Cambridge University Press, 1982), and MacIntyre, *After Virtue*.

18. John Stuart Mill, "On Liberty," in *Three Essays* (Oxford: Oxford University Press, 1975), 5–141.

19. Ibid., 45–47.

20. Ibid., 24–29.

21. Ibid., 79.

22. Ibid., 16.

23. David Edwards notes that one of the important supports for Mill's argument for free thought and discussion is its connection with the value of individuality. See Daniel Edwards, "Toleration and Mill's Liberty of Thought and Discussion," in *Justifying Toleration: Conceptual Historical Perspectives*, ed. Susan Mendus (Cambridge: Cambridge University Press, 1988), 87–113.

24. Mill, "On Liberty," 70.

25. Ibid., 78.

26. Herbert Marcuse, "Repressive Tolerance," in *A Critique of Pure Tolerance*, Robert Paul Wolff, Barrington Moore, Jr., and Herbert Marcuse, (Boston: Beacon Press, 1965), 81–123, especially 85–97.
Feminist criticisms of "free speech" follow a similar line. See, for example, Catharine MacKinnon, *Towards a Feminist Theory of the State* (Cambridge: Harvard University Press, 1989), 195–214.

27. Mill, "On Liberty," 92–93.

28. See John Horton, "Toleration, Morality, and Harm," in *Aspects of Toleration*, ed. John Horton and Susan Mendus (London: Methuen, 1985), 113–35.

29. Mill himself admits that its value is not supreme. In some circumstances, he says, we need to reign in individuality for the sake of order. See Mill, "On Liberty," 75.

30. For arguments along these lines, see Robert Bellah, et al., *Habits of the Heart* (New York: Harper & Row, 1985); MacIntyre, *After Virtue*; MacIntyre, *Whose Justice? Which Rationality?* (Notre Dame: University of Notre Dame Press, 1988); Sandel, *Liberalism and the Limits of Justice* (New York: Cambridge University Press, 1982); Roberto Unger, *Knowledge and Politics* (New York: The Free Press, 1975); and Charles Taylor, *Sources of the Self: The Making of the Modern Identity* (Cambridge: Harvard University Press, 1989).

31. Immanuel Kant, *Foundations of the Metaphysics of Morals*, trans. Lewis White Beck (New York: Macmillan, 1990), 47 (*Akademie* edition, 430).

In this work, Kant explicitly states his support for a form of toleration. See Immanuel Kant, *The Metaphysical Elements of Justice*, trans. John Ladd (Indianapolis: Bobbs-Merrill, 1965), 94–95 (*Ak.* 327–28).

32. John Rawls, *A Theory of Justice* (Cambridge: Harvard University Press, 1971), 205–21, 251–57, 541–48. A similar argument can be found in Richards, *Toleration and the Constitution*, 67–102.

33. This argument is suggested by D. D. Raphael, "The Intolerable," *Justifying Toleration: Conceptual and Historical Perspectives,* ed. Susan Mendus, 137–53.

34. For an example of an argument along these lines, see Peter Nicholson, "Toleration as a Moral Ideal,"*Aspects,* ed. John Horton and Susan Mendus (New York: Methuen, 1985), 158–73. See also Joseph Raz, "Autonomy, Toleration, and the Harm Principle," in Mendus, *Justifying Toleration*, 155–75.

35. Indeed, Rawls sometimes makes this commitment explicit. In the Dewey lectures, he assumes that on a Kantian view, moral persons have a "highest-order interest" in developing their "capacity to form, to revise, and to rationally pursue a conception of the good." See Rawls, "Kantian Constructivism in Moral Theory," *Journal of Philosophy* 77 (September 1980): 525. In *Political Liberalism*, however, Rawls distances himself from this form of constructivism. See Rawls, *Political Liberalism* (New York: Columbia University Press, 1993), 99–101.

36. The arguments in Rawls's more recent work have a rather different tenor, and they may not be subject to the same objections. In *Political Liberalism*, Rawls argues that toleration will be chosen, "because, given the fact of reasonable pluralism, a public and shared basis of justification that applies to comprehensive doctrines is lacking in the public culture of democratic society" (60–61). Thus, Rawls suggests that toleration depends crucially on a "political ideal of democratic citizenship that includes the idea of public reason" (62).

If I understand Rawls correctly, toleration is a product of a particular political milieu, and he thus defends a view similar to the one I offer in section 3. However, if Rawls means that the nature of rationality or respect requires a public reason that implies toleration, then it falls prey to the objections I have outlined here, because it presupposes a conception of reason or respect that would be rejected by the opponents of toleration.

37. This argument is suggested by Matthias Lutz-Bachmann, "One God or Many Gods?" lecture presented to the Aquinas Institute and to the department of philosophy at Saint Louis University, November 1992.

38. A number of people have tried to convince me that the choice between salvation and freedom is a false dichotomy, that salvation requires freedom. But the kind of freedom required for salvation is surely metaphysical free will, not political freedom. Otherwise, people who live in coercive societies could never be saved. Indeed, as Seyyed Hossein Nasr points out in his remarks in his chapter, Muslims often do not understand the Western obsession with political freedom, since it has nothing to do with the "Absolute."

39. I take the following suggestion from Don Herzog, *Happy Slaves* (Chicago: University of Chicago Press, 1989), 162–71.

40. Locke lived through the civil war and the Commonwealth as a young man. Later, as the personal secretary to the first Earl of Shaftesbury, the Whig's leader, he was closely involved in the movement for exclusion, and he may have participated in the planning for a general insurrection and the attempt to assassinate Charles that became known as the Rye House Plot. He had good reason to flee to Holland after the failure of the latter in 1683. See Richard Ashcraft, "Revolutionary Politics and Locke's *Two Treatises of Government*," *Political Theory* 8 (1980): 429–85.

Locke's interest in the issue of toleration was further piqued by the plight of the Protestant Huguenots in France after the revocation of the Edict of Nantes in 1685. (He refers to it at least twice. See Locke, *Second Letter*, 72, 87.) For the circumstances of Locke's writings on toleration, see Raymond Klibansky, "Preface," in Locke, *Epistola*, vii–xliv. See also Maurice Cranston, "John Locke and the Case for Tolera-tion," in *A Letter concerning Toleration, in Focus*, ed. John Horton and Susan Mendus, (London: Routledge, 1991), 78–97.

41. Locke, *Second Letter*, 52-55.

42. Locke's allies won only a partial victory. The 1689 Act of Toleration still officially recognized the Church of England, and it granted toleration only to Protes-tant dissenters who accepted the Trinity, so its "toleration" did not encompass non-Christians, Catholics, Deists, or Unitarians. And even the dissenters who were tolerated could not hold public office. Full toleration would await the Catholic Emancipation Bill of 1828, and the Anglican church has a privileged status in England to this day.

43. Ibid., 28.

44. Ibid., 26.

45. Ibid., 33.

46. For a more complete account of these changes, see Don Herzog, *Happy Slaves* (Chicago: University of Chicago Press, 1989), 39–71.

47. Of course, we have to be sure that the institutions we set up embody the goals we intend and that their structures do not undermine those goals.

48. This position does not, however, imply that toleration must be extended indefinitely. Toleration, like all virtues, has its limits. Those limits, like everything else, depend on the particular social context and the needs of a particular situation.

49. Defining these boundaries more exactly is, of course, a difficult task, one that I cannot tackle here. However, we should recognize that defining the exact bound-aries of other virtues, such as courage, temperance, and wisdom, is not any easier.

50. If I am right, then Nicholson's argument that toleration has two aspects—a negative duty to refrain from intolerance and a positive duty to respect others—is correct. However, Nicholson thinks that these two aspects are inherently connected,

but if I am right, the link between them, while substantive, is more complex. See Nicholson, "Toleration as Ideal," 163–68.

51. For this view of liberalism, see Michael Walzer, "Liberalism and the Art of Separation," *Political Theory* 12 (1984): 315–30.

52. If I am right, then liberalism is based neither on a perniciously individualistic psychology nor on a false conception of natural rights, but on the social processes that created modern "masterless men." Individual rights arise, not as a part of the natural structure of the universe, but as the social devices by which we guarantee the toleration of individuals. I discuss these themes at greater length in "Liberalism in Context," *Polity* 25 (Summer 1993): 565–82.

53. My claims in this section rely on a strong form of internalism; that is, I think that moral claims must be capable of motivating people, given their context and their background. Unfortunately, to define exactly—much less defend—this view goes far beyond the scope of this chapter.
For a measure of the complexities involved here, see William Frankena, "Obligation and Motivation in Recent Moral Philosophy," in *Readings in Ethical Theory*, 2d ed., ed. Wilfrid Sellars and John Hospers (Englewood Cliffs, N.J.: Prentice-Hall, 1970), 708-29; and Bernard Williams, "Internal and External Reasons," in *Moral Luck* (Cambridge: Cambridge University Press, 1981), 101–13.

54. See Bernard Williams, *Ethics and the Limits of Philosophy* (Cambridge: Harvard University Press, 1985), 156–73.

55. For the more recent of Locke's predecessors, see Richard Tuck, "Scepticism and Toleration in the Seventeenth Century," in *Justifying Toleration*, ed. Susan Mendus (Cambridge: Cambridge University Press, 1988), 21–35; and Quentin Skinner, *The Foundations of Modern Political Thought* (Cambridge: Cambridge University Press, 1978), 2:241–54.

56. However, this view does not imply that whatever people think is right is right. People often have a poor understanding of the goals that shape their environment. For example, segregation was not justified in the 1950s, even though most people accepted it, because it was not consistent with the deepest goals and values of American society. I defend this view at length in "Living with Contextualism," *Canadian Journal of Philosophy*, forthcoming.

57. This chapter owes a special debt to Connie Rosati, whose trenchant comments on an early version I have only begun to answer. It also owes a debt to Gerry Magill, Doug Williams, Andrew Valls, Jennifer Kwon, and the members of the interdisciplinary group on values at Saint Louis University.

12

Differences: Indifference or Dialogue

Gertrude D. Conway

At times the interconnectedness of philosophical theory and cultural practice seems strikingly evident. Ironically, the current interweaving of philosophical inquiry and popular culture seems most apparent at a time when philosophy's very purpose and worth are called into question. Postmodern philosophical theory and popular culture commentary both circle about a cluster of issues and problems which can be characterized as preoccupation with the recognition and acceptance of the other. Not surprisingly, such preoccupation also leads to the privileging of tolerance.[1]

Contemporary philosophy and life are to a great extent distinguished by a recognition of the existence of diverse, pluralistic traditions and beliefs. Postmodern thought has thematized the problem of the other, preoccupying itself with a critique of all attempts to exclude, reduce, conceal, or assimilate the alterity of the other, to diminish *difference*, otherness, and plurality. Deconstruction has identified itself as rooted in "an openness to the Other"[2] which calls us to "activate the differences."[3] Other contemporary philosophers, such as Gadamer and Habermas, similarly identify the pluralization of discourse as distinctly defining contemporary experience and as shattering the previously assumed "naive consensus."[4] But significant differences emerge concerning the response to such pluralism. Richard Rorty can be characterized as framing a philosophical account of the position played out in current cultural discourse regarding the celebration of pluralism and tolerance. It will be argued that such discourse merits serious reconsideration.

As entailing the recognition that not all beliefs, claims, and values can be harmoniously reconciled, pluralism gives rise to a consideration of tolerance.

As Aristotle recognized, "People cannot live together if they are not pleasant and do not enjoy the same things."[5] Lack of unanimity creates conditions in which tolerance becomes possible; we find ourselves at odds with the other, objecting to beliefs and practices and yet refraining from interference in or suppression of such alterity. But the characterization and justification of the tolerant response to such pluralism varies and carries significantly different implications.

With Rorty, lack of unanimity need not occasion concern. Rorty debunks foundationalism and its preoccupation with commensurability, with the project of discerning rules by which rational agreement can be reached.[6] Challenging the very assumption of and preoccupation with commensuration, he attempts to replace the seeking of consensus with the acceptance of dissensus, the agreement to disagree. Rather than continuing the threadbare Western philosophical preoccupation with "truth," "objectivity," "rationality," and "argumentation," Rorty proposes a delimiting of vision to what is simply "local and ethnocentric," to the traditions which build consensus within a particular community.[7] A spirited affirmation of pluralism defines this postmodern "liberal ironic" or "anti-anti-ethnocentric" viewpoint proposed by Rorty.[8] Whereas ethnocentrism posits the truth of its own parochial claims and anti-ethnocentrism is preoccupied with ahistorical, invariant truths, "anti-anti-ethnocentrism" disclaims any preoccupation with truth whatsoever.

According to Rorty, postmodern liberalism celebrates pluralism, affirming the existence of and further creative invention of diverse ways of coping with lived human experience. Characterized by a spirit of openmindedness, it extols but a single virtue—tolerance. Upon review, such tolerance appears to be ultimately grounded in the very groundlessness of all beliefs and claims. The Rortyian postmodern liberal resolutely accepts the utter contingency of beliefs and claims woven into a specific "story" or "final vocabulary."

> All human beings carry about a set of words which they employ to justify their actions, their beliefs, and their lives. These are words in which we formulate praise of our friends and contempt for our enemies, our long term projects, our deepest self doubts, and our highest hopes. They are words in which we tell, sometimes prospectively and sometimes retrospectively, the story of our lives. I shall call these words a person's "final vocabulary."[9]

One is called to respect the diversity of such "stories" and "final vocabularies," but only through recognizing their equally contingent status and lack of rational justification. Given the reduction of such vocabularies to the level of matters of preference rooted in historical contingencies, Bernstein maintains that Rorty leaves us merely commenting, "Here I stand (and I hope you will also stand here)."[10] Yet even such hope seems to take us beyond the postmodern liberal's acknowledgement of the other. Herein the other's stand *is* recognized, but only as equally arbitrary as one's own. Neither can justify his or her own stand or provide reasons for convincing the other to embrace this stand. There seems to be no motive for taking the other seriously or even oneself for that matter. In fact, Rorty's postmodern liberal is characterized by a distinct lack of seriousness—an aesthetic playfulness.[11]

Such playfulness affirms and celebrates the will to meaning which generates a plurality of meanings, an "ever expanding repertoire of alternative descriptions"[12] and discards what Nietzsche called the "spirit of seriousness" and any preoccupation with the truth or falsity of such meanings. One is left simply affirming the pluralism of such "final vocabularies," recognizing that "if doubt is cast on the worth of these words, their user has no non-circular argumentative recourse. Those words are as far as he can go with language; beyond them there is only helpless passivity or a resort to force."[13]

It seems that the basis for such tolerance is diminished esteem for one's own "final vocabulary." The dissolution of strongly held beliefs and commitments" serves then as the precondition for tolerance toward the other. But since the ironist has "radical and continuing doubts about the final vocabulary she currently uses . . . and realizes that argument phrased in her present vocabulary can neither underwrite nor dissolve these doubts; (and) insofar as she philosophizes about her situation, she does not think that her vocabulary is closer to reality than others,"[14] it would seem that the recognition of such pervasive skepticism would undermine confidence in and allegiance to one's basic commitments. Yet Rorty argues that such skepticism is in no way immobilizing, maintaining that "a belief can still regulate action, can be still thought worth dying for, among people who are quite aware that this belief is caused by nothing deeper than contingent historical circumstance."[15] Given that the other's "final vocabulary" is equally groundless, one wonders why one would take the other seriously, or be "impressed by other vocabularies, vocabularies taken as final by people or books (one) encounters."[16] Rather than effecting an increased spirit of tolerance, such skeptical playfulness would simply occasion the debunking of the accepted. Rather than increasing respect for other perspectives, one's own and the other's would be diminished in esteem. All would become leveled.

Upon review, Rorty's account delivers a very minimal understanding of tolerance as bordering on indifference. This spirit of tolerance delivers a single universal appeal, namely, that we accept pluralism, simply acknowledging its inevitable existence. Such a minimalistic account requires that we "live and let live," removing all impediments to and interference in the other's way of life. Since there is no basis for choosing between different final vocabularies, each community of discourse should be left alone to pursue its own differing and competing way. It offers no reason for attending to the other, for taking the other seriously, for welcoming such difference. Such tolerance is at best what Susan Mendus characterizes as a negative, passive virtue.[17] In the end Rorty leaves us with two extremes—an intolerant Objectivism, which maintains that there is a single, ahistorical Truth which I most certainly possess, or a tolerant skepticism, which maintains there is no truth to be possessed, so let us be playful and indifferent.[18] Intolerance stems from taking beliefs and commitments seriously; tolerance from the arbitrary groundless play of skepticism. Each leads to detached indifference to the other, providing no motivation for seeking exchange, dialogue, or the open conversation Rorty repeatedly calls for. Transformed into mutual indifference, such tolerance leaves us merely affirming pluralism, without attempting any engagement of differences.

It seems that such tolerance also leads to an unrestricted celebration and flourishing of pluralism. Given that the single universal call is to embrace tolerance, tolerance stands without limits.[19] When tolerance is honored as the sole virtue without any accompanying understanding of a shared human form of life, of respect for persons or truth, there can be no circumstances in which limits to tolerance might be reasonably drawn. Herewith it seems that, if anything at all were to be critiqued, intolerance characterized as fanaticism alone would qualify. We are then left tolerating all and any sort of diversity even that which, for example, entails the oppression and subjugation of persons. Herein tolerance seems to slide toward unbridled license. Rorty's casting of tolerance requires a posture of neutrality, a suspension of judgement regarding all other perspectives. Yet his own passionate condemnation of acts of cruelty toward persons and strong defence of democratic liberalism belie such neutrality. His stance embodies substantial moral claims and ideals, and yet his position seems to undermine their seriousness and thwart any condemnation of their violation. The postmodern liberal ironist seems to be either caught in performative contradictions or in a silent neutral passivity. Intellectual discourse concerning such unrestricted tolerance may prove more palatable than the observation of its practice.

An alternate understanding of tolerance can be drawn from other contemporary philosophical positions which also affirm pluralism. Although as equally concerned with the recognition of the other, Gadamer's understanding carries a significantly different response to pluralism, a response rooted in respect for persons and their seeking of truth.

Gadamer's inquiry originates in an awareness of the embeddedness of the human subject in a tradition among other traditions. All human understanding takes off from inherited ways of making sense of this human world. These inherited prejudgements which form the scaffolding of one's thoughts shape one's understanding of oneself and the world. Without them there could be no understanding. Each inquirer stands committed to a view of the world which shapes what can be taken seriously. Such confidence and partiality toward a tradition should not be mistaken for arrogance which unreasonably presumes the superiority of one's tradition over all others. Rather, one stands confidently and seriously committed to the truth of the tradition into which one has been initiated.

Once one recognizes the centrality of beliefs, claims, and practices to the shared life of one's own community and tradition, one must reasonably extend such recognition to other communities and traditions. One may find oneself far from agreeing with or appreciating and even closer to outright disapproving of such alien beliefs and practices. And yet from such a distance, one must still acknowledge their centrality within the alien tradition. Tolerance would thus be rooted in due respect for persons and traditions in their very diversity.[20] But rather than resting with the mere respectful acknowledgement of such diversity, Gadamer draws one toward engagement rather than disengagement, toward dialogue rather than indifference. Herein one seeks to understand the other, to reasonably explore basic differences, to engage in dialogue in a spirit of tolerance. Such dialogue is taken seriously and promoted only on the basis of respect for persons and the assumption that dialogue may disclose something of worth.

Gadamer brings us to understand the demands and worth of such dialogue. Attending to the other requires that we open ourselves to the other's claims in their very alterity. Postmodern thinkers bring us to recognize the great demands of even such minimal recognition of the other and the strong tendency to silence differences, exclude the alien, assume a "false consensus," assimilate what is alien to our own categories, and dismiss the alien as unintelligible nonsense.[21] But Gadamer's dialogue demands more than such minimal recognition and becomes possible only if one practices a cluster of hermeneutic virtues: an openmindedness which requires that we be receptive to the disclosure of the other, seeking to understand and do justice to what is disclosed; an imaginative empathy which allows us to conceive of the other in its very alterity;[22] and a courage which allows us to risk our own prejudgements. Such response demands that rival claims be taken seriously and presented in their strongest light. Rather than being primarily preoccupied with discrediting the other or winning debate, we seek to understand the other's standpoint and horizon, so "his ideas become intelligible without our having to agree with them."[23]

Gadamer affirms the worth of such dialogue. Only through encountering the alien does one come to true self-understanding. Being initiated into an inherited tradition, one "swallows whole" a cluster of assumptions which defines one's understanding of the world.[24] Encountering the other brings us to articulate and examine the tradition to which we belong, thus occasioning more reflective participation in that tradition. Herewith, we subject our claims to critical review, putting to test our most basic prejudgements. Mill similarly affirms such tolerant dialogue which leads to the eclipse of superannuated truths and the transformation of knowledge that comes through the critical view of claims. He emphasizes that an "intelligent and living apprehension of the truth requires the same condition as the discovery of the truth, namely, that one be confronted with ideas contrary to one's own and thus be compelled to reason."[25] According to Mill,

> The whole strength and value . . . of human judgement depending on the one property, that it can be set right when it is wrong, reliance can be placed on it only when the means of setting it right are kept constantly at hand. In the case of any person whose judgement is really deserving of concidence, how has it become so? Because he has kept his mind open to criticism of his opinions and conduct. Because it has been his practice to listen to all that could be said against him; to profit by as much of it as was just, and to expound to himself, and upon occasion to others, the fallacy of what was fallacious. . . . The beliefs which we have most warrant for have no safeguard to rest on but a standing invitation to the whole world to prove them unfounded.[26]

Facing the other brings us to articulate and examine our own prejudgments and prevents us from lapsing into thoughtless conformity. Dialogue with the other discloses our entrenched prejudgments, putting them at risk before the other, forcing us to justify our truth claims. Such encounters enable us to distinguish "blind (unjustifiable) prejudices" and "enabling prejudices" capable of justification. Self-referential, monological inquiry often fails to disclose such distinctions.[27]

Besides disclosing our own point of view, dialogue allows for the disclosure of that of the other as other. In seeking to understand the other, we recognize that we cannot simply shift horizons. Through dialogue, we articulate our awareness of our horizon, enlarged so as to include the disclosure of the other's claims in their own respective horizon. Herein, a "fusion of horizons" occurs.[28] It seems that tolerance is the precondition of the very possibility of such a fusion of horizons. Tolerance opens the possibility of such mutual attending to each other's claims, explicating of one's positions, discovering of insights and oversights, agreements and disagreements, and disclosing of what was previously unseen.

This interpenetration or "fusion" of horizons is only possible if both participants are situated within a horizon which encompasses both self and other. Dialogue requires mutual recognition both of identity and difference and of commonality and alterity. It hinges on the seeking out of that which rests in sameness and that which defines distance. Without such commonality in a shared form of life, there is no possibility of dialogue. Without significant difference, there is no need for dialogue. There is no dialogue, if no commonality; there is no recognition of an other, if no difference. Rorty's repeated denial of a human nature, any shared form of human life, thus seems to undercut the very possibility and point of such dialogue.[29] What is alien can only speak as such from within a shared form of life. For dialogue even to commence, the other must be recognized both in sameness and alterity. For the dialogue to continue, the participants must not rest content with the mere voicing of difference nor cancel differences in order to raise the dialogue to a desired unanimity. Dialogue intends mutual understanding of our very differences, the mutual questioning from the context of a situated horizon. The "fusion of horizons" is only possible if horizons, although limited, are not closed and are capable of being enlarged.

Within such a fusion of horizons, we mutually recognize that we are objects of tolerance to the other. Entering dialogue in such a spirit of tolerance, we stand both committed to our own point of view and open to the equally committed claims of the other. Such posture requires an understanding of our human finitude. Tolerance appears to rest in the realization of our fallibilism, in the insight that we may be wrong and the other right.[30] Tolerant dialogue is distinguished by a certain intellectual humility whereby one assumes one is not mistaken, yet remains humbly open to such possibility. We take seriously the other's truth claims as they bear on and question ours. Herein, the other's views are courteously acknowledged and judiciously heard. Such respect for the other does not require that we accept the other's claims but that we be open to the possible disclosure of their truth. We stand committed to the constellation of beliefs and claims which define our "final vocabulary" and at the same time remain open to their revision. Such "engaged fallibilistic pluralism"[31] recognizes that, as truth claims, our judgments are worth defending and at the same time corrigible. We open ourselves to dialogue with the other, avoiding both an overconfident dogmatism which refuses to subject itself to revision and a skepticism which concedes all is groundless. Through critical dialogue one seeks to reveal what is of worth. One tolerantly commences dialogue, recognizing the value of mutual criticism, its disclosure and refinement of our prejudgements, and the enlargment of our horizons. As Alasdair MacIntyre states, "To foreclose on tolerance is to cut oneself off from . . . criticism and refutation. . . . It is to gravely endanger one's own rationality by not admitting one's own fallibility."[32]

Bernstein identifies well what is needed in response to today's awareness of pluralism, namely, a recognition of our historical finitude and fallibilism. Fallibilism itself presupposes that there is a truth to be known. We can support our allegiance to a tradition by showing how it is rationally progressing according to its own historically developing strands of rationality and how it can meet challenges of rival traditions.[33] But as Bernstein emphasizes, such dialogue requires a public space "in which human beings can come together to debate and argue with each other. . . . public debate presupposes what Rorty seems to want to eliminate—that we can be locked in argument with each other."[34] With Rorty we are left with the mere creative flourishing of ever-inventive final vocabularies which provide no basis for dialogue. Such an account cannot offer a basis for valuing the articulation or engagement of our differences. With all positions traceable to fiat, and no position more justified than any other, all that remains besides the will to meaning is the will to power which allows one to enforce one's final vocabulary.[35] Bernstein provides a warning which speaks to the needs of our multicultural society and world. Today we are "threatened by a new form of tribalism in which difference and otherness are reified and where there is a failure to seek out [any] commonalities and solidarities."[36] We can all too vividly see the consequences of Rorty's vision, when we accept there is nothing more to be done than concede our differences, when "beyond that there is [but] helpless passivity or resort to force."[37]

Gadamer's position provides a response to the queries why and when be tolerant? Tolerance is grounded in respect for persons and rational inquiry as disclosing truth. Tolerance is rooted in and restricted by the overarching requirement that we respect persons and their beliefs and truth claims, even when they differ from our own. To respect persons is, *ipso facto*, to respect the ways in which as persons they differ from one another. Tolerance brings us to respectfully consider the significance and worth of other points of view and ways of life. The recognition of our own fallibilism and the worth of reasonable dialogue generate a presumption in favor of tolerance and a means of drawing limits to tolerance. The principle of respect for persons entails valuing diversity within a reasonable limit. It follows that one ought not to respect beliefs and practices which contravene tolerance and its underlying respect for persons and rational inquiry as disclosing truth. True tolerance fosters the practical wisdom of knowing how and when to be tolerant and when justifiably to be intolerant.[38]

The intending of dialogue in circumstances which risk misinterpretation and misunderstanding renders it a hopeful but realistic venture. We commence dialogue with the other, acknowledging that it may not lead to unanimity, to "our living together and enjoying the same things." We realistically recognize that dialogue may end with our facing a "nonreducible plurality of opinions."[39] But by engaging in dialogue, we promote conversation and reasonable discourse, activities Aristotle described as fostering and sustaining friendship and civility. The contemporary recognition of a plurality of rival traditions, claims, and beliefs places great responsibilities upon us. It seems our times call for more than a "live and let live" pluralism in which we prize our autonomy and noninterference with the other.[40] Rather, such times call for an open dialogue engaging our differences, sensitive both to the fragility and to the importance of such dialogue. Such times demand that we recognize and work to eliminate situations and conditions that thwart and distort dialogue, cultivate the host of virtues bearing upon tolerance (humility, courtesy, respect for persons and truth), and work to envision and actualize ways of fostering dialogue which lets "what seems to be far and alienated speak again."[41] Herein, we promote tolerance not as passive acquiescence to a regrettably inevitable pluralism but as the judicious promotion of the very mutuality of respect distinctive of rational persons and civil societies at their very best.

NOTES

1. Richard Bernstein characterizes learning to live tolerantly with the other as one of the most pressing demands of contemporary life. See Richard Bernstein, *The New Constellation: The Ethical-Political Horizons of Modernity/Postmodernity* (Cambridge, Mass.: MIT Press, 1992), 9.

2. Jacques Derrida, "Dialogue with Jacques Derrida," in Richard Kearney, *Dialogues with Contemporary Continental Thinkers* (Manchester: Manchester University Press, 1984), 124.

3. Jean-Francois Lyotard, *The Post Modern Condition: A Report on Knowledge*, trans. G. Bennington and B. Massumi (Minneapolis: University of Minnesota Press, 1984), 81–82.

4. Jürgen Habermas, "Questions and Counterquestions," in *Habermas and Modernity*, ed. Richard Bernstein (Cambridge, Mass.: MIT Press, 1985), 192.

5. Aristotle, *Nichomachean Ethics* 5.5.1157b.22–23.

6. Richard Rorty, *Philosophy and the Mirror of Nature* (Princeton: Princeton University Press, 1980), 316.

7. Bernstein, *The New Constellation*, 242.

8. See Richard Rorty, *Contingency, Irony, and Solidarity* (New York: Cambridge University Press, 1989); Rorty, "On Ethnocentrism: A Reply to Clifford Geertz," *Michigan Quarterly Review* 25 (Summer 1986): 525–34, and Rorty, "Solidarity or Objectivity," in *Relativism, Interpretation, and Confrontation*, ed. Michael Krausz (Notre Dame: Notre Dame University, 1989), 35–79. Such a position forces the liberal ironist to acknowledge that Western liberalism's distinctive claims regarding human equality and dignity are reducible to Western eccentricities or parochial biases which are no more justified in terms of the "nature of humanity" or "demands of rationality"

than any other claims. As Rorty states, herein freedom is substituted for truth as the goal of thinking and social progress (Rorty 1989, xiii). Yet Rorty himself promotes the ideals of liberalism as the "best hope of the species" (Rorty 1986, 532).

9. Rorty, *Contingency*, 73.

10. Bernstein, *The New Constellation*, 278.

11. See Richard Rorty, "The Priority of Democracy to Philosophy," in *The Virginia Statute for Religious Freedom, Its Evolution and Consequences in American History*, ed. Merrill D. Peterson and Robert C. Vaughan (New York: Cambridge University Press, 1988), 272. Rorty writes "Like the rise of . . . the insouciant pluralism of contemporary culture . . . such superficiality and light-mindedness helps along the disenchantment of the world. It helps make the world's inhabitants more pragmatic, more tolerant, more liberal . . . Moral commitment . . . does not require taking seriously all the matters that are . . . taken seriously by one's fellow citizens. It may require just the opposite. It may require trying to josh them out of the habit of taking these topics so seriously. There may be serious reasons for so joshing them. More generally, we should not assume that the aesthetic is always the enemy of the moral. I should argue that in the recent history of liberal societies, the willingness to view matters aesthetically—to be content to indulge in what Schiller called "play" and to discard what Nietzsche called "the spirit of seriousness" has been an important vehicle of moral progress."

12. Rorty, *Contingency*, 39.

13. Ibid., 73.

14. Ibid., Also see Richard Rorty, *Objectivity, Relativism and Truth* (New York: Cambridge University Press, 1991), 29, in which he writes, "I have been arguing that we pragmatists should grasp the ethnocentric horn of this dilemma. We should say that we must, in practice, privilege our own group, even though there can be no noncircular justification for doing so."

15. Rorty, *Contingency*, 189.

16. Ibid., 73.

17. In *Toleration and the Limits of Liberalism* (Atlantic Highlands, N.J.: Humanities Press, 1989), Susan Mendus develops such a negative account of tolerance without any reference to Rorty or to other postmodern accounts.

18. See Mendus, *Toleration and the Limits of Liberalism*, 77. Here Mendus considers at length a number of non-Rortyian liberal accounts of tolerance. One particular construal of modern liberalism entails a neutral posture which denies that there is any better way to live. Another maintains belief in intrinsically superior ways of living, but refrains from forcing such belief on others. The latter type of liberalism does affirm a conception of human nature and the good life but stresses the supreme value of autonomy, affirming that a chosen way of life is preferable to one which is externally imposed. Truth and self-determination are herein valued. See Glenn Tinder,

Tolerance: Toward a New Civility (Amherst, Mass.: University of Massachusetts Press, 1976), 83. Tinder argues that Mill's individualistic liberalism expresses indifference toward and disengagement from the other. The individual's supreme aim is preserving autonomy, the right to live as one pleases so long as one inflicts no harm.

19. See J. Budziszewki, *True Tolerance, Liberalism and the Necessity of Judgement* (New Brunswick: Transaction Books, 1992), xiii. He comments, "Tolerance is a virtue indeed; but if it is the only virtue, it can hardly be anything more than good conscience in our continuing lack of convictions."

20. As T. S. Eliot once said, "The Christian does not want to be tolerated," in the sense of being put up with. The Christian *does* want to be respected, valued, welcomed. See Susan Mendus and David Edwards, *On Toleration* (Oxford: Clarendon Press, 1987), 101.

21. Bernstein, *The New Constellation*, 51–52.

22. Heidegger offers an interesting contrast between empathy and indifference. In *Being and Time* (1.4.26), Heidegger grounds empathy in the more primordial existential possibility of Being-with-and-towards-one-another. He distinguishes an empathetic way of being with others which allows for "the possibility of understanding the other" and an "inconsiderate" being with others which reckons with them "without ever wanting to 'have anything to do with them'."

23. Gadamer, *Truth and Method*, rev. 2d ed., trans. and rev. J. Weinsheimer and D. G. Marshall (New York: Crossroad, 1989), 303.

24. Wittgenstein considers this point in *On Certainty* #141, "When we first *believe* anything what we believe is not a single proposition, it is a whole system of propositions (Light dawns gradually over the whole)."

25. See Tinder, *Tolerance*, 24.

26. John Stuart Mill, *On Liberty*, ed. C. V. Shields (New York: Bobbs-Merrill, 1956), 27.

27. Descartes provides such an example. Numerous prejudgments pass his monological methodic doubt unnoticed.

28. Gadamer, *Truth and Method*, 306–7. Gadamer speaks of the possibility and demands of such fusion. Such imagery suggests that far from being encircled by a closed boundary, understanding can incorporate what is initially foreign and seemingly incomprehensible. This fusion possibility applies to the overcoming both of historical and of cultural distance. But Gadamer does not address the possibility of conditions in which such a fusion may not be possible. Gadamer refers to texts which *initially* appear strange to us and resist interpretation. But could there be claims rooted in such radically different points of departure that understanding is precluded? It seems that Gadamer would argue that only if there is some fundamental common unity underlying multiplicity and diversity, can dialogue, comprehension, and translation be possible. Given such unity, there would be no fully closed, inaccessible horizons.

29. Rorty states, "The idea my sort of philosopher wants to get rid of, [is] the idea that the world or self has an intrinsic nature" (8). Rorty recognizes that this undercuts the liberal ironist's attempt to support the claim that cruelty is wrong. An empathetic response to the other's suffering builds the solidarity Rorty seeks, but the condemnation of cruelty and promotion of solidarity stand without justification. Rorty repeatedly disclaims any preoccupation with the idea of a human nature. Yet in *Objectivity, Relativism and Truth*, (215); he states, "The anthropologist and the native agree, after all, on an enormous number of platitudes they usually share about, for example, the desirability of finding waterholes, the danger of fondling poisonous snakes, the need for shelter in bad weather, the tragedy of the death of loved ones, the value of courage and endurance, and so on. If they did not . . . it is hard to see how the two would ever have been able to learn enough of each other's languages to recognize the other as a language user."

30. Mill argues that all silencing of disagreement in discussion rests on the assumption of infallibility (21–22). He also emphasizes that theoretical recognition of fallibilism is often not carried into practical judgement; " . . . While everyone well knows himself to be fallible, few think it necessary to take any precautions against their own fallibility, or admit the supposition that any opinion of which they feel very certain may be one of the examples of the error to which they acknowledge themselves to be liable" (22).

31. Bernstein, *The New Constellation*, 338–39.

32, Alasdair MacIntyre, *Marcuse* (New York: Viking Press, 1970), 104. MacIntyre develops his account of the intimate connection between tolerance and rationality amidst his critique of Marcuse. He envisions the transformation in Marxism from a rational to an irrationally maintained theory as rooted in Marxists' "cutting themselves off from possibilities of criticism and refutation." He argues that the "use of state power to defend Marxism as the one set of true beliefs in the Soviet Union produced the atrophy of Marxism and the irrationality of Soviet Marxism" (105).

33. Bernstein, *The New Constellation*, 64.

34. Ibid., 284.

35. See Charles Taylor, *Sources of the Self: The Making of the Modern Identity* (Cambridge, Mass.: Harvard University Press, 1989), 99. Taylor argues for the implausibility of neo-Nietzschean acccounts such as Rorty's. He writes that "the point of view from which we might constate that all orders are equally arbitrary, in particular that all moral views are equally so, is just not available to us humans. It is a form of self-delusion to think that we do not speak from a moral orientation which we take to be right. This is a condition of being a functioning self, not a metaphysical view we can put off or on." (99).

36. Bernstein, *The New Constellation*, 313.

37. Rorty, *Contingency*, 73.

38. R. J. Royce, "Pluralism, Tolerance and Moral Education," *Journal of Moral Education* 11 (May 1982): 179. Here Royce draws an insightful parallel between tolerance and loyalty. Neither in itself is worthy of acclaim; moral evaluation must take into account that toward which tolerance or loyalty is shown.

39. Richard Bernstein, *Beyond Objectivity and Relativism: Science, Hermeneutics and Praxis* (Philadelphia: University of Pennsylvania Press, 1983), 221–23.

40. Rorty characterizes such a situation as promoting "a world of moral narcissists, congratulating themselves on neither knowing nor caring what people in the club on the other side . . . are like." See Rorty, "On Ethnocentrism," 533.

41. Gadamer, "Practical Philosophy as a Model of the Human Sciences," *Research in Phenomenology,* 9:83.

13

Radicalizing Liberalism and Modernity

Henry L. Ruf

Tolerance obviously is better than intolerance. So is showing respect better than being disrespectful and seeking understanding better than perpetuating misunderstanding. However, I would suggest that none of them are adequate responses to the differences existing within ourselves and the worlds in which we and other people live. The indecent and poisonous contamination of everyone touched by intolerance, disrespect, and misunderstanding can be better resisted and lessened if we do not rest content with merely seeking tolerance, respect, and understanding, but if in addition we seek to move through them and beyond them by constituting new social practices and forms of subjectivity which incorporate a prizing of differences and inexplicable mysteries and a cherishing of things radically other than how we tend to see ourselves.

Merely tolerating those who are different seems grossly inadequate. Calling for toleration is not the only possible response to behavior-exhibiting intolerance, the unjustified refusal to let people who are different live in their differences. Toleration still implies that there is something wrong or inferior about that which is being tolerated.[1] We do not merely "tolerate" those we love and admire no matter how different they are from us. Sometimes we put up with things we disapprove of because it would cost too much to express such disapproval. Sometimes we do so because we recognize that we are fallible and might be wrong.[2] However, such prudential or epistemological warrants for tolerance still leave in place the original beliefs and attitudes of superiority, convictions which for many in our world do become dangerous justifications for coercing others into conformity or marginalization because they are convictions of those who have no doubt about the correctness of their position and who are willing to die and kill for their convictions. There is a better response to intolerance than tolerance. If one removes the tendency to judge as inferior others who are merely different, then one can move beyond both intolerance and mere tolerance.

Similarly, it does not seem to be enough merely to respect beliefs, perspectives, and ways of living with which we disagree or the right of others to hold such beliefs and to be different from us. Although this can be an important right, demonstrating that disrespect is not to be tolerated. This right may consist of no more than granting a negative freedom to be left alone. It too may be motivated only prudentially or in a recognition that one cannot prove these disagreeable beliefs false or this way of life inferior, even though one thinks they are. When you and I share the same beliefs, perspectives, and ways of living, we do not talk about respecting each other's positions. Some-times we recognize that had we been reared in the kind of situation in which people with different beliefs and ways of life were reared, then we too most likely would have held these positions which now seem so foreign to us. Thus, we should respect these differences even though these are not positions we would ever want to hold ourselves.[3] It is such a moral demand for respect for foreign cultures and ways of life that grounds the almost universal moral condemnation of imperialism today. As appropriate as this demand is, it is not sufficient to ground a moral condemnation of ethnic cleansing and all other efforts to cleanse one's own neighborhood of foreign and inferior influences, beliefs, practices, orientations, and ways of life.

So many today say, "Our situations are different; our ways of life are different; if someone doesn't like the way we live, let them go back home, let them stay with their own kind, let them stay in the closet. Everyone has a right to believe whatever they want, but if they are going to live here they are going to have to live as we live." As long as one prizes only what one takes oneself to be, talk about respecting others who are different will be insufficient in this world in which differences lie all around us and even within us. It is only when the inescapability of otherness in all persons and neighborhoods is recognized and prized that one can move beyond merely granting negative freedom to be left alone to those with differences we do not prize and go on to grant others and ourselves the positive freedom and power to resist the domination of exclusion and to be able to walk in many different, astonishingly rich, neighborhoods.

Finally, even seeking to understand differences may not be sufficient to minimize either domination or self-deception. The alternative to misunder-standings caused by interpreting others in terms of our interpretations and misinterpretations of ourselves is not just a matter of pursuing the goal of understanding others and ourselves better. It often involves a cherishing of incommensurate and inexplicable differences within the worlds in which we live and within ourselves. Some differences are so great that cherishing them requires moving beyond misunderstanding and understanding. Recognition that we never fully understand anything, even ourselves, often is needed in order to lessen the motivation to use self-interpretations in misunderstanding others. Misunderstanding, of course, is to be minimized in order that people are not miscategorized and thus mistreated. Knowing that one set of categories of interpretation is inappropriate, however, does not entail the availability of an alternative, appropriate set of categories in terms of which people can be interpreted and understood. Letting people be what they are may mean letting them be in that indeterminably rich and inexhaustibly mysterious materiality and particularity which never can be fully understood.

The pursuit of understanding can be overrated, and when it is it becomes an instrument fostering tendencies to exercise overpowering domination, as Nietzsche noted, and perpetuating self-misunderstanding, as the Buddha noted. The increased similarity of people throughout the world may be more a result of coercively producing such similarity than a matter of securing mutual understanding. As Foucault pointed out, one of the great dangers of the modern world is the belief that the totalization of normalization is possible and desirable.[4] People in love know how little they really understand each other and how exciting this makes life when they do not misunderstand each other. It would have been presumptuous of me to pretend that I understood the Buddhist monks enrolled in my philosophy classes in Thailand, but I did not have to understand them to know that my life had been enriched by having encountered them. Similarly, if we could come to prize diverse forms of sexuality, then we could let homosexuality, heterosexuality, bisexuality, autosexuality, and celibacy just be in others and in ourselves, even when they are so interwoven as to defy understanding.

Given what we know about the material, social, cultural, historical, and interpersonal fields in which people are constitutively located as unique individuals—individuals as decentered as these fields are filled with gaps, fractures, contradictions and incommensurabilities—and given what we know about the virtually unlimited ways in which people consciously and unconsciously work out responses to their constitution, environments, and other people, it would require a tragic blindness of the highest order for anyone to desire or presume that they could fully understand themselves or others. Compassionate acceptance of what one must work with in caring for oneself requires and permits one to move beyond self-deception, self-misunderstanding, and the desire for total understanding. It is such a morality of compassion for the idiosyncratic and descriptively inexhaustible character of all people that Edwards has shown that Wittgenstein endorsed.[5]

Two contemporary giants among the philosophical defenders of political liberalism, John Rawls and Ronald Dworkin, have published books in which they acknowledge the incommensurate differences that exist in various conceptions of the good life and in various judgments about the manner in which one should respect the intrinsic value of life. Both argue that accepting a liberal, procedural sense of justice which respects the right to choose to live differently is the only reasonable response to the dilemmas caused by such incommensurables.[6] These two books represent only the latest in a series of efforts by defenders of liberalism in the last decade to combine a defense of liberalism with a recognition of incommensurate moral ideals and judgments.[7] However, these recent defenses of liberalism fail to provide the response needed to defend liberalism against its many contemporary critics because they fail to appreciate the significance of such incommensurables, and the consequent need to radicalize liberalism and the principle of individual autonomy which lies at the heart of all forms of liberalism.

Moral ideals and judgments are often constitutive elements in people's understanding of their worlds and of themselves. Therefore, it should not surprise us that calls for respecting an individual's political right to have different moral ideals and judgments are going to be inadequate to morally motivate those who believe that such a purchase of social peace comes at too high a price—their moral integrity and the salvation of their souls.[8] Political liberalism cannot be justified to those who do not place highest value on individual freedom to choose among alternative conceptions of the good life, who do not prize above all else such a form of individual autonomy. As MacIntyre has pointed out, liberalism's neutrality is a constitutive element within a particular moral form of life and is not a context-free valuing of a space in which rival moral ideals can flourish in peace.[9]

Even Raz's effort to abandon neutrality and to commit liberalism to pursuing the good of maximizing a form of individual autonomy which makes room under its umbrella for alternative conceptions of the good life is not radical enough. Raz acknowledges that his ideal of maximizing personal autonomy does not spread a wide enough umbrella to make room for all ideals that might be pursued in some societies which would be capable of providing valuable and satisfying lives to its members.[10] He is thinking of the opposition which the Muslim minority in England would have to liberal efforts to use the schools to nurture students to be able to freely choose among alternative good forms of life. Raz recommends that the liberal state pursuing the moral ideal of maximizing autonomy tolerate such subcultural groups, as long as they do not harm those who prize autonomy, until they can be assimilated.[11] Such toleration and assimilation efforts seem to express gross disrespect for ways of life which are guilty only of being different.

It is autonomy itself which has to be radicalized if liberalism's umbrella is to become broad enough to do justice to moral and social incommensurabilities. Doing what one wants or thinks is right does not guarantee autonomy, and being autonomous does not entail modern, Western individualism. Liberals themselves have begun to recognize that individual autonomy consists only of relative independence from contingent social factors and that Kant's notion of a transcendentally autonomous person, giving laws to oneself while free from all nonuniversal social influences, is impossible.[12] Since all individuals making choices are socially constituted individuals of a particular, materially contingent sort, a host of moral issues arise which liberals only now are beginning to think through. Given that luck may have a great deal to do with determining the kind of moral socializing a person gains, liberal concepts of character traits and personal responsibility and merit are being rethought.[13] Given that individual wants, desires, and identities can be the result of socializing practices servicing the interests of such overpowering forces of domination as consumerism, cultural hegemonies, and a microphysics of disciplinary practices, maximizing autonomy must go beyond providing the negative freedom needed to be left alone to do what one wants; it must involve doing what is necessary to empower people with the positive freedom to refuse to be some of the things they have been socially constituted to be.

Maximizing autonomy means minimizing nonconsensual living, something it is extremely difficult to know one is doing because it requires one to make, as Habermas points out,[14] counterfactual judgments about what persons would give consent to if they knew what had been done to them, what practices they were participating in, and what consequences, intended and unintended, were occurring because of this history and these practices. However, it seems very likely that many people in forms of life different from modern Western liberalism would give informed consent to their own ways of life, accenting as they do community and tradition rather than the traditional liberal notion of critical individuality. This seems true for participants in some Islamic, Confucian, Buddhist, and communitarian Christian forms of life. If this is true, then prizing the autonomy of the participants in these ways of life requires prizing the existence of these different ways of living. Such prizing must go beyond that respecting which is only avoiding coercive disrespect. It must involve a very liberal and compassionate cherishing of different forms of life, different ways of being human, and different moralities and religions.

In one important respect such a cherishing of differences is still liberalism and not some form of postliberalism. The radicalization of liberalism and the autonomy principle recommended here require that communitarians and tradition-centered communities also be radical liberals. They too are bound to cherish the autonomy of other communities and their traditions, including the modern Western world. Many Buddhists and Confucians and some Muslims and Christians already are doing this. This form of radical liberalism endorses Foucault's very abstract principle of minimizing nonconsensual living as a universal norm binding all communities in their relations with other communities and in their treatment of dissidents within their own community.[15]

Foucault's principle seems to be what would result if one were to raise to the level of a universal principle of justice Rawls' principle of democratic reasonableness, which condemns comprehensive moral or religious doctrines which would authorize the use of state power in ways which could not be justified to all citizens who are seen as free and equal.[16] Peffer is right that Rawls unnecessarily ties his own hands when he reduces the position enunciated in *Justice as Fairness*[17] from a moral project to merely a democratic liberal project, thus making it impossible to morally condemn those who would legitimate their rejection of the need to justify all moral requirements to those who will be bound by them by claiming that they are not interested in being democratic liberals.[18] Peffer goes too far, however, in seeking to return Rawls' principles of justice, basic liberties and primary goods (in a slightly modified form) to the level of basic principles of social justice. Rawls is right about the fact that not all people who endorse the reasonableness principle will endorse the rest of the principles of *Justice as Fairness*. The reasonableness principle requires that no one be denied participation as full and equal voices in the dialogue which will constitute a people's morality. Young correctly points out that it is such universal access to the dialogue constituting social norms (a key aspect of Habermas' "Discourse Ethics")[19] which is the alternative to unreasonable bias in ethics.[20] Young also points out, contra to Habermas, that respecting such dialogical access does not guarantee that a single morality will be constituted, but it in fact requires respecting the differences that result. Endorsing Foucault's principle of minimizing nonconsentuality or elevating Rawls' reasonableness principle to the status of a universal principle of social justice does not exclude moral pluralism, but it does point out the parameters within which morally reasonable moralities must reside.

The acceptance of such a very abstract norm requires going beyond obedience to a law to a spirit of cherishing radical and never fully understandable differences. When such differences are not prized, the other will be seen as inferior or worthless and one will not believe that adherents are really informed in giving their consent. One must prove the worthiness of the differences, something one cannot do with incommensurables. This is probably why Taoists have insisted that the acceptance and the cherishing of the other must rest on and be justified by absolutely nothing.[21] There is much that is not unjustified that lies beyond the realm of the justified. Differences free of coercion need no justification. They can rest on nothing. Not indicting them as inferior or worthless means letting them be—resting on nothing, something people will do only if radical difference itself is cherished.

Cherishing incommensurate differences and an inexhaustible reservoir of aspects and relationships which transcend our finite abilities to describe, understand, explain, or justify requires not only radicalizing moral and political liberalism, but it also requires radicalizing Western modernity's very concept of rationality. The only alternative to being irrational, holding beliefs or performing actions for bad reasons is not rationality, holding beliefs, or performing actions for good reasons. The rationality practice of acting and holding beliefs on the basis of reasons (good ones or bad ones) is a practice which presupposes a whole background which need not be rationalized and which cannot be exhaustively rationalized. As Wittgenstein pointed out, the game of giving explanatory and justificatory reasons comes to an end in the way of life which gives the game a point.[22] Similarly, all of our descriptive vocabulary can be used to make distinctions and mark similarities only because they are used in shared linguistic practices in a context of other nonlinguistic practices against a background of a natural environment, learned skills and social practices which themselves cannot be exhaustively described.[23]

Instead of seeking reasons for everything, radicalizing modernity would shift presumption and ask the question, "Why always ask why?" Why are reasons always necessary? Explanatory reasons are needed only when anomalies turn up because of conflicting beliefs we hold. With most presumed states of affairs there is no need to say anything more than, "That's how things are," the claim we cannot help end up making when final explanations are given. Likewise, beliefs, desires, actions need justification only when there are reasons for thinking that they are in error. They are presumed innocent until a prima facie case can be presented for indicting them by showing how they conflict with what we accept as being not unjustified. Requesting and giving reasons is only a small part of human living. Some philosophers unfortunately believe that civilization will fall unless their vested interest in universalizing such rationalizing is acknowledged by all, especially our educational, legal, and moral institutions. Many holders and would-be holders of sufficient dominating power to determine criteria of rationality would like to see such a totalization of rationalization. Minimizing nonconsentuality requires refusing to restrict ourselves within the confines of such rationalizing.

As valuable as Habermas's reconstruction of modernity is, radicalizing modernity will require more. Rather than seeking Foucault's goal of a minimization of nonconsensuality, which calls for the public to open itself to inescapable and cherishable differences, Habermas in fearful avoidance of life-threatening irrationality pursues a goal of maximizing a consensual rationality that only leaves such room for difference and other as a consensual public permits to exist as private matters. Recognizing the need to go beyond modernity's absolutizing of individual subjectivity and ahistorical, asocial rationality, without falling into a nihilistic abyss of relativism and irrationality, Habermas surrenders to intersubjectivity and consensual rationality the authority to set the boundaries around everything acceptable.

Habermas believes that only seeking the Peircean goal of an ideal scientific community sharing the same descriptive and explanatory characterization of nature will serve the human interest in productively controlling natural raw materials in order to guarantee the continuing life of the species.[24] He further claims that only engaging in speech acts presupposing the universal pragmatic ideals of true representations of the world, truthful expressions of oneself, and rightful obedience to the consensually accepted norms of one's community will serve the human interest in securing the universal understanding necessary for the preservation of the identities of social communities.[25] Finally, according to Habermas, only critiquing ideologies in terms of what will be consensually agreed to after free and open debate and critiquing oneself in terms of consensual scientific understanding, life-world hermeneutics and consensually accepted norms will serve the human interest of emancipating oneself from coercion and self-deception.[26]

Through such a reconstruction, Habermas seeks to preserve modernism's project of liberation through rational enlightenment. I suggest that a much more radical change in modernism is needed if nonconsentuality is to be minimized. Even as modernity lacked enough of the social, so now Habermas's reconstruction of modernity leaves insufficient room for that which is other than the socially consensual. When everything is enclosed within consensual rationality, then the contextually dependent character of rationality itself is misunderstood and the non-rational becomes imprisoned rather than cherished and allowed to be free from explanations or justifications.[27]

That all worlds of subjects and objects are socially constituted does not mean that all social practices have as their point the maintenance and reproduction of the social. It is against just such a functionalist reduction that participants in artistic and religious practices have protested as they have attempted to remain faithful to the beautiful and the sacred rather than the useful. Although their demand for autonomy often has gotten caught up in irrationalisms and service to forces of overpowering domination, they nevertheless also always have been avant garde resistors of social domination in their efforts to practice artistic and religious freedom.

Social rationality itself always presupposes and points beyond itself to something other which also always remains constitutively located within such rationality itself. This is Derrida's great contribution to our appreciation of an inescapable otherness in our language and ourselves. The ideality of our linguistic signifiers and signifieds can never be freed from their contingent materiality. Power and domination are only two of these material factors. Signifiers are played with, and metaphors and interpretations of interpretations creatively open space for new language and new worlds. A host of chance occurrences determines how distinctions, family resemblances, vague boundaries, and language games are constituted and modified.[28] The very course of the history of the development of the social practices which constitute us as subjects and agents and the world of objects which we relate to is filled with inexplicable contingent ruptures. This is the freedom of the Being of beings to which the later Heidegger gives priority over human freedom in the constitution of worlds and which he calls for us to poetically cherish so that new worlds can come to be through us. It is just this radical contingency of the constitution of ourselves and our world that needs to be prized rather than dismissed as irrationally mystical.[29] Living then beyond all need to justify existence in order to avoid nihilism, no matter what results from the throw of life's dice, one can say with Zarathustra, " 'Over all things stand the heaven Accident, the heaven Innocence, the heaven Chance, the heaven Prankishness.' . . . you are to me a divine table for divine dice and dice players."[30] "Was *that* life? Well then! Once More!"[31]

Science, restricted to Habermas's consensual rationality, is a greatly restricted science, and the nature so studied is reduced to raw materials to be utilized in a very limited range of productive human activities. Incommensurate vocabularies and explanatory theories may never be rooted out by any ideal scientific community. Are we to speak of particles or fields, objects and substances, or Whiteheadean and Buddhist events and processes, or Deleuzian flows? Furthermore, scientists themselves often focus less on raw materials of service to human needs, biological or social, and more on the grandeur of butterflies, insects, orchids, and galaxies.

Nature, for many, never can be fully captured by human vocabularies, but will always remain the Heideggarian forest surrounding the worldly clearing which is the linguistic house of being or the Taoist's unnameable transcendent tao or the Shinto's Kami permeating mountains and rivers or the native American's Great Spirit hovering over all. Even toward the incarnate tao housed within human language many different attitudes toward so many worlds other than the technological world of usable objects exist to be prized. There is the world described by Thoreau on his nature walks. There is the natural world captured in paint and poetry by Western romanticists and Chinese masters. There is the bamboo leaf portrayed by the Zen artist after months of emptying himself of self-serving concerns. There is the holistic natural world of the ecologist which has intrinsic value on its own and is not to be seen merely in an anthropomorphic way as mere raw materials serving consensually recognized human needs.[32] There is our own materiality, as desiring machines[33] and the feminine body's "extra resource" and her baby's fragility and vastness as "possible's body,"[34] which always will be more than we can understand and control and which needs to be prized if in humility we are to keep efforts to control from becoming coercive. There is the very need to recall how blurred are the boundaries which supposedly differentiate the realm of the biologically natural from the realm of the socially constituted.[35] Finally, there are the Jewish, Christian, and Muslim worlds of God's creations. (It would be the height of presumptuous disrespect to attempt to reduce such religious approaches to the other to human psychological and sociological phenomena.[36])

These reminders about incommensurate approaches to nature already throw doubt upon Habermas's claim that it is the pursuit of universal common understanding that is the point of communication and the necessary condition for the preservation of social identities through historical change. The fractured social and cultural character of historical communities demonstrates that actual shared understanding is not necessary for historical continuity. Neither is the pursuit of an ideal of shared understanding necessary. Foucault has attempted to show that analyses of practices of seeking understanding, explanations, and justifications need to be located in a setting of practices of people overpowering other people with many power relations taking on the relatively permanent, asymmetrical character of domination.[37] A narrative of power being exercised and resisted is a crucial part of the story of social continuity. Political, economic, racial, and sexual domination have played a major role in constituting and reconstituting social phenomena even when understanding has been absent.

It is not enough to acknowledge the existence of social and cultural differences, as Habermas does, and then to claim in the name of Gadamer that such differences are to fuse through uncoerced dialogue.[38] Gadamer is correct that persons engaged in cross-cultural dialogue will be changed in unpredictable ways when they listen, do not force the other to speak with the voice of one's own prejudices but interpret the other in ways that give meaning which is new to all in the dialogue.[39] This is his insightful development of Heidegger's theme of the freedom of Being. However, fusion is often not the result of dialogue between individuals or traditions, partly because unity never existed within the partners in the dialogue and because social and cultural phenomena constantly produce unintended and unexpected historical effects. Witness how conflicting moral traditions live on in the Western world, and how religious traditions resist secularization, and how non-Western traditions resist Western cultural imperialism. Witness how the fully bilingual often end up at home in no world and unable to say what they any longer are. When fusion does occur in social and cultural worlds, it often parallels the fusion of hydrogen into helium. Tremendous force is applied, explosive and often destructive energy is released, and an uninteresting inert product is produced. Witness the oppressive globalization of neocapitalism and consumerism and the comparable global response to its emptiness with dogmatic and often irrational ontotheological fundamentalisms in most of the world's religions.[40]

Habermas's reconstruction of modernity's notions of individual self-realization and self-determination is likewise not radical enough.[41] Individuality, he claims, requires moving beyond mere social conventionalism and projectively locating oneself in an ideal universal community "in which everyone can take up the perspective of everyone else and count on reciprocal recognition by everybody . . . of my claim to uniqueness and irreplaceability,"[42] a projection which requires interpreting one's past and planning one's future so as to provide a unified narrative to one's life. Radicalizing modernity would mean recognizing and cherishing the uniqueness and irreplaceability of each person while recognizing the following: the indeterminately rich and incommensurate character of the physical, biological, and historical character of the materials making up that uniqueness; that there are different kinds of human individuation (the Japanese have a dozen first-person pronouns while in English we have one); that everyone cannot take up the perspective of everyone else; that multiple narratives are necessary for each person's decentered life, that our uniqueness lies in having no unified racial[43] or sexual identities;[44] that lives can contain radically different and wonderfully exciting stages. This does not mean that lives which are to be made into wonderful works of art are to have no unity of any kind. As Shusterman points out in his criticism of Rorty's tireless quest for the novel, styling oneself aesthetically requires harmonizing the many and the one, and this can be done by creatively adapting familiar roles and lifestyles to one's own individual circumstances.[45]

In reconstructing modernity, Habermas has not been radical enough and therefore does really remain faithful to that attitude which is so definitive of modernity itself and the enlightenment project. Foucault characterizes modernity as an attitude or ethos which both respects the reality of tradition's constitutive effect on us and breaks with it. He characterizes the enlightenment project as one which examines the place of the singular, the contingent, and the product of arbitrary constraints in what is given to us as universal, necessary, and obligatory in order to give new impetus to the undefined work of freedom by showing the possibility of no longer being, doing, or thinking what we are, do, or think and thus the possibility of resisting domination through the practice of freedom.[46] The radical liberal ideal of minimizing nonconsensuality is modernity's ideal; becoming enlightened about the nature and limits of consensual rationality is one necessary step toward that ideal. Not postmodernism but a radicalization of modernity is what is being recommended here.

Commitment to radical liberalism and modernity can give to every person a sense of identity which does not stand in opposition to any prizeworthy differences. When the ethical is seen as the minimization of nonconsentuality, then the radical, modern liberal can say with Kierkegaard, "I propose to will the ethical with all my strength, . . . and I propose to will absolutely nothing else."[47] Because resistance to domination is never extinguished, no total homogenization of our constitution is ever possible. We can refuse to be aspects of what we are, and we can resist what others coercively take us to be. We can maintain multiple, incommensurate self-interpretations and multiple, radically different projects, rejoicing in our schizophrenia[48] and life changes. We can strategically see ourselves as the racial, gender, and class persons that we are treated as by dominating others as part of a project to lessen the impact of such treatment and to empower us to resist these very classification systems and the disrespect they show to our uniquely individual and cherishable differences.[49] Such a commitment to oppose domination and to practice freedom can bind people together in the form of solidarity needed to empower such an opposition. As Bell Hooks urges us, we can answer the question, "Who am I?" with the answer, "I am one opposed to all forms of domination."[50] Minimizing nonconsensuality means seeking to nurture this identity in all people, in all places, and in all times.

Movements aimed at liberating us in one fell swoop never succeed, and thus resistance movements in which freedom is practiced are always needed. Living free in a celebration of differences is central to that practice. Exposing ideologies used to strengthen domination is never enough to resist domination. It is necessary to resist the disciplinary practices which empower such ideologies and mold our very identities. Exercising resistance and practicing freedom are at the heart of Foucault's ethic of caring for the self and seeking to minimize non-consentuality.[51] Heaven on earth is not our destiny, but lessening the hell on earth caused by coercive political, economic, cultural, racial and sexual domination is our calling.

NOTES

1. See Joseph Raz's analysis of tolerance in *The Morality of Freedom* (Oxford: Clarendon Press, 1986), 401–7.

2. Alasdair MacIntyre offers such an epistemological justification for showing tolerance toward alternative moral forms of life in *Whose Justice? Which Rationality?* (Notre Dame: University of Notre Dame Press, 1988), 388.

3. A similar analysis of respect presented by Charles Larmore, *Patterns of Moral Complexity* (Cambridge: Cambridge University Press, 1987), 61–65.

4. See Michel Foucault, *L'Impossible prison*, ed. Michelle Perrot (Paris: Editions du Seuil, 1980), 37, quoted in Michel Foucault, *The Foucault Reader*, ed. Paul Rabinow (New York: Pantheon Books, 1984), 20.

5. See James Edwards, *Without Philosophy: Wittgenstein and the Moral Life* (Tampa: University Press of Florida, 1982), chapter 6.

6. John Rawls, *Political Liberalism* (New York: Columbia University Press, 1993); Ronald Dworkin, *Life's Dominion* (New York: Alfred A. Knopf, 1993).

7. See Joseph Raz, *The Morality of Freedom* (Oxford: Clarendon Press, 1986); Michael Walzer, *Spheres of Justice: A Defense of Plurality and Equality* (New York: Basic Books, 1983); Charles Larmore, *Patterns of Moral Complexity* (Cambridge: Cambridge University Press, 1987); T. E. Hill Jr., *Autonomy and Self-Respect* (Cambridge: Cambridge University Press, 1991); and Hill, "Symposium on Pluralism and Ethical Theory," *Ethics* 102, no. 4 (July 1992).

8. See John Gray, review of *Political Liberalism*, John Rawls, in *The New York Times Book Review*, 16 May 1993, 35; and Lawrence Tribe, review of *Life's Dominion*, by Ronald Dworkin, in *The New York Times Book Review*, 16 May 1993, 1 and 41.

9. Alasdair MacIntyre, *After Virtue* (Notre Dame: University of Notre Dame Press, 1981); MacIntyre, *Whose Justice? Which Rationality?* (Notre Dame: University of Notre Dame Press, 1988); and MacIntyre, *Three Rival Versions of Moral Enquiry* (Notre Dame: University of Notre Dame Press, 1990).

10. Raz, *The Morality of Freedom*, 395, 423.

11. Ibid., 423–24.

12. See Hill, *Autonomy and Self-Respect*, 47; Larmore, *Patterns of Moral Complexity*, 80–86; and Raz, *Morality of Freedom*, 369–78.

13. See Bernard Williams, *Moral Luck* (Cambridge: Cambridge University Press, 1981).

14. See Jürgen Habermas, *Postmetaphysical Thinking*, trans. W. M. Hohengarten (Cambridge, Mass.: MIT Press, 1992), 145–146; and Habermas, *Legitimation Crisis*, trans. T. McCarthy (Boston: Beacon Press, 1975), 89–90.

15. Michel Foucault, "Politics and Ethics: An Interview," in *The Foucault Reader*, ed. Paul Rabinow (New York: Pantheon Books, 1984), 379.

16. See Rawls, *Political Liberalism*, 60–62, 138–39.

17. John Rawls, *Justice as Fairness* (Cambridge, Mass.: Harvard University Press, 1971).

18. See R. J. Peffer, *Marxism, Morality, and Social Justice* (Princeton: Princeton University Press, 1990), 299–305.

19. See Jürgen Habermas, *Moral Consciousness and Communicative Action* (Cambridge, Mass.: MIT Press, 1991).

20. See Iris Marion Young, *Justice and the Politics of Difference* (Princeton: Princeton University Press, 1990), 106.

21. See David Wong, *Moral Relativity* (Berkeley: University of California Press, 1984), 206–8.

22. Ludwig Wittgenstein, *On Certainty* (Oxford: Basil Blackwell, 1969), sections 110, 192, 204–5.

23. Wittgenstein, *Philosophical Investigations* (New York: The Macmillan Press Ltd., 1953), sections 206, 211, 217, 241, 242, 244, 257. See also Hubert L. Dryfus, *Being-in-the-World: A Commentary on Heidegger's Being and Time, Division I* (Cambridge, Mass.: MIT Press, 1991), 16–23, 102–7, 115–21.

24. Jürgen Habermas, *Knowledge and Human Interests*, trans. J. J. Shapiro (Boston: Beacon Press, 1971), 308ff.

25. Jürgen Habermas, *Communication and the Evolution of Society*, trans. T. McCarthy (Boston: Beacon Press, 1979), 59–65, 116–23.

26. Ibid., 69–94.

27. O. K. Bousma applies the label *miracle* to the nonrational: "To regard it as a miracle . . . is neither to have found an explanation nor to have failed in finding an explanation. It is to be filled with wonder at such an event - and not to question it. In this sense the ordinary, a drop of water or a grain of sand, may strike us not as extraordinary, but as miracles." See O. K. Bousma, *Without Proof or Evidence* (Lincoln: University of Nebraska Press, 1984), 13.

28. For an excellent study of the similarities between Wittgenstein's critique of Platonism and Derrida's critique of logocentrism, see Henry Staten, *Wittgenstein and Derrida* (Lincoln: The University of Nebraska Press, 1984).

29. Habermas dismisses the later Heidegger as a totalitarian mystic and Derrida as a Jewish Cabalist mystic. See Jürgen Habermas, *The Philosophical Discourse of Modernity*, trans. F. G. Lawrence (Cambridge, Mass.: MIT Press, 1987), 151–60, 181–84.

30. Nietzsche, "Thus Spoke Zarathustra," in *The Portable Nietzsche*, trans. William Kaufmann (New York: Penguin Books, 1954), 278.

31. Ibid, 269.

32. For a liberal's defense of such an attribution of intrinsic value to nature, see Thomas E. Hill, Jr., "Ideals of Human Excellence and Preserving Natural Environments," in *Autonomy and Self-Respect* (Cambridge: Cambridge University Press, 1991), 104–17.

33. See Gilles Deleuze and Felix Guattari, *Anti-Oedipus: Capitalism and Schizophrenia*, trans. R. Hurley, M. Seem, and H. R. Lane (Minneapolis: University of Minnesota Press, 1983), 1–50.

34. See Helene Cixous and Catherine Clement, *The Newly Born Woman*, trans. B. Wing (Minneapolis: The University of Minnesota Press, 1986), 83–100.

35. See Alison Jaggar, "Human Biology in Feminist Theory: Sexual Equality Reconsidered," in *Beyond Domination: New Perspectives on Women and Philosophy*, ed. Carol C. Gould (Totowa, N.J.: Rowman & Littlefield, 1984), 21–42; and Sandra Harding, *The Science Question in Feminism* (Ithaca, N.Y.: Cornell University Press, 1986), 92–102.

36. For a critique of all attempts to reduce religious language games to supposedly primitive scientific or psychological and sociological language games, see D. Z. Phillips, *Religion without Explanation* (Oxford: Basil Blackwell, 1976). Phillips is developing the critiques offered in Wittgenstein, "Remarks on Frazier's *Golden Bough*, in *Wittgenstein: Sources and Perspectives*, ed. C. G. Luckhardt (Hassocks, Suxxes: The Harvester Press, 1979), and by E. E. Evans-Pritchard, *Theories of Primitve Religion* (Oxford: Clarendon Press, 1965).

37. Michel Foucault, *Discipline and Punish*, trans. A. Sheridan (New York: Vintage Books, 1979), 135–69; Foucault, *Power/Knowledge*, trans. C. Gordon, L. Marshall, J. Mephan, and K. Soper (New York: Pantheon Books, 1980), 55–63, 109–133; and Foucault, *The History of Sexuality*, trans. R. Hurley (New York: Vintage Books, 1980), 1:135–59.

38. Jürgen Habermas, "The Unity of Reason in the Diversity of Its Voices," in *Postmetaphysical Thinking*, trans. W. M. Hohengarten (Cambridge, Mass.: MIT Press, 1992), 115–48.

39. Hans Gadamer, *Philosophical Hermeneutics* (Berkeley: University of California Press, 1976).

40. This warning against the danger of seeking to fuse the heterogeneous into the homogenous remains relevant even if Hoy is right in saying that Gadamer's talk of fusing horizons is really a reminder not to eliminate the strangeness of what we read or hear by forcing it into the framework constitued by our prejudgments but instead to let such voices from others make what is too familiar to us seem strange enough to warrant reconsideration. See David Hoy, "Is Hermeneutics Ethnocentric?" in *The Interpretive Understanding*, ed. David R. Hiley, James F. Bohman, and Richard Shusterman (Ithaca, N.Y.: Cornell University Press, 1991), 164–65.

41. Jürgen Habermas, "Individuation through Socialization: On Mead's Theory of Subjectivity," in *Postmetaphysical Thinking*, trans. W. M. Hohengarten (Cambridge, Mass.: MIT Press, 1992), 183–93.

42. Ibid., 186.

43. See Gerald Early, ed., *Lure and Loathing: Essays on Race, Identity, and the Ambivalence of Assimilation* (New York: Penguin Books, 1993).

44. See especially Iris Marion Young, "The Ideal of Community and the Politics of Difference," in *Feminism/Postmodernism,* ed. Linda J. Nicholson (New York: Routledge, 1990), 300–23.

45. See Richard Shusterman, *Pragmatic Aesthetics: Living Beauty, Rethinking Art* (Oxford: Basil Blackwell, 1992), chapter 9.

46. Michel Foucault, "What Is Enlightenment?" in *The Foucault Reader*, ed. Paul Rabinow (New York: Pantheon Books, 1984), 32–50.

47. Søren Kierkegaard, *Concluding Unscientific Postscript*, trans. D. Swenson (Princeton: Princeton University Press, 1944), 123.

48. For a positive characterization of schizophrenia, see Deleuze and Guattari, *Anti-Oedipus: Capitalism and Schizophrenia*, chapter 4.

49. Sandra Harding's recommendation in *The Science Question in Feminism,* 243–47.

50. Bell Hooks, *Feminist Theory: From Margin to Center* (Boston: South End Press, 1984), 43–65; and Hooks, *Yearning: Race, Gender and Cultural Politics* (Boston: South End Press, 1990), 145–53.

51. Michel Foucault, "On the Genealogy of Ethics: An Overview of Work in Progress," in *The Foucault Reader*, ed. Paul Rabinow (New York: Pantheon Books, 1984), 340–72.

IV

Ethics

14

On the Difference between Non-Moral and Moral Conceptions of Toleration: The Case for Toleration as an Individual Virtue

Robert Paul Churchill

Hate the sin and love the sinner.
—Mohandes Karamchand Gandhi

INTRODUCTION

The debate in recent years over "political correctness" and rising alarm over hate speech have reignited the controversy over the place of toleration in a liberal, democratic society. Must a liberal, pluralistic society tolerate (verbal) behavior that is intended to undermine the values that make liberal democracy possible in the first place? Certainly not, say some commentators, and they believe this shows that toleration cannot itself be a primary social value. Thus these commentators revive the position taken by some (e.g., Herbert Marcuse)[1] during the stormy "anti-establishment" days of the 1960s, proclaiming that rather than representing a moral posture, toleration is wrong (or immoral) because it is permissive of racism, sexism, antisemitism, or other aspects of bigotry, discrimination, and subordination that undermine respect for persons.

In my view, this line of argument is confused. It is certainly wrong to tolerate racism, sexism, and bigotry. But this admission offers no evidence for the view that toleration, when correctly understood, is not an individual virtue or a public good. On the contrary, this admission is a recognition of several pervasive facts about our moral and social lives: first, that virtuous dispositions and moral principles may sometimes be misapplied or lead to untoward outcomes (just as efforts to promote another's welfare paradoxically may result directly in her suffering a loss),[2] second, that political efforts to set limits to what the government, or body politic, should tolerate are in some cases extremely difficult to answer; and third, that an extraordinary degree of confusion surrounds our conceptions of toleration.

I shall not focus on the political correctness or the hate-speech controversies. Instead, my concern will be with the conceptual and logical properties of toleration. In particular, my objectives are the following: (1) to clarify and to distinguish the various conceptions of toleration that arise from the ways we speak and think about tolerant and intolerant behavior, and especially to distinguish among the respective conceptions of toleration as moral indifference, permissiveness, endurance, and neutrality; (2) to identify and defend the defining characteristics of a further conception of toleration, namely, toleration as a moral virtue; and (3) to defend toleration as a moral virtue by dissolving the so-called "paradox of toleration." In particular, I shall try to fulfill this last objective by showing why there is no logical inconsistency between moral disapproval of certain beliefs or behavior and moral approval of, or respect for, the persons whose beliefs or behavior one disapproves of.

It is often thought that toleration has a very special place in the liberal tradition. Indeed, liberals are frequently defined as people who value liberty and the toleration necessary for the promotion of pluralism.[3] Moreover, it is within the liberal tradition that toleration has received the most robust and extensive of defenses as a public good. Whatever may be the best justification for toleration understood as neutrality,[4] or even liberalism, I believe that arguments over neutrality and liberalism would be benefited greatly by closer scrutiny of conflicting conceptions of toleration and a better appreciation of the differences between toleration as an individual virtue and toleration, or neutrality, as a political principle. Should we not have a better grasp of toleration as an individual virtue affecting relationships between discrete individuals before considering how toleration, or neutrality, might function as a regulatory principle for a just society? It is just this concern that has led me to focus in this chapter on setting out and defending a concept of toleration as a moral virtue.

The need for this project arises from the general failure to distinguish among different notions of toleration, and especially to mark off ways of thinking and talking about toleration most central to our moral reflections *about personal virtues* from various other ways of regarding toleration in discussions of social behavior and political theory. Once these concepts are properly clarified, we will be better able to appreciate the vast difference between toleration as a special kind of moral virtue and the many other ways expressions of tolerant behavior are relevant to liberal politics. Moreover, it will be easier to see that most of the behaviors, attitudes, or dispositions that are indiscriminately referred to as "toleration" but that abet bigotry and other forms of repression are better described (and condemned) as varieties of moral indifference, permissiveness, or the sheer endurance of what one dislikes.

Liberals also generally argue that toleration, or neutrality, is morally grounded in respect for persons, and therefore, that toleration as a moral principle bids us give equal consideration to others as autonomous agents.[5] While justificatory arguments for neutrality, and liberalism itself, are highly controversial, I believe that the connection between toleration, respect for persons, and autonomy is ultimately correct and defensible. I indicate as much in the exercise that follows. However, it must be emphasized that this chapter does not attempt to answer the question, Why should we value toleration? or more specifically, Why should we cultivate toleration as a moral virtue? Rather, I am concerned with the more restricted, but prior question: How is a concept of toleration as a moral virtue possible? Thus I am primarily concerned to demonstrate the logical coherence of the concept of toleration as a moral virtue and to defend the concept from a paradox some believe to be inevitable and to vitiate its coherence as a concept. Thus, although I believe my argument could have important consequences in the storm over liberalism and neutrality for the defense of toleration as a central value in a just society, it is intended primarily as an exercise in conceptual analysis rather than theory construction. This is a bit of academic spade work on the intellectual landscape over which liberals and their critics rush too quickly in their battles over the great, theoretical strongholds.

TOWARD CONCEPTUAL CLARITY

In *Toleration and the Limits of Liberalism,* Susan Mendus has made a good start at identifying the "circumstances of toleration . . . [that] isolate the conditions under which we may properly speak of toleration as opposed to liberty, license, or indifference."[6] She notes,

1. Toleration arises "in circumstances of diversity," i.e. when people are aware of salient differences existing among them.
2. Toleration is a matter of leaving others alone or refraining from persecuting them, either through the law or by means of what John Stuart Mill called the "tyranny of public opinion."[7]

But Mendus notes (drawing on Cranston[8]) that these necessary conditions alone are not sufficient to distinguish toleration from liberty, license, or indifference. Nor are these first two conditions enough to distinguish toleration from compelled or coerced restraint. For example, we do not consider a person tolerant who restrains her desire to slander or libel a lesbian if she is restrained only by her fear of a subsequent law suit for defamation. Hence, toleration also requires:

3. Voluntary forbearance or voluntarily leaving others alone when the diversity itself gives rise to forms of offense such as disapproval, dislike or disgust.[9] Moreover,
4. The tolerant person exercising forbearance must be in a position to be able to interfere with the behavior of the tolerated; that is she has the ability to suppress, disrupt, or censure the offending speech or behavior, but refrains from doing so.[10]

All four of these conditions are necessary for toleration, but are they jointly sufficient? Interestingly, the way in which we answer this question will determine whether or not we regard toleration as morally commendable and as a moral virtue. My view is that Mendus's four conditions greatly advance our understanding: they ought to be regarded as necessary for any *correct* use of the concept of toleration. Nevertheless, we need to distinguish among significantly different but generally prevalent conceptions of toleration which, although different, have some claim to legitimacy in ordinary usage. To appreciate the need for further distinction, consider two different types of cases of toleration, where each type satisfies the four necessary conditions. In the first type, a tolerant majority takes the view that a minority whose behavior they tolerate have broken certain tacit rules of conduct in the community or have failed to live up to the standards expected of them. In these cases, the tolerance of the majority is consistent with the belief that, although there are standards binding on all concerned, it is better, all things considered, that some violations or failures should be overlooked, excused, or grudgingly allowed. Thus, far from being based on respect for diversity of belief or practice, tolerance is based in these cases on some combination of social efficiency (e.g., avoiding social strife), concessions to human weakness, or pity. Tolerance in these cases is compatible with disrespect, even contempt for those tolerated.

By contrast, in the second type of case, the members of a community share the view that the diversity of people's views and choices are to be tolerated because such toleration is required by fundamental respect due to persons as moral agents. In these cases, the tolerant majority believes that respect for persons as morally autonomous requires that we give equal consideration to others' beliefs, interests, and choices as manifestations of their conceptions of the good life. This equal consideration does *not* entail approval of the ideas, interests, and behaviors expressing this diversity in the sense that the tolerant believe they are right or believe that there is no way to determine what is true or right (as some cultural and ethical relativists might believe). On the contrary, although they may disapprove of what they tolerate, tolerant persons in this second type of case accept the view that the beliefs and choices they tolerate may be regarded in good faith by those who hold these beliefs and make these choices as being central and fundamental to the latter's conceptions of the good life. More specifically, tolerant persons concede that what they believe they should tolerate may occupy a place in others' conceptions of the good life as central as the place occupied by the cherished beliefs and practices manifesting the tolerant persons' own conceptions of the good life.[11] Hence, in cases of this second type, when an individual *A* tolerates *B*'s belief *X*, *A*'s disapproval of belief *X* does not entail disrespect for *B*. On the contrary, *A* can consistently believe *X* to be false, even morally wrong, and yet respect *B*'s believing *X* as a worthy effort to discover the truth, find meaning in life, or to be a morally autonomous, self-directing person.[12]

Now, one thing to learn from these contrasting cases of toleration is that both types satisfy Susan Mendus's four necessary conditions. Nevertheless, toleration identified in the first case is perfectly compatible with moral indifference, permissiveness, and forbearance understood as endurance, whereas toleration in the second case is *not* equally compatible with these other concepts. These differences are sufficiently significant to warrant a brief but more precise exploration of the ways in which toleration understood as moral indifference, permissiveness, or endurance all differ from toleration understood as a moral virtue.

TOLERATION AS MORAL INDIFFERENCE, PERMISSIVENESS, OR ENDURANCE

Moral indifference refers to those cases in which the tolerant do not take sides because, although they do not care for what they tolerate, they just do not care enough *about the persons whose behavior they tolerate or about persons adversely affected by that behavior* to do anything about it. In the first instance, the tolerant person (in this restricted sense of the word) is indifferent toward those whose behavior he tolerates, for he does not care enough to desire improvement of their well-being. Second, and more ominously, the tolerant person is morally indifferent to those who may be the victims or "targets" of the expressions and practices of those he tolerates when those tolerated speak and behave in prejudiced, demeaning, and intimidating ways, as some do in "hate speech" cases, for example. It is just not worth the trouble, from the viewpoint of the morally indifferent; or worse yet, although they may regard the beliefs and practices they tolerate (e.g., allowing religious fundamentalists to expose their children to poisonous snakes) as not only wrong but as dangerous to those who share them, they are unable psychologically or unwilling to intervene, to support state intervention, or even to attempt persuasion.

In either event, it must be clear that the morally indifferent are not people who have decided against interference on the basis of *principle*. On the contrary, they approach these cases without principles, or even scruples, and avail themselves, when possible, of psychological defense mechanisms that enable them to block awareness of the possible harms suffered because of behavior they claim to tolerate.[13] In addition, the beliefs or practices tolerated by the morally indifferent rarely pose serious risks to the tolerant themselves.[14] This is the sense in which it might be correct to say that many residents of large American cities tolerate the behavior of homeless people who refuse shelter on even the coldest winter nights, or tolerate sexist slurs as "just the way men talk," or tolerate the recreational use of crack cocaine (although the toleration of such practices may also have additional explanations as noted below). It is in its most extreme form the kind of moral indifference with which a majority of non-Jewish Germans responded to the gradual but intensifying persecution of the Jews by the Nazis in the 1930s,[15] or (again to take a modern example), the moral indifference of many Europeans and North Americans to the actions of the Pol Pot regime in Kampuchea or of the Serbs and Croats in Bosnia.[16] These last examples may seem to explode the comparison I am making just because they are so extreme. Yet I believe that research in social psychology allows us to conceive of them as simply more extreme examples of behavior on a continuum of indifference ranging from lack of concern about neighbors or the plight of the homeless all the way to the moral blindness implicated in a failure to understand and oppose genocidal policies.[17] Clarity in communication would be well served in discussing such cases by the consistent replacement of "toleration" with "moral indifference," but conceptual confusion will persist, I fear, just because "toleration" is a euphemism for moral indifference, and the morally indifferent will prefer to mask the reality of their failure of concern behind the more positive connotations of "toleration."

Tolerance as permissiveness refers to cases of either of two types. The first is the tolerant who attempt, when they are of a nonchalant, carefree attitude, to be as expansive and accepting as possible, regarding nothing, or almost noting as "beyond the pale," and refusing to pass judgments of any kind. There is the motto that "nothing human is foreign." But when this optimistic nonchalance and expansive attitude is absent, the permissively tolerant ignore, or try to ignore what they find offensive and disagreeable, retreating to a "live and let live" outlook. Unlike the morally indifferent, the permissive often base their tolerance on *principle*, however inchoate it may be in expression. In particular, the permissive may embrace some version of extreme relativism, subjectivism or skepticism as a matter of principle. When not based on positive belief in relativism or skepticism, permissiveness seems to be motivated by extreme pessimism about the possibility of "cross-cultural" agreement, or an extreme lack of confidence in one's own beliefs and values—the kind of insecurity that leads one to believe that she is without warrant for standing up for what she believes and arguing against what strikes her as wrong. But whether based on principle or not, permissiveness differs from moral indifference because the permissive do care: they regard untrammeled diversity as a positive good, or contrariwise, and an undesirable, but inevitable fact of life.

Toleration occurs as endurance when the necessary forbearance is experienced as difficult or painful under the circumstances. In this case the tolerant person has a certain fortitude; she is able to put up with, and endure what she finds highly disagreeable, repugnant, or even condemnable. Hence she is unlike the morally indifferent person who expresses no opinion, and unlike the permissive person with her "live and let live" outlook. Indeed, this tolerant person endures what she would prefer to have stopped. Some cases of sexual harassment, such as the harassment endured by Anita Hill while under Justice Thomas's influence, offer examples of this type of tolerance. Possibly victims (real or self-described) fear the consequences of resistance or interference, or may feel that protest is useless, or they may adopt the view that some "give and take" is necessary to avoid conflict; for example, as a member of a minority that is often the target of discrimination, one may believe that unless she occasionally endures what she dislikes, others will not endure what they may strongly dislike about her.[18]

As illustrated by the first type of case discussed in this section, toleration, when regarded as moral indifference, permissiveness, or endurance, is logically compatible with disrespect for those tolerated. This is manifestly clear in the cases of moral indifference and endurance and the negative version of permissiveness. And while it is true that permissiveness in the more positive sense—the carefree, nonchalant love for difference—could be married to a deep-seated respect for the human bearers of this diversity, I doubt that this respect can plausibly be offered as a *justification* for permissiveness. The difficulty is to show how extreme relativism and extreme skepticism—the refusal to apply moral or epistemological criteria to beliefs or practices (and hence the view that they are on the same general epistemic or moral plane)—can generate respect for any belief or practice. If everything is equally true or good, then everything is, by the same (lack of) measure, equally untrue and bad. It is doubtful that beliefs and practices of such dubious moral or epistemic status can be *worthy* of respect. Therefore, the respectful among the permissive may indeed respect persons who bear diverse characteristics, but they cannot respect them *for the reason that* they hold a diverse view or engage in an unusual practice. And this must be the case even if they value diversity as a good in itself. It also follows that even carefree, permissive persons may disrespect the other whose exotic presence titillates them. This might be the case, for example, when diversity is sought for the arousal or excitement it occasions, and the exotic other is regarded as a mere means to that end.

Unlike the first, the second type of case presented earlier offers a stark contrast. Just because toleration, as exemplified in this type of case is *logically implied* by respect for persons, toleration understood in this special, moral, and "respect laden" sense is logically incompatible with moral indifference, permissiveness, and endurance.[19] I believe that failure to note the fact, that toleration as a moral concept is logically distinct from other conceptions of toleration lies behind such wholesale condemnations of toleration as that expressed by Thomas Paine when he declared that "toleration is not the opposite of intolerance, but it is the counterfeit of it. Both are despotisms. The one assumes itself the right of withholding liberty of conscience, the other of granting it. The one is the pope armed with fire and faggot, the other is the pope selling or granting indulgences."[20] A similar confusion over toleration lies behind Robert Paul Wolff's argument in *A Critique of Pure Tolerance*.[21] In "Beyond Tolerance" Wolff suggests a paradox similar to Rousseau's (in)famous claim that "it may be necessary to force men to be free," by claiming that society will become more tolerant if certain things are *not* tolerated. This paradox easily dissolves as soon as we recognize that it is indeed morally wrong to *endure*, to *permit*, or to be *morally indifferent* about many things. Indeed, if discriminatory, intimidating, and manipulative practices (not to mention outright violations of rights) were stopped, then we would enjoy a more liberal and richly pluralistic way of life. However, what this argument shows, is only that toleration should not be embraced as a fundamental value for members of a liberal society *if* toleration is understood as equivalent to moral indifference, permissiveness, and endurance. It does not show, however, that there is any irreconcilable conflict between the values of a liberal, pluralistic democracy and toleration understood in its richer, moral sense.

ON THE CONFUSION OVER NEUTRALITY

Before turning to a fuller exposition of toleration as a moral concept, we must attend, however briefly, to the confusion over toleration understood as neutrality. As noted in the Introduction, some liberals identify toleration with neutrality, and almost all liberals would agree that neutrality is a defining feature of liberalism.[22]

Despite their differences, all liberals share the view that a just society provides a neutral arena within which a great variety of different and opposing ways of life may be pursued. Hence, neutrality is presented as the principle that governments must be neutral as between competing conceptions of the good,[23] or as Ronald Dworkin puts it, "Political decisions must be, so far as is possible, independent of any particular conception of the good life, or of what gives value to life."[24] Thus, as the "practical manifestation of liberalism,"[25] neutrality is a guiding principle for political *institutions*. The principle of neutrality sets limits on what state institutions and private organizations supported by law may legitimately do and therefore specifies the *public* limits of or scope of toleration.

Even this brief account reveals the difference between neutrality and toleration as a moral virtue. First, the latter concerns morally commendable individual behavior, whereas neutrality concerns public policy: restraints on state and institutional actions. Obviously, one can exist without the other: individuals can be virtuously tolerant even in nonliberal, repressive societies; likewise, neutrality regulates public behavior even in the absence of moral toleration, which always only requires voluntary forbearance (based on moral grounds as explained below). By contrast, in some circumstances neutrality may require more than restraint or forbearance, depending on one's conception of the primary justification of neutrality. If the justification of neutrality is, as Dworkin believes, equality expressed as ensuring *equal* respect and consideration for persons, then neutrality may require that governments sometimes act positively to assist persons in realizing their visions of the good life when doing so is (at least theoretically) nonprejudicial to alternative conceptions of the good.[26] Finally, and most important, neutrality logically cannot be toleration as a moral concept, for the former is the principle that government *cannot disapprove*, whereas toleration necessarily requires disapproval plus forbearance.

These considerations, as incomplete as they may be, show that there can be no simple equivalence between toleration and neutrality. Although itself morally defensible, the principle of neutrality is not some collective, public expression of toleration. Members of any collectivity, however liberal they may regard themselves, will differ widely on what they feel prepared to tolerate, and some things will inevitably be regarded by large numbers as beyond the bounds. Hence there is the need for some principled way of working out and fixing—at the societal level—the (shifting) boundary between what is and what is not legally acceptable. This is where the principle of neutrality comes in: it insists that boundary drawing must, as far as practical, give all members of society an equal opportunity to pursue their conceptions of the good life. Toleration is one thing; neutrality is a principle about the scope and limits of toleration to be recognized by public institutions.

Having said this, it may be conceded, first, that individuals sharing a liberal ideology will want neutrality as a guiding principle for their social institutions, and second, that both toleration and neutrality may derive their justification from the same grounds.[27] But it must be stressed that much of the controversy over neutrality is controversy over "line drawing" (as distinct from controversy over neutrality's justification), and therefore, that charges that too much is tolerated—such as, hate speech—are complaints about where the line should be drawn. We should avoid confusing arguments over the merits or demerits of a certain "scratch line" as arguments over the moral value of toleration. (Although there can be no doubt that boundary-line arguments *are* arguments over what should be endured or permitted.)

TOLERATION AS A MORAL CONCEPT

As we have seen, the four conditions identified earlier are all necessary, but hardly sufficient for toleration as a *moral* concept. What are the most plausible candidates for the missing conditions? Obviously more must be said about the logical relationship between toleration and respect. We should first note several considerations preliminary to exploring that important connection, however.

The first might be said to concern the proper *subject* of ascriptions of "toleration" and "tolerance." Does the term *tolerance,* like its obverse *intolerance,* properly refer to behaviors and acts as well as to attitudes and dispositions that may prompt and support antidiscriminatory (or discriminatory) behavior? In other words, is a person's tolerance (in the moral sense) primarily a feature of the individual's psychology—her character, virtues, disposition, and so on—or primarily a feature of the consequences of her forbearance? Common parlance offers no help in answering this question; nor does most written reflection on toleration. For example, the UN Declaration on the Elimination of All Forms of Intolerance and of Discrimination Based on Religion or Belief (adopted by the UN General Assembly in November 1981) treats intolerance as synonymous with discrimination at one point (appendix, article 2.2) but suggests that the two are different at another point (appendix, article 4.2).[28] For the sake of clarity we ought to use the term *discrimination* to refer to acts and *intolerance* to describe the emotional, psychological, philosophical, and religious biases and attitudes that may prompt such acts of discrimination.[29] Yet, in fact, whereas certain social conditions—the presence of overt practices of persecution and discrimination—might be easily identified and distinguished from the attitudes and dispositions underlying them, it is hard to draw the line between such social conditions and outward expressions of intolerant attitudes such as taunting, insulting, and inflaming speech.

If one wishes to explore the potential of toleration as a *moral concept*, however, then toleration cannot be identified as the consequential actions or the results of certain beliefs, feelings, motives, and attitudes. Rather, the term must have as its primary designations cognitions and affects that make certain behavioral dispositions subject to guidance and modification by moral reflection. Unless this restriction is made, it is logically impossible to distinguish belief, speech, or behavior that is tolerated due to moral considerations (i.e., respect) from belief, speech, and behavior that is not interfered with for the sorts of nonmoral reasons noted earlier: because it is endured or suffered with ill will, for example, or because it is excused or overlooked as a failing, or simply because those who witness it respond permissively or with indifference.

If those who are tolerant are to be morally commended for their toleration, then, at a minimum, they must forbear from interference because they believe or feel that such interference would be wrong morally. Indeed, as we shall see, they believe that interference would be a manifestation of disrespect for those tolerated. These considerations thus yield a fifth necessary condition:

5. Toleration is an attribute of moral character; it pertains to the attitudes, motives, and behavioral dispositions of those who voluntarily forbear from interference with speech or conduct of which they disapprove.

Closely related to this condition is another, also bearing on toleration as a morally commendable character trait. This can be a sixth condition:

6. As a moral virtue, toleration pertains to what an individual morally disapproves of based on reasons rather than on simple dislikes, negative feelings, or biases.

Alternatively, and for the sake of economy, condition 3 can be reformulated to reflect the moral basis of disapproval as follows:

3. Voluntary forbearance from interference when diversity itself gives rise to moral disapproval, that is, disapproval based on reasons rather than on simple dislikes, negative feelings, or biases.

One can concede much to Aristotle's account of the formation of the moral virtues through training and habit, while insisting that, to be morally commendable, toleration must be more than voluntary control over the expression of one's dislike or disgust. To be truly commendable as moral, toleration must be voluntary forbearance from interference with what one morally disapproves on the basis of judgment and the possession of reasons over which moral argument is possible.[30]

Thus when we approve morally of a person's toleration, we approve not only of her voluntary forbearance but also of the exercise of this forbearance in the face of behavior we believe the tolerant person disapproves of on morally relevant grounds, and therefore, might have felt justified in trying to suppress. It is surely good to check one's irritation, or control one's tendency to express or act on feelings of dislike or disgust. But such restraint against one's prejudices and contingent feelings of liking or disliking are relevant to explanations of *why* a person is or is not inclined to be tolerant. But toleration is a matter of moral choice *both* as to the forbearance *and* the reasons why forbearance is morally appropriate or especially called for in a particular situation. Hence, if toleration reflects a moral position, it would be extremely odd to regard one's bare emotions, feelings, and sentiments as supplying sufficient reason for qualifying one's forbearance as moral.[31] One's toleration is truly moral then only when one can present reasons for feeling justified in disapproving of the tolerated behavior.[32]

Just as further reflection about the subject of toleration has led us to condition 5 and the reformulation of 3 above, deeper reflection about the "object" of toleration is also illuminating. What is the "object" of toleration? Can it be persons as well expressions, beliefs, behaviors, and practices the tolerant find offensive?[33] It is not uncommon to hear of someone's tolerating a person she does not like. But this takes us back to the nonmoral notion of toleration. If toleration is to be a moral concept, and if we are to be able to rule out expressions such as *tolerant racists*, or tolerant sexist as nonsensical oxymorons, then we must agree that persons themselves cannot be the objects of toleration.

The argument for this claim is fairly straightforward. Condition 3 as reformulated establishes the rational basis for toleration as a moral virtue. One tolerates what one disapproves of on the basis of reason. It follows, therefore, that one can tolerate morally only what one can regard as subject to change or alteration. Moral disapproval signifies belief in the responsibility of others for the behavior tolerated. It would hardly be rational to tolerate (morally) what cannot be altered or what is beyond anyone's control. (Of course, we do speak of tolerating such things as the frailties of old age, and the ravages of weather and incurable diseases, but only when we slip back to the notion of toleration as endurance.) To speak of tolerating another, in the moral sense, implies that it is to her discredit that she does not change that feature of herself that is the object of toleration.[34] Where something is unalterable, no praise or blame may properly accrue. This is a simple application of the principle that "ought" implies "can." And thus only those things subject to alteration by agents are the legitimate objects of toleration: individual behavior certainly (whether speech or action) and beliefs and practices (to the extent that they are not resistant to individual's efforts to change them). But such ascriptive characteristics as eye or skin color, gender, physical condition at birth, origin of birth, or ethnicity, are beyond individuals' control. It is absurd to imagine that one's gender or race is malleable like cultural identity or life style. It follows, therefore, that no one can be held responsible for such characteristics as race or gender, and that it is incoherent to select them as the grounds for moral disapproval. But the racist and sexist want to disapprove of persons just because they are of a particular race or gender, And this is why the notion of a "tolerant racist" or "tolerant sexist" is nonsensical from the moral point of view.

It follows from these considerations that the following condition is also necessary (stated as a new sixth condition):

6. The objects of toleration, as the expression of a moral virtue, are not persons per se, but beliefs, attitudes, behavior (including verbal), and practices subject to change or alteration by the persons who hold these beliefs and attitudes or exhibit or participate in the behaviors or practices in question.

The distinction between persons and their "deeds" is crucial to the understanding of the final condition necessary for toleration as a moral concept. This last condition addresses directly the relationship between toleration and respect for persons alluded to elsewhere in this chapter. The condition can be stated as follows:

7. Toleration is a manifestation of respect for persons; more precisely, it is the manifestation of the disposition to subject one's moral disapproval of another's belief or behavior to one's respect for the other's attachment to the belief or behavior in question.

Note that there is a very important distinction between the justification of condition 7 *simpliciter* and its justification as logically necessary. That is, one can demand answers to two quite distinct questions: What is the justification for respecting persons who behave in ways one morally disapproves of? and Why is respect for persons identified in condition 7 logically necessary for the concept of toleration as a moral virtue? The second question is easier to answer. It just is the case that, given moral disapproval of the objects of toleration, there must be sufficient grounds for voluntary forbearance. The distinction between the doer and the deed, identified in condition 6, points toward the only appropriate grounds for forbearance that can be chosen morally, namely, the relative priority one assigns to conflicting moral sensitivities. For, as condition 7 indicates, moral toleration involves a tension between one's moral disapproval of some belief or behavior and appreciation (perhaps even approval) of the importance the other assigns to the object of this belief or behavior. Respect, especially when understood as respect for the autonomy of the other, supplies the grounds for one's decision to assign greater weight to the other's attachment to the belief or behavior in question than one assigns to one's disapproval of it.

The first question, what is the justification for this respect? or more broadly, what is the justification for moral toleration? would lead us into an extensive consideration of the various grounds offered by liberals, from John Locke and John Stuart Mill to John Rawls, Bruce Ackerman, Ronald Dworkin, and Joseph Raz, among many others, as well as critics of liberalism, such as David Miller and Susan Mendus who nevertheless value toleration.[35] This debate is complicated not only by the common failure to notice differences among the concepts of tolerance employed but by failure to distinguish between toleration as an individual virtue and toleration as a public or social good (i.e., as resulting from principles regulating the conduct of public life). While I cannot enter fully into this enormous body of complex and controversial argumentation, I hasten to add that I believe a satisfactory case can be made for neutrality as a political principle as well as for toleration as an individual virtue, otherwise I would not have been at pains to clarify the concept of toleration as a moral virtue.

The necessary conditions so far identified can be summarized briefly as follows: (1) awareness of diversity; (2) voluntary forbearance; (3) moral disapproval; (4) power to suppress or interfere; (5) attribute of moral character or moral disposition; (6) directed against alterable beliefs, attitudes, behaviors, and so on; and (7) based on respect for persons. These seven conditions are, as far as I can discern, also jointly sufficient. This means simply that they jointly satisfy criteria roughly (very roughly) analogous to the tests of "finality" and "self-sufficiency," or "completeness" Aristotle employed in identifying happiness as the *summum bonum*. Aristotle meant that happiness possessed "finality" in the sense that it was never chosen as a means to something else. In the present case, the concept defined by our seven conditions possesses "finality" in the sense that it uniquely marks out the moral sense of toleration: it could not correctly be chosen for contexts in which notions of toleration as moral indifference, permissiveness, or endurance apply. In addition, the concept is self-sufficient or complete in the sense that nothing more needs to be added to establish the concept of toleration as a moral virtue: all that plausibly could be implied by the concept has been accounted for.

THE PARADOX OF TOLERATION

It might be thought that the concept of toleration as a moral virtue involves a logical inconsistency. How can it be thought right to tolerate that which we believe to be wrong? The philosophy of D. D. Raphael raises this issue pointedly:

> To disapprove of something is to judge it to be wrong. Such a judgment does not express a purely subjective preference. It claims universality; it claims to be the view of any rational agent. The content of the judgment that something is wrong, implies that the something may properly be prevented. But if your judgment is reasonably grounded, why should you go against it at all? Why should you tolerate?[36]

It might be thought that Raphael's remarks only pose a paradox—just the *appearance* of an inconsistency. Indeed, this response is likely to be congenial to liberals. In the liberal perspective, we ought to tolerate others' behavior (within limits) even when we believe it is morally wrong because autonomy is a positive good, toleration is necessary for the promotion of autonomy, and individuals cannot be truly autonomous agents unless each is free to act as he or she thinks best, even if the others' "best" is what we believe to be immoral. But this liberal response does not adequately respond to the logical difficulty Raphael believes to arise from the logical property disapproval possesses *as a moral judgment*. Moral judgments claim universality. That is, if I believe that something is morally wrong, say hunting for recreational purposes, then consistency requires that I regard all cases of recreational hunting as morally wrong. The attitudes of the Amish, or other sectarians, when they claim that certain practices are immoral for themselves but acceptable for "people of the world," do not express toleration as a moral concern. Moral judgments entail universalizability and therefore do not permit such exemptions. It therefore follows, the critic might claim, either that I do not really tolerate morally what I disapprove of (although I may be indifferent, permissive, or endure it), or that my disapproval is not genuine moral disapproval, but a matter of dislike.

Raphael could be correct about a real logical inconsistency in the concept of toleration, but *only if* we allow him to characterize tolerance as incompletely as the quoted passage suggests. Raphael claims of the moral disapproval, "The content of the judgment, that something is wrong, implies that the something may properly be prevented." But this way of making the point glosses over a critical distinction. What judgment, more precisely, does Raphael have in mind? I cannot consistently judge that X is morally wrong for some persons and that the same X is morally permissible for other persons, given the same relevant conditions. But there is no inconsistency between judging, first, that *A*'s doing *X* is morally wrong (and would be for anyone in similar circumstances), and second, that only *A* can exercise the executive decision to do or not to do *X*. For example, there is no inconsistency in my judging both that *A*'s smoking and hunting swans is morally wrong, and my judging that only *A* is appropriately situated to determine whether she will in fact smoke and shoot at swans. My moral disapproval of *A*'s conduct commits me only to consistent disapproval; it does not end if and when *A* begins to smoke and to shoot at swans. To suppose, as Raphael does, that the content of my judgment entails the belief that it is proper to interfere is to confuse my judgment about the morality of *A*'s action with a further judgment about the appropriateness of my action. But, as a general rule, it does not follow logically from my belief that *X* is morally wrong that I must suppress, or interfere with *X,* or even contrary to the expectations of many ethicists, that I must be *disposed* to suppress or interfere with *X*.[37]

This last point is supported by the contributions of the philosopher Thomas Wren in enlarging our understanding of moral *motivation*, or "conscience" (as distinct from moral motives), as constituting a metacognitive "moral domain."[38] Building on the research of Piaget and Kohlberg on the psychology of moral development,[39] Wren conceives of moral motivation as a "deep structure" determining or regulating moral motives (reasons for action as well as attitudes and affective responses), and hence, an agent's moral action tendencies.[40] Wren concludes that Piaget's and Kohlberg's research data on the differences between the cognitive capacities of individuals and their respective stages of moral development, *especially concerning the different bases for individuals' experience of the "necessity" for moral action*, requires that we recognize that action judgments about what it is right (or wrong) to do are actually global, or executive, judgments made up of (often unacknowledged) combinations of two different types of judgment. Thus the "moral domain" constituting an agent's motivational basis for moral action includes secondary, "responsibility" judgments as well as primary, "deontic judgments." The latter are judgments about what it is right or wrong for the individual to do, whereas the second-order "responsibility judgments" represent a follow-through function: a judgment of responsibility to act on what has judged to be right or wrong.[41]

The distinction between deontic judgments and responsibility judgments explains why toleration as a moral conception does not succumb to the logical inconsistency suggested by Raphael. Wren's analysis shows that there is a "space" between evaluative cognition, affect, and disposition, on the one hand, and the decision to act, on the other hand. Moreover, responsibility judgments are supervenient upon deontic judgments;[42] what is distinctive about the former, *but not the latter*, is the conviction that an action is necessary for one as an existent individual, that is, necessary to one's "present personal Moral cognition"[43] knowing what is right (or wrong) and even feeling that a course of action is right (or wrong) are, in themselves, not sufficient to motivate performing (or abstaining from) the moral (or immoral) act.

In the absence of "congruence" or consistency between one's deontic judgments and responsibility judgments, an agent will refrain from acting on her deontic judgments, despite the presence of powerful conative and affective motives for action. For example, I will be morally motivated to interfere with *A*'s smoking and shooting at swans if I believe both that what *A* desires to do is morally wrong, based on my deontic judgments, and that my interference is justified, based on my responsibility judgments. Thus moral toleration is possible because it sometimes happens that there is a special kind of incongruence or "dissonance" between our deontic and our responsibility judgments; namely, the combination in which we judge both that something is morally wrong *and* that it is not morally right to interfere.

There is an odd, perhaps cruel, paradox in the recognition that the same gap or "space" between deontic and responsibility judgments that makes moral toleration psychologically possible also accounts for many cases of moral indifference: the failure of agents to do what they judge is right due to incongruence between their deontic and responsibility judgments. In a sense, moral toleration represents the positive aspects of the moral domain as a "deep structure,"[44] whereas moral indifference may represent its negative, dysfunctional aspects. But critics might wonder why, if both moral toleration and moral indifference arise from the same psychological processes, we should regard toleration as a virtue after all. Does not my failure to interfere with *A*'s smoking and shooting at swans represent the same kind of moral failure characteristic of moral indifference? Answering this question for particular cases depends upon what kinds of background assumptions we are prepared to make: for instance, whether in virtue of my relationship to *A* (perhaps as her husband or father) I have a duty of care for her health; whether the swans are rare, or pets, or endangered as a species, and whether the hunting is legal, and so on. But there need be no concern about our ability to establish the *general distinction* between morally virtuous restraint and morally condemnable or pathological failures of moral behavior. This distinction rests on what influences or determines our responsibility judgments. In the case of moral toleration, these judgments flow from judgments we attach to the value of autonomy, our respect for the other as worthy of equal consideration, and similar considerations. By contrast, empirical research shows that in cases of moral indifference, responsibility judgments are blocked, infected by, or overridden by extrapersonal influences ranging from situational stimuli that elicit inherent tendencies such as the tendency to obey authority,[45] to social pressures that create "pluralistic ignorance" and the "diffusion of responsibility,"[46] and even to pathological processes resulting in such severe forms of dissociation as "physic numbing" and "doubling."[47] Thus, although the *capacities* both for toleration and for indifference may arise out of the same psychological mechanisms, they represent markedly different outcomes—not unlike Kant's distinction between autonomy and heteronomy—based on clearly different explanations for the behaviors in question.

This defense of the logical consistency of toleration as a moral concept has led into some deep reflections about the psychological bases of moral action. A fully developed account of moral psychology is obviously out of place here. Thus it is appropriate to return to the key point about the psychological "space" between our deontic and responsibility judgments. Why is it desirable that there be a need for congruence between our deontic and responsibility judgments, given the risks of moral failure? The most obvious answer is so that we do not act as automatons programmed to try to enforce whatever we believe to be right. It must be remembered that, while it is certainly not true that "anything goes" with respect to moral beliefs (moral beliefs must meet at least minimal criteria such as universalizability), it is unfortunately notorious that persons can hold and defend as moral beliefs what many reasonable people would regard as egregious error.[48] The less obvious but equally important answer arises from the need to appreciate our complexity as human beings; contrary to the efforts of some ethicists to demonstrate the completeness and consistency of some one supreme principle, moral pluralism marks the reality of our lives. We have multiple and diverse moral reasons for the choices we make and the goods we pursue. This is not to suggest that consistency is not also a moral value, but rather that it is too much to expect that our moral motives and moral judgments can always be shown to fit within a single comprehensive scheme. There are tensions, for example, between our drives for autonomy or moral independence and the feelings of separateness and distance associated with them, and our desire for solidarity, for wanting to belong and to be welcomed into various communities. Toleration as a moral virtue is an inevitable and welcome consequence of our acceptance of this moral pluralism and moral tension: it allows us as individuals to decide moral issues in such a way that they are *properly* our own,[49] while at the same time feeling confident that those with whom we seek to join our lives are persons whom we can respect, not just because they share our values, but because in choosing to share these values they manifest a character worthy of respect. For Mill was indeed right regarding this point: "It really is of importance, not only what [people] do, but also what manner of [people] they are that do it."[50]

NOTES

1. "Repressive Tolerance," in Robert Paul Wolff, Barrington Moore, Jr., and Herbert Marcuse, *A Critique of Pure Tolerance* (Boston: Beacon Press, 1965), 81–123.

2. Ironies of this kind are immortalized by Boccaccio's tale of Federigo's falcon in the *Decameron* (1348–1358) and by Guy de Maupassant's (1850–1893) short story, "The Gift."

3. For example, see John Rawls, *A Theory of Justice* (Cambridge, Mass.: Harvard University Press, 1971); Anthony Arblaster, Publishers, *The Rise and Decline of Western Liberalism* (Oxford: Blackwell, 1984); Joseph Raz, *The Morality of Freedom* (Oxford: Clarendon Press, 1986); Jeremy Waldron, "Theoretical Foundations of Liberalism," *Philosophical Quarterly* 37 (1987): 127–50; and Joseph Raz, "Autonomy, Toleration and the Harm Principle," in *Justifying Toleration: Conceptual and Historical Perspectives*, Susan Mendus (Cambridge, Mass.: Cambridge University Press, 1988).

4. See Joseph Raz, "Liberalism, Autonomy, and the Politics of Neutral Concern," *Midwest Studies in Philosophy* 7 (1982): 89–91.

5. See, for example, John Rawls, *A Theory of Justice*; Bruce Ackerman, *Social Justice in the Liberal State* (New Haven: Yale University Press, 1980); Ronald Dworkin, "Liberalism," in *A Matter of Principle* (Cambridge, Mass.: Harvard University Press, 1985), 181–204; and P. Jones, "The Ideal of the Neutral State" in Susan Mendus, *Liberal Neutrality*, ed. Robert Goodwin and Andrew Reeve (London: Routledge, 1989).

6. *Toleration and the Limits of Liberalism* (Atlantic Highlands, N.J.: Humanities Press, 1989), 8. I have also been assisted in formulating the following four conditions by Peter P. Nicholson, "Toleration as a Moral Ideal," in *Aspects of Toleration*, ed. John Horton and Susan Mendus (London: Methuen, 1985), 158–73.

7. From Mill's *On Liberty* and cited by Mendus, *Toleration and the Limits of Liberalism*, 8.

8. Maurice Cranston, "John Locke and the Case for Toleration," in *On Toleration*, ed. Susan Mendus and David Edwards, (Oxford: Clarendon Press, 1987), 101.

9. Mendus, *Limits of Liberalism*, 8. Although not explicitly stated, Mendus must surely mean that such forbearance is voluntary.

10. Mendus, *Limits of Liberalism*, 9.

11. Liberals have attempted to account for our valuing toleration on various grounds. John Locke addresses the irrationality of attempting to coerce belief in *A Letter Concerning Toleration*, ed. J. Tully (Indianapolis, Ind.: Hackett, 1983). John Stuart Mill attempts to make the case for diversity as an inherent value and presents an argument for autonomy in *On Liberty*, ed. G. Himmelfard (Harmondsworth: Penguin Books, 1978). Joseph Raz also argues persuasively for toleration founded on autonomy in *The Morality of Freedom* (Oxford: Clarendon Press, 1986). John Rawls related neutrality to justice by deriving neutrality from the original position in a *Theory of Justice*. Ronald Dworkin argues for a foundation for liberalism, and hence toleration, in a principle of equality understood as equal concern and respect in *A Matter of Principle*.

While there is every reason why each of these values central to liberalism—diversity, autonomy, justice as fairness, and equality—(as well, of course, as such fundamental moral principles as Kant's categorical imperative) can supply reasons for attaching moral value to toleration, I believe the best explanations for the respect manifest in toleration have to do with our capacity to see ourselves in the place of the other, and to appreciate how deeply "anchored" in our lives are the commitments for which we (and others as we imagine ourselves in their place) demand respect. On this point Bernard Williams observes quite correctly: There are points of resemblance between moral and factual convictions; and I suspect it to be true of moral, as it certainly is of factual convictions, that we cannot take very seriously a profession of them if we are given to understand that a speaker has just decided to adopt them. . . . We see a man's genuine convictions as coming from somewhere deeper in him than that (See Bernard Williams, *Problems: Problems of the Self.* [Cambridge, Mass.: Cambridge University Press, 1973], 227).

And in support of this line of reasoning H. L. A. Hart argues that there is no significant distinction (no logical stop) between those cases in which we would want tolerance and those in which others want tolerance. The point is obviously not that there are differences between the *weight*, or standing, group A gives to its ends and interests, as served by certain beliefs and acts, and the weight group B gives to its ends and interests, as served by persecuted beliefs and acts. See H. L. A. Hart, *Law, Liberty and Morality* (Stanford: Stanford University Press, 1963) 46–47. Working from a different philosophical tradition, Maurice Mandelbaum reaches a similar conclusion in *The Phenomenology of Moral Experience* (Baltimore, Md.: The Johns Hopkins Press), 277–90. Mandelbaum argues that we must tolerate other's views of certain types (e.g., religious) if it can be shown that these views have arisen from a bona fide type of experience (e.g., religious) analogous to the bona fide experiences we credit with grounding and validating our beliefs.

12. That this *appears* to be an inconsistent set of beliefs generates the "paradox of toleration" discussed later in this chapter.

13. For discussions of these defense mechanisms, see Robert Jay Lifton and Eric Markson, *The Genocidal Mentality* (New York: Basic Books, 1990), and Douglas V. Propora, *How Holocausts Happen* (Philadelphia: Temple University Press, 1990).

14. There may be exceptions produced by some combinations of cultural traditions, willful ignorance, delusion, and self-interest. Very troubling, for instance, are the cases of those Jews who cooperated with the Nazi regime or who refused to believe reports about the death camps. In some instances the line between toleration of Nazi persecution as indifference and actual complicity was crossed; in other instances, what psychiatrist Robert Jay Lifton calls "atrocity-producing situations" provided self-interest in cooperation in the vain hope of buying time. Neither of these kinds of cases can be described properly as exhibiting indifference. Yet there remained instances in which some of the victimized were tragically indifferent bystanders psychologically incapable of appreciating that the fate of those whom they failed to assist also awaited them.

Serious discussion of the extent and causes of Jewish complicity and indifference began with Hannah Arendt's *Eichmann in Jerusalem: A Report on the Banality of Evil* (New York: Viking Press 1963). Helpful discussions of the issues can be found in essays by Rainer C. Baum, Lawrence L. Langer, Abigail L. Rosenthal, John K. Roth, and others in *Echoes from the Holocaust: Philosophical Reflections on a Dark Time*, ed. Alan Rosenberg and Gerald E. Myers, (Philadelphia: Temple University Press, 1988), as well as in Abigail L. Rosenthal's extensive reflections in *A Good Look at Evil* (Philadelphia: Temple University Press, 1987). Robert Jay Lifton's account of cooperation (compliance) and indifference at the death camps is to be found in *The Nazi Doctors: Medical Killing and the Psychology of Genocide* (New York: Basic Books, 1986).

15. See Rainer C. Baum, "Holocaust: Moral Indifference as *the* Form of Modern Evil," in *Echoes from the Holocaust*, 53–90.

16. For an examination of the moral indifference of citizens of the United States to U. S. government-supported massacres in El Salvador and elsewhere in Latin America, see Douglas V. Propora, *How Holocausts Happen: The United States in Central America*.

17. For an explanation of how such a "coninuum of destruction" forms and operates, see Ervin Staub, *The Roots of Evil: The Origins of Genocide and Other Group Violence* (Cambridge, Mass.: Cambridge University Press, 1989).

18. I have been greatly aided in making the distinctions between permissiveness and endurance by Thomas K. Hearns, Jr., "On Tolerance," *Southern Journal of Philosophy* 8 (1970).

19. It does not follow from this logical point that there will not be "mixed" cases, i.e., cases in which the tolerant person feels, for example, both that she respects the persons whose beliefs she tolerates and that she feels unhappy about the need to endure the expression of those beliefs. The key to the distinction is in the clarity of the reasons she would give for her tolerance: if respect alone is sufficient ground, then her tolerance is based on moral virtue (to be explained below) even though her attitudes and motives might be quite mixed.

20. Quoted in Robert L. Ketchum, "James Madison and Religion: A New Hypothesis" in *James Madison on Religious Liberty,* ed. Robety S. Alley (Buffalo, N.Y.: Prometheus Books, 1985), 187–88.

21. See "Beyond Tolerance," 3–52.

22. Mendus, *Limits of Liberalism,* 117.

23. For example, John Rawls, *A Theory of Justice*; Bruce Ackerman, *Social Justice in the Liberal State*; and Joseph Raz, "Liberalism, Autonomy, and the Politics of Neutral Concern."

24. Dworkin, "Liberalism," 191.

25. Mendus, *Limits of Liberalism*, 142.

26. Dworkin, "Liberalism," 195.

27. That is to say, we may answer the questions, Why should we cultivate toleration as an individual virtue? and Why should we promote neutrality as a regulatory principle? by appealing to the same values of autonomy, justice as fairness, and equality.

28. David Little, *Ukraine: The Legacy of Intolerance* (Washington: United States Institute of Peace, 1991), xvi–xvii.

29. Donna Sullivan, "Advancing the Freedom of Religion of Belief through the UN Declaration on the Elimination of Religious Intolerance and Discrimination," *American Journal of International Law* 82 (1988): 505.

30. Peter P. Nicholson, "Toleration as a Moral Ideal," 160.

31. See ibid., 160–61.

32. Two further points deserve attention. First, adding this condition intensifies the "paradox of toleration." Second, Mary Warnock obviously disagrees, proclaiming, "The intolerable is the unbearable. And we may simply feel, believe, conclude without reason that something is unbearable and must be stopped," (see Warnock, "The Limits of Toleration," in *On Toleration,* 126). Susan Mendus and David Edwards, eds. (Oxford: Clarendon Press, 1987), 126. But Warnock is, in my view, really addressing the other conceptions of toleration identified above, especially toleration as endurance. Warnock's major reason for disagreeing is her concern (inherited from Hume) that no sharp line can be drawn between what we dislike and what we disapprove of (127). I believe a line can be drawn that is "sharp enough" to sustain this point, but I cannot pursue this metaethical issue here.

33. This question is raised by Mendus in *Limits of Liberalism*, 16–17.

34. Mendus, *Limits of Liberalism*, 16, 149–50.

35. For the works of the liberals cited, see notes 3, 4, and 5. For the critical commentary see David Miller, "Socialism and Toleration," in *Justifying Toleration,* D. D. Raphael, and Susan Mendus, *Limits of Liberalism,* 69–162.

36. "The Intolerable," in *Justifying Toleration,* 139.

37. This does not mean, of course, that there are not cases in which moral judgments entail correlative obligations. Obviously, these are most clear when it is appropriate to speak of *rights* or of special duties or obligations acquired as a result of voluntary choice. For example, if one believes that a fetus has a right to life, then one must also believe that (at least some) others are obligated to prevent the abortion of the fetus. But, of course, one may believe abortion is morally wrong without believing that fetuses have a right to life.

38. Thomas E. Wren, *Caring about Morality: Philosophical Perspectives in Moral Psychology* (Cambridge, Mass.: The MIT Press, 1991).

39. In particular, Wren draws on Jean Piaget, *The Moral Judgment of the Child*, trans. M. Gabin (New York: Free Press, 1965); Piaget, *The Origin of Intelligence in Children* (New York: International Universities Press, 1952); Piaget, *Intelligence and Affectivity: Their Relationship during Child Development* (Palo Alto, Calif.: Annual Reviews, 1981); Piaget, *Biology and Knowledge: An Essay on the Relations between Organic Regulations and Cognitive Processes* (Chicago, IL.: University of Chicago Press, 1971); Lawrence Kohlberg, "Stage and Sequence: The Cognitive-Developmental Approach to Socialization"; Kohlbert, "The Six Stages of Justice Judgment" all collected in Lawrence Kohlberg, *Essays on Moral Development: Vol. 2. The Psychology of Moral Development* (New York: Harper and Row, 1984).

40. Wren, *Caring about Morality,* 9–10.

41. Ibid., 144.

42. Ibid., 145.

43. Anthony Blasi, "Moral Cognition and Moral Action: A Theoretical Perspective," *Development Review* 3 (1983), 178–210.

44. Wren, *Caring about Morality*, 9–10.

45. See Stanley Milgram, *Obedience to Authority* (New York: Harper and Row, 1969), and Herbert C. Kelman and V. Lee Hamilton, *Crimes of Obedience: Toward a Social Psychology of Authority and Responsibility* (New Haven: Yale University Press, 1989).

46. See Propora, *How Holocausts Happen*, 15–38 and Robert B. Cialdini, *Influence: The New Psychology of Modern Persuasion* (New York: Quill, 1984), esp. 15–202.

47. See Robert Jay Lifton and Eric Markson, *The Genocidal Mentality: Nazi Holocaust and Nuclear Threat* (New York: Basic Books, 1990), and Robert Jay Lifton, *The Nazi Doctors: Medical Killing and the Psychology of Genocide* (New York: Basic Books, 1986).

48. A clear example is the view of some Muslim women on female circumcision. From a Western perspective, this practice represents barbaric mutilation, but women who approve of it can present reasons for regarding it as harmful not to undergo such treatment. We may abhor the views of male domination and female sexuality that this perspective implies, but that it arises out of a distinct and the supposed universality of our concepts of harm. For a fuller discussion of this point, see John Horton, "Toleration, Morality and Harm" in *Aspects of Toleration*, 113–35.

49. Mill, *On Liberty,* 126.

50. Ibid., 123. (Were he alive today, Mill certainly would accept the substitution of the term *people* for *men.*).

15

Concerning Moral Toleration

Jeff Jordan

If there is any moral stance which is widely recognized and generally applauded, it is toleration. There are various kinds of toleration: religious, cultural, political, what we could call "stoic"—"I can barely tolerate this heat"—and the kind that is often thought to be the most basic of all: moral. Moral toleration involves a person in tolerating some behavior or some state of affairs which she finds morally problematic. Like the other kinds of toleration, 'moral toleration' is widely seen as a morally praiseworthy act.[1] But what has not been recognized at all is that the concept of 'moral toleration,' when conjoined with a plausible moral principle, generates a conceptual puzzle.[2] In short, given the analysis of moral toleration, and given the principle that it is morally wrong to abet, knowingly and freely, the wrongdoing of another, it follows that by being morally tolerant one is doing a morally wrong act. But, accepting the widespread belief that moral toleration is morally praiseworthy, then by being morally tolerant one may be doing a morally praiseworthy act which is morally wrong.

Resolving this conceptual puzzle has an important consequence: the widespread idea of moral toleration being both morally praiseworthy and morally obligatory is erroneous and should be excised from the canons of respectable intellectual ideas. Though we toss this idea out, it does not follow that intolerance will rule the day. There are many kinds of toleration, variously incorporating rationality, prudence, social utility, or even aesthetic values, which are distinct from moral toleration. Hence, if toleration should be obligatory in some context or another, it will be an imperative that is not moral in nature.

THE ANALYSIS OF MORAL TOLERATION

Consider the following sentence:

1. S morally tolerates P's doing X
   where S and P are placeholders for persons and X stands for some action. How are we to understand (1)? An analysis of (1) reveals four conditions. If (1) is true then:

   A. S believes that the doing of X is morally wrong.

   And,

   B. S believes that she has it within her power to interfere with P's doing of X. And,

   C. S takes no steps to interfere with P's doing of X.

   And,

   D. S believes that she is doing a good thing by doing nothing (being morally tolerant).

Each of the conditions, (A) through (D), require comment. The first point to notice is this: moral toleration is not merely a matter of disliking something. The disliking of something is found, for instance, in the concept of 'cultural toleration.' Jones may find a certain exotic cultural practice bizarre; indeed he may immensely dislike the practice (perhaps it is a culinary practice) without it being the case that Jones finds anything morally problematic about it. Moral toleration is a matter of believing that something is morally wrong, that something is morally impermissible. Of course, one may in fact find the action distasteful as well as wrong. But disliking is not an essential component of the concept of moral toleration.

A second point is this: to believe sincerely that something is morally wrong entails two features. First, it entails that one believes that the world would be better off if that act or that state of affairs were not to obtain, all other things being equal. This point holds whether one takes a consequentialist approach to morality or a deontological one. A consequentialist holds that rightness and wrongness are defined by virtue of whether the act in question maximizes or diminishes the good. A hedonic act utilitarian, for instance, holds that those acts which maximize pleasure are those acts which are morally right. So, if a consequentialist believes that X is wrong, then she believes that the doing of X (or perhaps the occurrence of X) lessens the amount of good in the world. A deontologist would hold that an immoral act is one done in violation of one's duty. And the failure to do one's moral duty would clearly not make the world a better place than it would have been if the duty had been satisfied. A second feature is that if one believes that P's doing of X (in circumstance C) is morally wrong, then one believes that anyone's doing X (in similar circumstances) is morally wrong. Beliefs about wrongness and rightness have a universal scope and not a limited one.

We should note here also that moral toleration does not entail moral skepticism, nor does it entail any strong view of moral uncertainty. One does not morally tolerate something if one is unsure about the moral status of the act. If Jones is doubtful about the act being wrong, and if, on the basis of that epistemic uncertainty, Jones believes it best to give the benefit of the doubt, Jones is not engaging in moral toleration. Jones may be engaged in some other kind of toleration, but it is not moral. Moral toleration entails the sincere belief that the act in question is morally wrong.

Third, one does not morally tolerate what one believes is entirely out of one's hands. If it is not within one's power to prevent X, or, at least, to interfere with X, then one cannot be said to morally tolerate X. However, it is a characteristic of stoic toleration that one can be said to tolerate that which is beyond one's control: this humidity is stifling. But moral toleration involves, at the minimum, a belief that one can interfere with the problematic act, even if that belief should turn out to be false. What is relevant, then, is the belief that prevention is possible and not that one really can, in fact, prevent the act in question.[3]

Notice that moral toleration is an individual act. Political states can be tolerant, of course, but states cannot be morally tolerant. Toleration as practiced on a collective, political level constitutes a kind of toleration different from moral toleration. Moral toleration involves a belief that the act in question is morally wrong. Since beliefs cannot be attributed to states, states cannot be considered morally tolerant.[4]

Moral toleration, because of the large role which beliefs play, is describable either as an act or as an attitude.[5] Moral toleration is best described as an act and not, at least not primarily, as an attitude. This is so, first, because moral toleration is episodic in nature: one is morally tolerant about X at some time. Attitudes are not episodic in nature. A second reason to think that moral toleration is best described as an act is that one can be morally tolerant about X at one time, and at some later time not be morally tolerant about X without changing any of one's beliefs, expectations, or preferences— That is to say, without changing any of those intellectual features which constitute attitudes.

A third reason to hold that moral toleration is best describable as an act is that persons with contemptuous (and indeed, contemptible) attitudes can nonetheless be morally tolerant. Just because one person views another in a disdainful light does not entail that the first cannot be morally tolerant toward the second. The point here can be expressed this way: even a racist can be morally tolerant. This person may hold that others of a different color are typically immoral because it is their nature to be violent, promiscuous, or oppressive. But if the racist never acts on his beliefs, and given that conditions (A) through (D) hold, then the racist is morally tolerant.[6] It would be odd indeed to attribute to such a person both racist attitudes and the attitude of moral toleration. Though it is not erroneous to describe moral toleration as a virtue, it is a derivative description since the act of morally tolerating something is conceptually prior to that of moral toleration as an attitude.[7]

A last point about the analysis of moral toleration is that the tolerator believes that by being morally tolerant she is doing the right thing. This may appear to indict the concept of moral toleration with a charge of internal incoherence: the moral agent believes, as per (A), that the world would be better off morally if the problematic act did not occur; and the agent believes, as per (D), that by allowing the problematic act to occur, she is doing a good thing: the world is better off by her toleration. But any appearance of incoherence here is illusory. The idea of moral toleration is coherent. The coherence can be seen as follows: let M stand for the world if the problematic act did not occur; let N stand for the world given the occurrence of the tolerated act with the act of toleration; and let O stand for the world in which the moral agent prevents the act in question; and let the symbol > stand for the binary relation of "one state of affairs being morally better than another." According to the concept of moral toleration, the agent's moral preferences can be seen as: $M > N > O$. The world in which the problematic act does not occur is the best; but a world with moral toleration is better than one without.

Before leaving the analysis of moral toleration, a widespread claim about moral toleration should be noted. This widespread claim is that

2. moral toleration is morally praiseworthy.

Typically, the friends of (2) hold it not because they think that moral toleration is supererogatory; generally (2) is held because it is thought that (3) is true:

3. moral toleration is a morally obligatory act.

Is (3) true? Many people certainly think that it is. Indeed, something like (3) seems to be an important part of the orthodoxy of classical liberalism.[8] Proposition (3) is false if moral toleration is not a morally obligatory act. One can show that an act is not morally obligatory by showing that there is some reason to think that the act is, in fact, morally wrong. Further, since the performance of morally praiseworthy deeds is morally additive in the sense that doing a good deed adds to one's goodness, an act is not morally praiseworthy if it, in fact, lessens one's moral goodness. Below, I argue that moral toleration suffers from both of these defects and, hence, is neither obligatory nor morally praiseworthy. The argument against (3) involves a principle that I argue is true. The case against (2) involves what I call the "puzzle of moral toleration." Simply put, the argument against (2) is that rejecting it is the most plausible means available of resolving the puzzle of moral toleration. Before formulating the puzzle of moral toleration, a word or two needs to be said about the plurality thesis.

THE PLURALITY THESIS

According to the plurality thesis:

4. there is no unified concept of toleration; toleration comes in several distinct kinds.

The various toleration concepts share a family resemblance between them since there is no single essential property shared by all the concepts.[9] The most likely candidate of a common essential property is that one allows or permits, does nothing, in tolerating whatever is tolerated. But even this minimal feature is not found in all the concepts: in stoic toleration, for example, one endures that which is tolerated; while in moral toleration one does permit that which is tolerated.

The plurality of concepts arises from three features: the object tolerated, the reason given as the justification of the toleration, and the view involved of the object of toleration. The object tolerated concerns what is tolerated, whether it is a political view, or behavior, or religious practices, for example. The reasons given as justification variously include moral duty, autonomy, prudence, social utility, or rationality. The view involved of what is tolerated would include whether one dislikes the object or finds it morally problematic, theologically heretical, or politically dangerous. The different kinds of toleration include, in addition to moral toleration, cultural toleration, religious toleration, and political toleration.

The plurality thesis is supported by two considerations. First, think of Locke's famous case for religious toleration. Locke's argument is based not on morality but on rationality. Because belief is largely involuntary, Locke argues, it is irrational to try to coerce someone into believing a religious proposition. Since the means employed are not efficacious for the desired end, religious intoleration is irrational. There is no appeal to morality in Locke's argument at all; and, clearly enough, Locke's concept of toleration is legitimate. Second, some concepts of toleration do not involve moral disapproval at all. One can dislike something or have to endure something which she does not find morally objectionable. Moral toleration is not only distinct from the other kinds of toleration, it is not even basic or conceptually prior to them. Some concepts of toleration, like Locke's, are entirely independent of moral toleration.[10]

THE PUZZLE FORMULATED

There is a plausible moral principle which, if conjoined with the concept of moral toleration, generates a conceptual puzzle concerning it. By *principle* I mean a general proposition which provides a judgment about particular acts. Principles are either necessarily true or necessarily false (or, if one prefers, valid or invalid). A true principle would be a principle which has no genuine counterexamples; a false one would not accommodate all the relevant facts. An example of an obviously true moral principle is the claim that

6. it is morally wrong, all other things being equal, to knowingly and intentionally kill a human being.

According to (6), homicide is wrong in the absence of a morally good reason. The inclusion of the ceteris paribus clause allows that there may be situations in which homicide is morally justified. So, for example, if capital punishment were morally permissible, this would be compatible with (6).

Consider the following principle:

7. it is morally wrong to abet, knowingly and freely, another's wrongdoing.

According to (7), if one assists or facilitates another in the commission of some wrongdoing, then one is doing something which is itself immoral. The abetting of another's wrongdoing is itself an act of wrongdoing. Of course, if one is coerced to aid another, or if one does not realize that the act in question is wrong, then (7) is not applicable. What (7) entails is that, to take a particular case, if Jones knows that Smith's contemplated action is wrong_ robbing the corner market, say—and Jones aids Smith in that action—he gives her a gun for example—then Jones' said is itself immoral. Principle (7) is not a principle about "moral spillover." Principle (7) does not entail that one shares in the blame resulting from some immoral act; (7) entails that abetting another in the performance of wrongdoing is itself wrong.

It might be tempting to restrict the scope of (7) to acts which involve some causal component. Given this view, one is morally responsible only if one's aid causally contributes to the occurrence of the act. Principle (7), under this construal, is a principle about shared responsibility resulting from shared causation. And further, shared causation implies the active commission of an action. Since inactions are not typically taken to be causally efficacious, then, under this restriction, principle (7) applies only to actions and not to inactions.

This restrictive view should be rejected, however. The ordinary understanding of moral toleration is that it involves omissions, the doing of nothing, as per (C). Moreover, omissions can facilitate another's action. If Jones knows that Smith is planning to do X, and she also knows that X is wrong and that she can, with very little effort prevent Smith's doing of X, and Jones does nothing, then Jones has facilitated Smith's doing of X. It is a necessary condition of the performance of any action that no one who feasibly could interfere with the doing of that act actually does so. The use of the term *feasibility* here is supposed to restrict the relevant scope to only those cases in which one could plausibly be said to know about the action, and to have a belief about the moral status of the action, and to be in a position to interfere with the action.[11] An omission which meets these conditions we can call a "facilitating omission" (or just a "facilitation"). Facilitating omissions are morally significant since the wrongdoing could occur only if the facilitation takes place. Principle (7), therefore, properly includes within the scope of abetting, facilitating omissions as well as cases of active assistance.[12]

Is (7) true? It clearly seems to be. But support for this can be gleaned from four arguments.[13] These arguments, though distinct, have a certain conceptual overlap. The cumulative effect of the four is to provide good reason for thinking that (7) is true. And, if there is good reason to think that (7) is true, then there is also good reason to think that (3) is not true. The first argument makes use of the concept of 'permission.'

Imagine two people, such that the first commits an immoral act A, which the second knew about and could have easily and safely prevented but does not. Though the second person is not morally responsible for A, the second person is morally blameworthy for permitting A. If Jones could have stopped the robbery committed by Smith and does not, then Jones has done something wrong. Permitting an action is morally significant since it seems clear enough that, if one permits another to commit an evil act, the one who has given permission is morally culpable for having done something wrong. The explanation of why permission is morally significant requires the concept of 'facilitating omissions'. Permitting an immoral act is just the facilitation of that act.

The second argument involves several thought cases, that is, cases, which generate certain moral intuitions that are explainable only if we suppose something like (7) to be true. The first case is called the "bus driver" case: Suppose A is a citizen bus driver in Nazi occupied Poland, who finds out that the passengers in his bus are being taken to a concentration camp from which they will never return, and A does nothing. Further, A stays with the job for the duration of the war, never having done anything; though he could have, with some small risk, quit the job. (Contrast here the case of Oskar Schindler who rescued over a thousand Polish Jews from the Nazis.)

A second case is the "bystander" case: Suppose B happens to look out her back window and witnesses in the alley below Jones viciously beating Smith. B could, with very little effort and with no risk to herself, report the assault to the police, or she could call out her window for help, perhaps frightening Jones off. Instead, B does nothing. (Think here of the famous 1964 Kitty Genovese case in which thirty-eight people watched the thirty-minute assault and murder of Kitty Genovese without calling the police or attempting in any other way to prevent the attack.)

The third case is the "taxi driver" case: suppose C is a taxi driver who finds the viewing of pornographic materials immoral (let us stipulate that the viewing of pornography is wrong). Suppose that one of C's passengers directs C to take him to the nearest blue theater, and C takes him there and lets him out of the taxi. Further, if C would have refused her passenger, it is likely that C would have lost her job.

The bus driver case and the bystander case both generate strong and determinate intuitions concerning (7). In the first case, our intuitions are that A, even though he did not intern any one in a camp himself, is nonetheless morally responsible for having enabled another, even if in a small way, to do something that is wrong. That is to say, A assisted in the immoral act. The bystander case, though it involves facilitation and not active assistance, generates intuitions just as strong and determinate as the first case: B is morally culpable for not intervening. Because B does not interfere with the beating, she has done something wrong. This point is important because it explains why we believe that bystanders who could have prevented or interfered with an evil act and do not are morally culpable of wrongdoing. By not involving herself, the bystander has facilitated the immoral act.

The taxi driver case, however, does not generate any determinate intuitions. Indeed, one might suppose that something like the taxi driver case presents a counterexample to (7). But the relevant difference in the intuitions generated by the first two cases and the third is explained by the fact that the third case situates the person in an employment situation and involves an immortality which is not very weighty in nature. Since C takes the voyeur to the pornographic theater only as a part of her job, and since it involves a kind of wrongdoing which is relatively harmless, and because C could very well lose her job over the matter, it is fairly clear that this case lies outside the scope of (7).[14] The taxi driver case in fact helps us see that there are important constraints on the relevant application of (7).

A third argument in support of (7) involves the principle that

8. for all persons S, if S does an act which is morally inferior to some other act which S could have done, then it is possible that S could have been morally better than she is.

Principle (8) has to do with the moral status of a person which accrues from one's acts.[15] Principle (8) is true, even if the acts involved are not themselves morally wrong acts. If two acts, M and N, are each supererogatory acts, such that M is morally better than N, and if all other things are equal, it follows that if one does N rather than M, then, by (8), one is not as good a person as one could have been. And this is so even though one did nothing wrong in doing N rather than M.

Is principle (8) true? It seems abundantly clear that (8) is true since the actions one does determine, in large part, one's moral status. Given this, how does (8) support (7)? The first point to notice is that (8) does not entail (7). However, proposition (8) does, provide us with some reason for thinking that (7) is probably true. The support provided by (8) can be seen as follows: suppose that one brings about a state of affairs, K, which is morally inferior to another possible state of affairs, J. K involves a morally wrong act, while J is, roughly, the same as K, except J does not include the wrong act. By permitting K, instead of bringing about J, one has brought about a state of affairs which is morally inferior to a state of affairs one could have brought about instead. Hence, by facilitating K, one is less morally good than one could have been otherwise. Of course, it does not follow from this that one has done a wrong act, but it does follow that facilitating a wrong act makes one less good than one otherwise would have been in the absence of the facilitation. Principle (8), therefore, supports (7), because (8) makes it clear that by facilitating or by actively assisting an immoral act, one's own moral status is affected.

A fourth argument makes use of the notion of perpetuating an evil. Consider the following proposition:

9. it is morally wrong to perpetuate, wittingly, an immoral state of affairs.

If one knows that X is wrong and one knows that one can prevent or at least hinder X, and one does nothing, then it is fair to say that one has perpetuated X. Perpetuating evils is commonly and widely thought to be wrong (for example, think of the common admonition to not stand silent in the presence of a sexist or racist comment). The explanation why perpetuating an evil is wrong entails the concept of facilitation. Sense can be made of why we believe that perpetuating a wrong is itself wrong only if we suppose that (7), or something quite similar to (7), is in fact true.

Provided that the foregoing arguments are sound, then we have good reason to hold that (7) is true. Conjoining (7) to (A) through (D) entails that the tolerator is doing something which is morally wrong. How so? The tolerator could prevent an act which she believes is wrong, and she does not. By not preventing what she might, the tolerator permits a wrong act to occur. By permitting the wrongdoing, the tolerator facilitates the wrongdoing of another. This facilitation is, as per (7), itself an act of wrongdoing. And, of course, it follows from this that (3) is false.

One might object that the tolerator is not plausibly charged with an act of wrongdoing because her moral views would be that, by being morally tolerant, the world is better off than if she were morally intolerant.

The first thing to notice here is this: even if one accepts the objection, moral toleration does not come out as well as is commonly thought. If one accepts the objection, one must see moral toleration as a kind of necessary evil, and it seems clear enough that necessary evils are not intrinsically good acts, nor are they morally praiseworthy.[16]

However that is, there is good reason to reject the reasoning involved in the objection. One may in fact believe that a world with moral toleration and the wrong act is morally better than a world with moral intolerance and the act prevented. But how is that relevant? Given the analysis of moral toleration and given the plausibility of (7), we see that by being morally tolerant one is facilitating a wrong act. This result obtains whether or not one believes that moral toleration, is justified. It may be true that one is not blameworthy because of one's beliefs, but it does not follow from this that the person has not done anything wrong. Analogously, a person may murder another without realizing that the killing was murder. The ignorance may diminish the blameworthiness of the act, but it does not change the fact that the act was wrong.

The puzzle of moral toleration is generated by conjoining (7) with (A) through (D), and adding (2) to the mix: by being morally tolerant one is preforming a morally praiseworthy act that is morally wrong. It is clear that one of the propositions, (2) or (7) or any of (A) through (D) must be rejected as being false. Assuming that the analysis of moral toleration is largely problem-free, then either (2) or (7) must be rejected. When one examines the principles (2) and (7), it is (2) which appears to be the principle that has obvious counterexamples. There are all sorts of morally wrong acts which are morally intolerable. If we are to reject one of those principles in order to defuse the puzzle, then the likely candidate is (2) and not (7).

A RIGHT TO DO WRONG?

Do persons sometimes have a moral right to do wrong? If they do, then (3) and possibly (2) may yet be salvaged. There is a claim, often repeated, that autonomy is a great good that requires or, perhaps, presupposes that moral toleration is generally practiced.[17] In the absence of moral toleration, that is, persons are less likely to be free autonomous moral agents than would otherwise be the case. It is not entirely clear what to make of this claim, but perhaps an objection can be formulated by conjoining the claim with the observation that the argument of section 3 presupposed that the proposition:

10. S's doing A is morally wrong entails the further proposition that

11. it is morally permissible, all other things being equal, to interfere with S's doing A.[18]

Perhaps, however, there is a way of blocking the inference of (11) from (10). The objection could be constructed as follows. Suppose that autonomy requires that:

12. S has the right to do A.

It would, then, follow that it would be morally impermissible to interfere with S's doing A. In other words, the inference of (11) from (10) is invalid, and there is reason, therefore, to reject the argument presented above against (2) and (3). If persons really do have a moral right to do wrong, then there may well be a correlative moral duty of moral toleration.[19]

Can there be a right to do something which is immoral? Well, yes and no. There certainly can be a legal right to do something which is immoral. For example, if hate speech is wrong (and given the constitutional right to free speech), it is clear that one can have a legal right to do something which one morally ought not do. However, there is good reason, to hold that there cannot be a moral right to do something which is immoral. To suppose that one could have a moral right to do a moral wrong leads to a contradiction. If action A is immoral, then it follows that

13. it is morally impermissible for S to do A, all other things being equal.[20]

And, supposing for the moment that (12) refers to a moral right, then it would be true that

14. it is morally permissible for S to do A, all other things being equal.

Holding the placeholders constant, and despite the fact that they both contain ceteris paribus clauses, (13) is the denial of (14). Since (13) and (14) are contradictory, we know that at least one of suppositions whence they were derived must be false. Because the inference of (13) from the claim that A is wrong seems unimpeachable, then we have reason to hold that if an act is immoral, one cannot have a moral right to do that act.

One might try to block the reductio of the idea that one can have a moral right to do wrong by claiming that (12) does not entail (14); though it does entail that

15. it is morally wrong for anyone to interfere with S's doing A, all other things being equal.

And, of course, since (15) is quite compatible with (13), the reductio is not generated. The problem with this contention is that it is incomplete and implausible. While it may be true that (12) entails (15), that is only part of the story since it would be extremely implausible to hold that one can a moral right to do X but that it does not follow that one morally can do X. It is certainly true that if one has a legal right to do X, it does not follow that one can morally do X, but that provides no plausibility to the idea that (12) does not entail (14). It is safe, then, to conclude that the reductio escapes unscathed. Hence, one may have a legal right to do a wrong, but one cannot have a moral right. Since the objection is cogent only if it involves a moral right to do wrong, it is unlikely that any appeal to rights will provide a cogent objection to the argument contra (2) and (3).

WHY BE TOLERANT ON MORAL MATTERS?

If moral toleration is not morally obligatory nor morally praiseworthy, there may appear to loom the threat of a society so rigid and Puritanical in its moralistic interferences that one must wonder about the plausibility of the foregoing. In this section I try to alleviate this worry by sketching a theory that explains and justifies the practice of moral toleration. It will be a theory that not only provides a pragmatic justification of moral toleration, but also explains and makes sense of many of our beliefs involving moral toleration. There are three ingredients necessary for formulating the theory. The first is a rejection of the "omni-riding" thesis concerning morality:

16. Moral considerations always take precedence over other grounds of choice.

According to (16), moral claims override, they trump, any and every other consideration. That is to say, suppose there are two claims, A and B, such that A is a person's moral right, whereas B is, say, an economic consideration. According to (16), A should be considered the more important and more deserving of respect and recognition than B. And it is not just that moral considerations override other considerations, moral considerations are themselves unsurpassable because they do not admit being overridden. Proposition (16) entails that moral claims are omni-riding in their scope and weight. The reason why (16) is often thought to be true is that we commonly take morality to be of supreme value and to be the most important of the demands made of us.

However, there is good reason to think that (16) is false. The falsity of (16) follows from a recognition of what has been called the "problem of dirty hands." The problem of dirty hands is usually formulated in a political context with the assumption that important political goods such as liberty, peace, and prosperity, can be gotten sometimes only by violating common morality (from a practical point of view given historical events).[21] We can list several historical examples of what might be considered cases of dirty hands: think of Lincoln's suspension in 1861 of the Constitutional right of Habeas Corpus in Maryland. Being president, Lincoln had sworn an oath to uphold the Constitution, and yet, in trying to protect the Constitution, he violated it. Or think of Grant's repeated and bloody assaults on the trenches of Cold Harbor in 1864. In trying to end the war, Grant engaged in a brutally costly campaign in which tens of thousands died. Or again think of Edith Wilson's de facto running of the executive branch after her husband suffered a stroke in 1919. Her usurpation of democratic power was done for political stability and public order. Or, more controversially, think of Reagan's attempt in what is known as "Irangate" to circumvent congressional oversight in order to free Americans being held hostage. These cases and others involve persons doing morally problematic actions, violating oaths or duties or sanctioning questionable activities, in order to bring about some desirable end. Given that dirty hands cases do occur, we have reason to reject (16) as false: there are occasions in which morality may be properly superseded by other considerations.

The second ingredient necessary is the concept of 'moral weight.' Consider the two acts of stealing a banana and of murder. It is clear that we find the murder of a human of much greater consequence than we do the act of stealing a banana. Both acts are wrong; yet they nonetheless differ in their moral weight. Murder is of a much greater moral weight than is stealing a banana. There is an instructive analogy here with the legal concepts of 'misdemeanors' and 'felonies.' While both misdemeanors and felonies are crimes, the latter are of much greater gravity. Likewise, some acts of wrongdoing carry much greater moral weight than do other acts. A judgment of the relative moral weight of an act would typically involve considerations such as the amount of harm which results from the act, whether the act is public or private, whether the act entails a violation of a right, and whether the act is singular or commonplace. Let's call those acts which are relatively heavy in their moral weight as "deep" immoral acts and those acts which are not morally weighty "shallow" acts of wrongdoing. Though no precise criterion of the cutoff between the deeply wrong and the shallow act of wrongdoing has been formulated, the idea is understandable enough for its employment here.

The third element is the prudential preference to be left alone. This preference is captured well by the slogan Live and let live. This preference encompasses nonmoral matters, including how one uses one's time, one's money, and one's talents. This preference also involves, and this is crucial, shallow acts of wrongdoing. We do not care to have others hovering over our shoulders, witnessing and judging the perhaps infrequent, yet embarrassingly common acts of shallow wrongdoing that we commit. Though shallow acts are wrong, we desire the moral space to make our own choices and our own mistakes free from the reproach and the constant evaluation of others. The desired moral space can be had only if something like the distinction between deep and shallow is recognized and only if we extend toleration to the shallow.

It is important to note that this prudential preference is compatible with the claim that (7) is true. Though morally tolerating another's act of shallow wrongdoing is itself wrong, it is itself only a case of shallow wrongdoing. And if we do have the prudential preference of live and let live, then the toleration of cases of shallow wrongdoing is an unavoidable cost of achieving that preference. Moral toleration, therefore, is a low-grade case of dirty hands. In order to reach the goal of being left alone, one must allow oneself to be "stained" with shallow wrongdoings.

Given these ingredients, the support for the claim that one should (prudentially) engage in moral toleration is as follows: we comply with a tacit treaty that we should leave others alone so that they will likewise leave us alone.[22] The idea here is a decision-theoretic one. By complying with the tacit treaty to leave one another alone, we wager that others will also comply. Because we prefer a society that is not severely Puritanical in its interferences, we exchange our moral purity for a relatively generous scope of being left alone. Since interference breeds interference, if we were to interfere constantly with other people, we would find ourselves likewise suffocated by others' interferences. By preventing the shallow wrongdoings of others, it becomes more likely that our own acts of shallow wrongdoing will be prevented and, indeed, that many of our nonmoral acts will also come under the heel of interference. Once shallow acts are fair game for interference, nonmoral acts will also become likely targets. Moral intoleration of shallow wrongdoing increases the likelihood of other sorts of intoleration and, as a consequence, diminishes the likelihood that we ourselves will be left alone as much as possible.

The treaty does not cover deeply immoral acts, but it does cover shallow wrongdoings, as well as nonmoral cases.[23] The idea is not that it is permissible to do shallow acts of wrongdoing. Shallow acts are immoral acts. Complying with the tacit treaty to live and let live just makes it likely that we will live in a society free from Puritanical interferences. Hence, moral toleration has a place in the guidebook of how we should live.[24] However, it is not a place of honor but a place of expediency, of prudence. To get what we want requires that we morally tolerate some things which we find immoral.

One advantage of this theory over any morality-based justification of moral toleration is that a pragmatic-based theory avoids a common version of the paradox of moral toleration—should one tolerate the intolerant? Given a morality-based theory, problems loom whether the answer given is affirmative or negative. If yes, then one is permitting evil; if no, then one may be engaged in the very kind of action that one finds morally problematic. But the idea of a decision-theoretic tacit treaty provides a ready answer. Should one tolerate the intolerant? Since intolerance constricts the desired moral space, the answer is no. Notice there is no threat of self-incrimination or self-refutation here. Because the habitually intolerant are not party to the tacit treaty, interfering with them (the intolerant) does not violate the treaty. By not being party to the treaty, one loses all claim on any reciprocal benefit which may otherwise result from it.

CONCLUSION

Given principle (7), it follows that by being morally tolerant, one is either doing a morally wrong act or one is morally less good than one otherwise would have been. Either way the result is not what follows if (2) is taken to be true. Since principle (7) appears to be beyond reproach—because it is plausible, and because it has survived scrutiny—the problem lies with proposition (2). Though this is different from the prevailing view, moral toleration appears neither to be morally obligatory nor morally praiseworthy. We have reason, in other words, to no longer tolerate the idea that moral toleration is morally praiseworthy. If we want something like the concept of moral toleration to guide our affairs, we ought best to look toward the resources of rationality and prudence to supply us with what we want.[25]

NOTES

1. Philosophical friends of moral toleration include Peter Nicholson, "Toleration as a Moral Ideal," in *Aspects of Toleration*, ed. John Horton and Susan Mendus (London: Methuen, 1985), 158–73; and Thomas Nagel, *Equality and Partiality* (N.Y.: Oxford University Press, 1991), 154–68.

2. There are several different puzzles involved with moral toleration. Susan Mendus in her *Toleration and the Limits of Liberalism* (London: The MacMillan Company, 1989), 18–21, discusses what she calls the "paradox of toleration." This paradox is different from the puzzle discussed in this essay. Her discussion concerns why one should tolerate what one finds morally problematic. Another puzzle concerning moral toleration would have to do with the propriety of not tolerating the intolerant. Is that itself an instance of intoleration? The puzzle discussed here concerns the consequences which result from conjoining the concept of moral toleration with a plausible moral principle.

3. Can moral toleration take the form of refraining from criticizing someone for an immoral act after the fact (the act already having been done)? It is clear that moral toleration is a proactive stance, can it also be reactive? If moral toleration can be reactive in nature, then (B) would have to be revised to incorporate that fact. I ignore this possible problem here.

4. The claim that collectives and states cannot properly be considered morally tolerant is quick. A state may, in fact, have a moral duty to be morally neutral or impartial between its citizens and their respective life projects and, in that way, may be practicing a kind of moral toleration (assuming, and this is a big assumption, that collectives can have duties). If that is correct, it is a kind of moral toleration different from what individuals are said to practice.

5. Let me make some stipulations. I use the terms *acts, actions,* and *omissions* as follows. Acts are either actions or omissions. An action is an event in which a human agent engages in an activity. Omissions are inactions. An omission is an event in which a human agent deliberately refrains from acting (though there are omissions which are not deliberate—I ignore those here).

6. Of course, racists usually base their views on something they dislike, rather than on something they find morally problematic.

7. It has been suggested that the word *toleration* should be used for acts and that *tolerance* should be reserved for attitudes. For such a proposal, see Nick Fotion and Gerard Elfstrom, *Toleration* (Tuscaloosa, Ala.: The University of Alabama Press, 1991).

8. See, for instance, Nagel, *Equality and Partiality*, 154–68; and John Rawls, *Political Liberalism* (N.Y.: Columbia University Press, 1993), 194.

9. For a proponent of what could be called the unitary thesis:

5. there is a single, overarching unified concept of toleration

see Susan Mendus, *Toleration and the Limits of Liberalism*, 18–21; and see Peter Nicholson, "Toleration as a Moral Ideal," 158–173.

10. Contra D. D. Raphael, "The Intolerable," in *Justifying Toleration: Conceptual and Historical Perspectives*, ed. Susan Mendus (Cambridge: Cambridge University Press, 1988), 137–53.

11. It should be emphasized that (7) has to do only with those who are in a relevant (or feasible) position to interfere with the act. My failure to prevent a wrongdoing in France is in no way culpable, since I am not in a feasible position to prevent it.

12. Can (7) be revised so that it concerns the abetting of good acts, such as:

7'. the free and knowing abetting of another's praiseworthy act is itself morally praiseworthy.

Though I cannot defend it here, it does seem plausible that something like (7') is in fact true.

13. The relevant scope of (7) is set by the following conditions. Principle (7) is applicable only if: (i) only minimal action is required to interfere with the wrongdoing; (ii) the action required is relatively risk free both for the agent and for others; (iii) the agent can perform the action independent of anyone else; and (iv) the action required to interfere with the wrongdoing is neither excessive nor morally disproportionate.

14. More precisely and fully, principle (7) should read:

7'. necessarily, for all persons S and P, if S believes that P's doing an action A is wrong and S is in a feasible position such that S could, with a minimal effort that is risk-free and proportional, interfere with P's doing A, and S does nothing, then S is morally culpable for doing nothing.

15. Proposition (8) is first formulated by Philip Quinn in his essay, "God, Perfection and Possible Worlds," in *The Problem of Evil*, ed. M. Peterson, (Notre Dame, Ind.: University of Notre Dame Press, 1993).

16. An instance of evil E is necessary just in case E is an essential part of bringing about some good G which is greater than E (G>E); or E is an essential part of avoiding some other evil E', such that E' is at least as serious an evil as E (E'>E).

17. For instance, see Susan Mendus, *Toleration and the Limits of Liberalism*.

18. Jeremy Waldron argues that (10) does not entail:

11'. it is morally permissible to interfere with S's doing A.

Waldron's major objection to the inference of (11') from (10) is that there are situations in which (10) may be true, while (11') is false: though lying is wrong, one may have an overriding reason why one should not, in a certain circumstance, interfere with the lying. But the introduction of a ceteris paribus clause is enough to defeat Waldron's argument against the inference of (11') from (10). While it may be true that the permissibility of interfering with a wrong can be overridden, it will still be true that interfering with a wrong is prima facie permissible. See J. Waldron, "A Right to Do Wrong," *Ethics* 92 (October 1981): 21–39.

19. The question of whether one can have a moral right to do a wrong played a leading role in the Lincoln-Douglas debates concerning political sovereignty of the late 1850s. Lincoln held that there could be no such right, while Douglas contended that there could be. For an interesting discussion of the issue, see Richard George, *Making Men Moral* (Oxford: Clarendon Press, 1993), 110–28.

20. The factors held constant include whether the action is a case of necessary evil or not and whether or not one realizes what she is doing is wrong.

21. For more on the problem of dirty hands, see Michael Walzer, "Political Action: The Problem of Dirty Hands," *Philosophy and Public Affairs* 2 (1972): 160–80. For an argument against the possibility of "dirty hands problems," see Alan Donagan, *The Theory of Morality* (Chicago: University of Chicago Press, 1977), 180-89.

22. I borrow the idea of a tacit treaty from David Lewis, "Academic Appointments: Why Ignore the Advantage of Being Right?" in *Morality, Responsibility and the University*, ed. S. Cahn (Philadelphia: Temple University Press, 1990), 239–41.

23. The other concepts of toleration—political, religious, and cultural—could also be brought under the terms of the treaty.

24. More precisely, a kind of moral toleration will have a place since we would need to revise the analysis of moral toleration to incorporate the rejection of (2) and (3) and to put in place the prudential underpinnings of toleration. The revision requires that we replace (D) with: D'. S believes that she is doing an advisable thing by doing nothing (by being morally tolerant).

25. I should like to thank David Haslett, Gordon Graham, Robert McKim, and Kristen Seal for helpful comments on earlier versions of this chapter.

16

Toleration as a Form of Bias

Andrew Altman

INTRODUCTION

Group bias is a pervasive feature of human life. Wherever humans live, they form in-groups and out-groups. Group bias systematically favors the interests of the in-group members and/or disfavors those of the out-group members. Many people would argue that fighting group bias is an important moral priority for any society at the close of the twentieth century and for humanity as a whole. They would point, quite correctly, to the moral horrors to which group bias has led throughout human history and especially in this century. Avoiding repetitions of these horrors seems to require a vast reduction or elimination of group bias.

Combatting bias, then, is generally regarded as a high moral priority. I do not quarrel with that assessment. However, I believe that we need a better understanding of what we can reasonably hope for and work toward in the battle. I do not regard the elimination of bias and the attitudes that underlie it as a realistic or even a desirable goal. Instead, we should work toward eliminating the most harmful consequences and most vicious forms of bias, while at the same time recognizing that bias in some form is here to stay. I shall argue that this amounts to a strategy aimed at establishing intergroup toleration. Though it may seem paradoxical, my argument is that toleration is a form of bias. Even more paradoxically, I argue that, despite being a form of bias, toleration is nonetheless a genuine moral virtue.

ANALYZING BIAS

Social psychologists disaggregate bias into two components: prejudice and discrimination.[1] While prejudice is regarded as a matter of attitude, discrimination is taken to be a matter of action. Attitudes are said to be inner psychological states, while actions consist of external behavior. The attitude-action distinction has been proved to be an important one in light of the many studies showing that there are often discrepancies between the attitudes people express toward others and the ways in which they behave toward them.

The attitude component can itself be further broken down into two aspects: cognitive and affective. The former is a matter of the way we process and retrieve information about the social world and of the social beliefs we form as a result. The latter is a matter of the feelings and desires we have toward others. Clearly, the cognitive and affective dimensions of bias are closely intertwined. The feelings and desires we have about others are typically a function of the beliefs we hold about them. And it may be that many, or even all, human emotions have both cognitive and affective dimensions.

In analyzing the cognitive dimension of any form of bias, it is important to distinguish the beliefs that are *constitutive* of that form of bias from the beliefs that *contribute* in some way to the existence of the bias. What I am calling "group bias" has a characteristic kind of constitutive belief, namely, the belief that the interests of the members of a certain sociologically defined group(s) should count less than the interests of some reference group. The contributory beliefs are those that support the constitutive belief. They are typically beliefs that ascribe deficient intelligence and defective moral character to the out-group members. Thus, anti-Semitism is characterized by the constitutive belief that the interests of Jews should count less than those of the members of other religious groups. This constitutive belief is, in turn, supported by the belief that Jews are greedy, dishonest, and the like.

Group bias comes in different degrees and forms. Thus, the affective components can be more or less intense. One could have an especially strong aversive feeling toward the members of a particular social group, or only a mild aversion, or something inbetween. The desire component can vary on two dimensions: the content of one's desires could represent a more or a less serious harm to the interests of the out-group members, and the strength of one's desire could be greater or lesser. Similarly, the cognitive component of bias can vary according to whether the constitutive belief represents as morally correct a more or less serious discounting of the interests of the out-group members.

Suppose we have a case where an intense aversion is combined with a strong desire to see very serious harm done to the basic interests of an out-group, and all this is conjoined to a constitutive belief that represents as correct the severe discounting of the basic interests of the out-group. We can call such a case a paradigm of group "hate." Such hate has been —and continues to be — a bane of human history. It bears a substantial portion of the responsibility for the twentieth-century genocidal horrors. We can and should work to eliminate it. But this should not obscure the fact that there are forms of bias that are different in degree and form from its most vicious manifestation in hate. The elimination of group hate would not by itself eliminate other forms of group bias or prejudice.

GROUPS AND HUMAN INTERESTS

Group bias is a pervasive and historically important phenomenon because group life is so central to human life. Although it is often portrayed as purely irrational, the fact is that group bias is connected to important human interests. We will fail to understand the nature and persistence of group bias unless we have some framework for understanding those interests and the role groups play in serving them.

There are two interconnected aspects of human existence from which our basic interests derive. First is our existence as biological organisms needing adequate nourishment, rest, and shelter in order to survive. Second is our existence as conscious beings who strive to find meaning and purpose in our lives. These two dimensions of our existence dictate what our most fundamental interests are.

Our existence as biological organisms means that to live well we must enjoy a certain level of material well-being. What counts as the appropriate level for any given group of people will vary depending on the social and historical context. But there is no escaping the conclusion that human beings have a basic interest in material well-being.

Our existence as conscious beings who seek meaning and purpose entails that to live well we must have some conception of who we are and why our lives are important, a conception that gives us the sense from within our own lives that they are valuable. Without that inner sense of identity and value, life takes on the character of a meaningless struggle, and our psychological well-being is destroyed.

Satisfying one's basic human interests in material and psychological well-being is almost never an exclusively individual effort. *Groups* construct and perpetuate systems of labor and exchange for ensuring that material needs are met. *Groups* construct and perpetuate frameworks of thought and belief for giving meaning and purpose to life. This entails that group membership is a logically derivative but crucially important interest of humans. It is logically derivative because being a conscious, biological organism is logically prior to being a member of any group.[2] It is crucially important because, given the hardwiring of the human brain and the environments humans are condemned to inhabit, it is for all practical purposes a universal truth that humans are unable to satisfy their fundamental interests well if they do not belong to groups that are organized to serve those interests.

This universal truth is a large part of the explanation for why humans typically conceive of their own identity, value, and worth as tied (in part or in whole) to their membership in some group or set of groups. The pride that people feel in belonging to a certain ethnic, religious, racial, or national group is a manifestation of that tie. So is the willingness of individuals to take personal risks and accept sacrifices for the good of the group.[3] Such attitudes bespeak more than some external, adventitious attachment to the group; rather they suggest that the person conceives of her group membership as (partly) constitutive of her identity as a being with inherent value and with a dignity that demands the respect of others. Group attachments are taken to be part of one's moral personality.[4]

On account of this way of experiencing group connections, there is no perception of a clear separation between self-interest and altruism. Promoting the interests of certain groups is not seen merely as an instrumental good for individuals who take their interests to be definable independently of their group connections. To serve the interest of the group is, apart from any instrumental effects, to serve their individual interests, as they conceive of themselves.

In the early days of human history, before the invention of such technologies as writing and the development of highly abstract thinking abilities, morally significant groups were strictly local phenomena, constituted by face-to-face interactions. Technological and cognitive developments made it possible for groups to extend well beyond the range of the local, face-to-face encounters. Humans could think of themselves as belonging to groups organized around a certain set of beliefs, values, and goals. It did not matter if any given member never had concrete interactions with the bulk of the other members of the group. Their tie was not a concrete one, but it was no less a tie for its abstract character. In the modern world, virtually all morally and sociologically significant groups are abstract entities in the sense that they extend beyond a set of individuals who are in concrete, face-to-face interaction with one another.[5] Yet, the crucial importance of group life in serving the interests in material and psychological well-being remains. Moreover, the abstract groups with which people identify morally are almost always much less inclusive than all of humanity and, in most cases, exclude people living in the same society as the individual. This stems from the fact that the groups that have served the material and psychological well-being of persons have been relatively exclusive, even when they have extended well beyond face-to-face communities.

CONFLICT AND BIAS

The forms of bias that are morally and sociologically important stem from the individual's moral identification with groups. Such identification leads ineluctably to placing the interests of one's in-group and its members above the interests of out-groups and their members. This privileging of the interests of the in-group in turn increases the chances of conflict with out-groups. And conflict further intensifies bias on all sides. Bias both fuels and is fueled by intergroup conflict.

There are a number of conditions that exacerbate intergroup conflict and bias. Below I enumerate four such conditions.

First, competition for scarce economic resources and opportunities is a widely noted variable that intensifies group bias and conflict. Hobbes famously invoked competition as one of his three main causes of quarrel among individuals, but it extends quite naturally to quarrel among groups.[6] If out-groups are perceived as threatening an in-group's ability to provide for the material well-being of its members, the threat strikes at one of the fundamental human interests that group life is organized to serve. There is a powerful imperative to combat such a threat by any means necessary.

Second, bias and conflict clearly are intensified when one group acts to harm another, leading the injured group to desire some form of retaliation. The situation is worsened by the fact that this desire for retaliation can be perpetuated over generations, festering and even intensifying as time marches on. This is because among the important features of group life are the collective memories that are passed from generation to generation. While these memories preserve the distinctive values and beliefs of a group, they also preserve the memories of past victimizations at the hands of other groups. And the preservation of these memories perpetuates and in some cases intensifies the desire for retaliation.

Third, bias and conflict are also exacerbated by distrust of the intentions of other groups who are (perceived to be) in a position to inflict harm. Again, the Hobbesian analysis of diffidence as a cause of quarrel naturally extends to group interaction.[7] Distrust among groups may be based upon past harms done or simply suspicions about future ones. In any case, it can easily lead to a preemptive strike in self-defense. "Better safe than sorry" reasoning imposes sure costs on other groups to avoid possible costs to oneself and one's own group. In doing so, it escalates the level of bias and conflict.

Fourth, virulent bias and conflict often stem simply from knowing of the existence of a group of people who are organized around a fundamentally different conception of life's meaning and purpose. The existence of such a group can be interpreted as constituting a challenge to the validity of one's own conception. If other people are surviving and perhaps even living well, then it might be reasonable to think that they have superior ideas about life's meaning and purpose. Yet, acknowledging the superiority of a group to which one does not—and perhaps cannot—belong is not an open option for most people. The strong tendency is to think that the values and beliefs of the groups with which one morally identifies are the best. This tendency can provoke a desire to subjugate these recalcitrant others, or to ensure in some other way that they do not live well or do not live at all. The realization of such desires could then be interpreted as the pragmatic proof of the inferiority of their conceptions of life's meaning and purpose. And the failure to realize the desire can be interpreted as the result of their evil designs. Thus virulent intergroup antagonism can exist, even when economic scarcity plays little or no role.[8]

TOLERATION

I do not think that there are any interesting a priori principles dictating which kinds of groups persons will identify with and regard as part of their moral personality. It is an obvious fact of human history that religious affiliation is very often so regarded. But some people give up their religious affiliations: sometimes because they become convinced that another religion is superior, sometimes for reasons of convenience, and sometimes because they become agnostics or atheists. In modern history, national groupings have taken on great importance, but how long this will last cannot be determined.

What will last for the foreseeable future is the moral identification of individuals with groups that are far less inclusive than all of humanity and, in many cases, exclusive of large numbers of persons living in their own society. This moral identification means that individuals will regard the interests of such groups and of the persons belonging to them as more important than the interests of out-groups and their members. Because of this, group bias will last. Persons will not treat the interests of all humans as having equal weight, but will put first the interests of the groups with which they morally identify.

Michael Walzer uses the term *tribalism* to refer to the moral identification of the individual with some group considerably smaller than the whole human population. He claims that tribalism "is a permanent feature of human social life. He also says that "Our common humanity will never make us members of a single universal tribe. The crucial commonality of the human race is particularism."[9]

I think that Walzer may be overstating the point when he claims that we will *never* be members of a single universal tribe. It is more justifiable to claim that any transcendence of tribalism would require leaps of technological and moral development that are at present virtually unimaginable. We should be very wary of equating what we cannot at present imagine with what will never happen, since we enjoy only a very limited understanding of human psychology and the possibilities of technological advancement. But on the practical moral and political point Walzer is quite right when says of tribalism that it breeds "parochialism" (i.e., a disproportionate concern for the interests of one's own groups) and that we must try to accommodate this parochialism rather than eliminate it.[10]

Acknowledging that group bias will last well into the foreseeable future does not mean that the most vicious forms of group bias will persist at the level that has characterized this century. A goal that is both realistic and desirable is to replace the more virulent forms of bias with more benign forms.[11] This is what Walzer is getting at when he advocates accommodation, and it is here that toleration plays its crucial role.

Toleration is a virtue tailor made for a situation in which group identification and the biases that go with it are inescapable features of life. As I understand it, toleration does not involve treating everyone's interests as having equal weight: that would amount to going beyond toleration to some kind of universal brotherly/sisterly love. Instead, toleration is a matter of placing certain limits on the ways in which one favors the groups with which one identifies. It does not eliminate but it does moderate the disproportionate weight given to the interests of those groups.

In order to understand this view of toleration more clearly, let us consider the practice of toleration as it emerged out of the religious warfare in Western Europe during the early modern period. Those thinkers such as Locke who advocated a strategy of religious toleration did not expect that the worshippers of different creeds would relinquish or transcend their commitment to their own church. People would still think that their own church and its form of worship were superior. They would still work to support and strengthen their own church, to put its interests above those of other churches. But the strategy of toleration did impose an important set of constraints on the way such interests were pursued; for example, people would be required to relinquish any effort to capture state power and use it for the purpose of imposing their own creed and rituals on everyone else. Thus, the strategy of toleration "lowered the stakes of religious conflict," as Walzer writes.[12] It did not seek to eliminate the conflict entirely by demanding that people repudiate their religious allegiances. But it did call on people to moderate what they were willing to do to others in the name of those allegiances.

My suggestion is that we take this practice of religious toleration as our model for understanding intergroup toleration. We need to generalize a bit from the practice, since our understanding of toleration should extend beyond religious conflict and the particular problems that were of concern in the sixteenth and seventeenth centuries. But if we do generalize appropriately from the model of religious toleration, then we get the following picture.

Toleration involves placing first the interests of the groups with whom one identifies, but it also puts morally important limits on how one may favor those groups. At a minimum, toleration does not allow an individual to favor her in-groups in ways that violate certain fundamental moral duties owed to all human beings. These would include the duties prohibiting murder, torture, and other forms of physical aggression, as well as the duty to respect the conscientious beliefs of others so long as those beliefs do not pose a threat to civil order.

I believe that there are also more generous forms of toleration that involve the recognition of some (imperfect) positive duties to aid those in out-groups. Such duties to aid would apply when the cost to oneself is small and the threat to the others is very serious. It is even possible for a form of toleration to involve expansive positive duties of aid, although those duties will fall below what the individual regards as owed to his in-groups.

When one treats some out-group as having interests every bit as weighty as those in the in-group, one is in effect abolishing the in-group/out-group distinction and embracing within the in-group those who were formerly members of an out-group. This is, of course, possible to do with respect to some out-groups, but it is a step beyond toleration to caring or brotherly/ sisterly love. Toleration is thus a form, of bias, but it is a nonvirulent, moderated form and that is precisely its virtue. It is also why some have argued that it is not virtuous enough. For these critics of toleration, the aim should be to eliminate group bias, to make the in-group so inclusive that any distinction between in and out groups becomes inapplicable and all humans become embraced within the circle of brotherly/sisterly love. This can be done only by treating the interests of all humans as having equal weight.

However one may judge a world where universal love reigned and each person treated everyone's interests as having equal weight, it would be a mistake to regard such a world as an end-in-view to guide our political and moral choices in the here and now. The problem is the general recalcitrance of the phenomenon of identification with in-groups. Perhaps those who criticize toleration for not being virtuous enough are themselves able to transcend in-group/out-group distinctions and embrace all humanity in brotherly or sisterly love. The rub is that they have no way of getting most other people to do the same. And this fact generates a very substantial risk which history warns us to avoid. The risk is that utopian reformers, unable to realize their ideals by voluntary and peaceful means, will adopt coercive ones to compel recalcitrant human beings to conform to their understanding of the ideal. Thomas Nagel puts the point clearly: "The danger of utopianism comes from the political tendency, in pursuit of the ideal of moral equality, to put too much pressure on individual motives and even to attempt to transcend them entirely through an impersonal transformation of social individuals."[13] In the context of efforts to eliminate group bias, the danger is that, unable to persuade people to give up their in-group attachments voluntarily, there will be a resort to coercion and violence: if people will not relinquish those attachments voluntarily, then they will be forced to do so through the destruction of the material and cultural infrastructure of their groups. That is the unacceptable danger that stems from treating toleration as insufficiently virtuous.

MAKING TOLERATION WORK

The strategy of toleration is a feasible one and does not carry the unacceptable risks attending the utopian strategy of eliminating bias. The successful practice of toleration depends on keeping in check those forces that exacerbate group bias, and accomplishing that does not require draconian measures. Western liberal democracies have had some measure of success in pursuing the practice of toleration. Although there is clearly room for improvement and some reason to worry about whether there will be significant backsliding in the future, it is illuminating to examine the features of liberal democracy that have helped to make toleration work to a very significant degree. There have been non-Western civilizations in the past that have successfully practiced toleration, and I am by no means suggesting that toleration can only work in a liberal democratic context.[14] I do believe, however, that in the contemporary context, liberal democracy has some important lessons to teach about making toleration work.

The relatively widespread distribution of political power characteristic of liberal democracy has played a substantial role in this regard. It has given the different groups in society an incentive to refrain from political actions aimed at seriously harming other groups: a group that acts to harm another is itself vulnerable to retaliatory harm and alienates a potential coalition partner for the future. Unfortunately, some groups have been largely frozen out of the pluralist political process and have not had a fair opportunity to bargain, to deal, to form coalitions, and to threaten retaliation. These are the groups Justice Stone called "discrete and insular minorities" in a famous footnote to a Supreme Court decision.[15] It is no accident that the out-groups that are the object of the most destructive biases are precisely the ones that have been denied to the greatest extent a fair chance at participating in the political process. Exclusion from such a chance is the product of bias, but it also helps to strengthen those very biases: in-group members are reinforced in their view that they have no common interests with the vilified out-groups, and that makes more intense vilification all the easier. Thus, an important part of the fight against the most harmful forms of bias will seek to integrate out-groups more fully into the political process.

The legal system has played an important role in the successful practice of toleration in several ways. First, when illegal actions are taken to harm the members of certain groups and their group membership is perceived as part of the explanation for the harmful action, the rule of law substitutes legal punishment for uncontrolled retaliatory vengeance. The state's punishment of the perpetrators provides some satisfaction to the afflicted group and, com-bined with the threat of legal prosecution should they take the law into their own hands, helps remove the incentive for the group to take vigilante action in retaliation. The rule of law thus helps cut off at an early stage what could otherwise be an escalating cycle of vengeance, violence, and hate.

The legal systems of liberal democracy also provide important consti-tutional guarantees that protect individuals even when they are members of vilified out-groups. These guarantees provide protections not dependent upon the vagaries of the political process. There are ways in which existing con-stitutional protections need to be expanded, but the idea of legal protections for individuals that are beyond the reach of the normal political process remains a crucial part of the successful practice of toleration in liberal democracies.

Toleration will not work well if certain groups interpret the existence of other groups organized around very different beliefs and values as a challenge that must be responded to with force and violence. Liberal democracies have done a fairly good job of making sure that the various groups within them do not put that type of intolerant construction on things. The political and legal systems have undoubtedly played their role in fostering more tolerant inter-pretations of the existence of groups with competing beliefs and values. But I believe that much broader cultural forces have been at work in fostering such tolerant interpretations: schooling, the media, and the market, with its amazing diversity of goods and services, have all combined to send the message that the simple existence of other groups organized around very different beliefs and values is not a challenge that needs to be met with force and violence.

Relativism represents one way of putting a tolerant construction on the existence of other groups organized around very different conceptions from those of one's own group. If truth and right are relative to the person and/or the groups with which she identifies, an individual has no reason to construe the existence of other groups as any kind of challenge at all to the validity of the beliefs of his in-group, much less a reason to respond with force and violence against the out-groups.

Skepticism represents another way of placing a tolerant construction on the existence of other groups. If knowledge is not attainable by humans, then the fact that other groups have different beliefs from mine is no real challenge to the validity of my beliefs: we have simply chosen different paths, and no one can know which is the right one.

Secularism represents another way of interpreting group differences in a tolerant manner. By the term *secularism* here I mean the belief that only those interests that concern life in this world should play a role in determining with whom one can live peaceably.[16] Groups that pose no threat to such secular interests need not be perceived as a challenge requiring force and violence. "Live and let live" is the correct response. Toleration legitimately gives way to intolerance *only* when groups threaten to harm secular interests.

Within liberal democracies, there are strong cultural strains of relativism, skepticism, and secularism, and these strains help to make toleration work. But there is another, though less common, way of putting a tolerant construction on the existence of other groups with very different beliefs and values. It involves regarding the existence of such groups as a kind of challenge, but not one that is to be responded to with force or violence. Rather, they represent a challenge to be met by reasoned discussion and argument. The aim is not so much to arrive at a consensus across groups on fundamental issues. That would amount to the elimination of group differences, a prospect I have previously discounted. Instead, the aim is to exercise and develop one's rational powers and thereby to gain a better understanding of one's own beliefs and those of out-groups.[17]

Some mix of relativist, skeptical, secularist, and reasoned responses to group differences is a good thing for liberal democracy. Each has its role and its limitations. Relativism combats overly restrictive and uniform conceptions of the human good, but it is logically incoherent when applied to all beliefs and stifles the development of our rational powers when applied promiscuously. Skepticism combats dogmatism and promotes a healthy fallibilism, but in its most extreme forms it can lead to intolerance as much as to toleration.[18] Secularism has effectively prevented the worst excesses of religious intolerance, but it is sometimes difficult or impossible to convince believers that a line can be drawn between the secular and the spiritual. Reasoned discussion promotes the lesson that reason rather than force is often the best response to difference, but it is not always desirable or possible. It is not desirable when force is morally necessary, and it is not possible when groups reject reason as a legitimate tribunal before which their ideas can be brought and judged.[19] Making toleration work in liberal democracy will continue to require these different strategies, appropriately limited, for interpreting group differences in a benign way.

Finally, I would like to say a word about the role of economic factors in making toleration work. Historically, economic growth helped to keep in check group biases. As the pie grew, intergroup conflict and bias moderated. In recent years, we have seen the flip side of this phenomenon: as the size of the pie has failed to increase, conflict and toleration have intensified. This is especially troubling in light of the fact that the prospects for future economic growth in many existing liberal democracies are quite uncertain. Yet, we should beware of exaggerating the dangers. The practice of toleration still remains strong, when seen in historical perspective. Economic stagnation will not, by itself, destroy the many political, legal, and cultural forces that foster toleration. However, such stagnation may create a kind of slack that must be picked up by those other forces. This means that efforts must be made to strengthen and to extend the political, legal, and cultural factors that have helped make toleration work.

TOLERATION AND HUMANE MORALITY

I have argued that toleration is a form of bias, distinguished from other forms by its relatively less virulent nature and by its willingness to refrain from violating certain fundamental moral duties owed to every person. I have also described toleration as a virtue. But it may be argued that I cannot have it both ways: toleration cannot be both a virtue and a form of bias. It seems that I am regarding it as a virtue simply because it is less vicious than other forms of bias. But that would only make it a less serious vice. In addition, the most fundamental principle of morality is a principle of impartiality that requires us to regard the interests of all as having the same weight. Toleration may not flout that principle to the same degree that more vicious forms of bias do, but it clearly does flout the principle nonetheless. Thus, it again seems that we are not dealing with a form of virtue here at all but only with a less vicious vice. Or so the argument goes.

The foregoing criticism gains some of its cogency from an equivocation regarding the principle of impartiality. It is one thing to say that a basic moral principle of impartiality holds that the interests of all people are of equal value. It is another to say that such a principle requires each person to treat everyone's interests equally. The first interpretation construes impartiality as a moral fact about the relative importance of the interests of different people, claiming that they are equally important across all persons. The second interpretation moves from this (alleged) moral fact to a claim about how persons morally ought to act. It is easy to think that the equal moral importance of interests entails that each person should act in a way that treats everyone's interests equally. But that easy inference makes a big—and questionable—assumption. It assumes that there are no other moral principles or morally relevant facts that could pull in a different direction from requiring each person to treat equally the interests of all.

Samuel Scheffler has recently argued that there *is* a fact that pulls strongly against such a requirement and that the best understanding of morality must integrate that fact with the idea of impartiality. The fact is that, despite the equal importance of interests from some impersonal stance, "each person's interests nevertheless have a significance for him or her that is out of proportion to their importance from an impersonal standpoint."[20] Thomas Nagel has made a very similar point, arguing that "from his own point of view within the world each person, with his particular concerns and attachments, is extremely important to himself. . . . The personal standpoint must be taken into account directly in the justification of any ethical or political system which humans can be expected to live by."[21]

Although there are some differences of emphasis and detail, for both Scheffler and Nagel the best understanding of morality regards it as accommodating and integrating both the impersonal standpoint from which the interests of all count equally and the personal standpoint from which one's own interests count disproportionately. The kind of morality that accomplishes this will provide relatively broad moral permissions for the individual to pursue with disproportionate concern those commitments, attachments, and projects she regards as most important to her. But, of course, it will also place some limits on such pursuits, limits that reflect the importance of the interests of others. Such a morality will thus be responsive to the claims both of the impersonal and of the personal standpoints.

Scheffler describes this kind of morality as one that reflects an "Ideal of Humanity," and opposes it to a much more stringent morality that rejects as immoral the individual's disproportionate concern with her own commitments, projects, and attachments. The stringent morality reflects, in his terms, an "Ideal of Purity."

It is not my aim here to argue for the superiority of the ideal of humanity over the ideal of purity, though I do find Scheffler's arguments persuasive. Instead I shall conclude with two points. First, the above argument that toleration is not a virtue but merely a less vicious vice assumes the superiority of the ideal of purity. Second, if one accepts the ideal of humanity as superior, toleration can be seen as a virtue precisely because it answers to and accommodates both of the factors to which that ideal seeks to be responsive. Toleration is responsive to the individual's disproportionate concern for the interests of the group with which she identifies, but it places important limits on how that concern can be expressed. Toleration is thus a humane virtue, even if it is not a pure one. And humanity is, I think, the best for which it is reasonable to hope.

NOTES

1. See, e.g., Robert A. Baron and Donn E. Byrne, *Social Psychology: Understanding Human Interaction*, 5th ed. (Boston: Allyn and Bacon, Inc., 1987), 151.

2. To call this interest "logically derivative" is not to say or imply anything about its relative motivational power. It is perfectly possible, as I note below, for this logically derivative interest to be motivationally more powerful than our logically fundamental interests in material and psychological well-being.

3. The willingness of an individual to risk life and limb for the good of the group shows that her interest in promoting the good of the group can be motivationally more powerful than her logically more fundamental interest in material well-being.

4. See Michael Sandel, *Liberalism and the Limits of Justice* (New York: Cambridge University Press, 1982). Unlike Sandel, however, I am not suggesting that group attachments really are part of one's moral identity. For the purposes of this chapter, I remain agnostic on that point and merely note that, as a matter of the phenomenology of moral experience, persons conceive of their attachments in that way.

5. See, e.g., Benedict Anderson, *Imagined Communities* (London: Verso Editions, 1983).

6. Thomas Hobbes, *Leviathan*, ed. M. Oakeshot (New York: The MacMillan Company, 1962), 99.

7. Ibid., 98–99.

8. Hegel makes a similar point in the context of conflict among individuals. See G. W. F. Hegel, *Phenomenology of Mind*, trans. J. B. Baillie (New York: Harper Torchbooks, 1967), 229–40.

9. Michael Walzer, "The New Tribalism," *Dissent* 39 (Spring 1992): 171.

10. Ibid., 169.

11. For current purposes, I leave open the interesting issue recently raised by Paul Gomberg of whether there are certain kinds of group identification which invariably manifest themselves in the most vicious forms of bias. Gomberg suggests that identification with racial groups and with national ones invariably manifest themselves in such a way. He makes his claim in the course of critiquing Stephen Nathanson's contention that racial and patriotic loyalties can be "moderate." Nathanson's moderate forms of patriotism and racial loyalty are closely connected to what I describe below as toleration. See Paul Gomberg, "Against Racism, against Patriotism," *American*

Philosophical Association Newsletter 92 (Spring 1993): 18–19; and Stephen Nathanson, "Is Patriotism Like Racism," *American Philosophical Association Newsletter* 91 (Fall 1992): 9–11. Also see Nathanson, "In Defense of Moderate Patriotism," *Ethics* 99 (April 1989): 535-52; and Gomberg, "Patriotism Is Like Racism," *Ethics* 101 (October 1990): 144–50.

12. Walzer, "New Tribalism," 169.

13. Thomas Nagel, *Equality and Partiality* (New York: Oxford University Press, 1991), 24.

14. See, e.g., the interesting discussion of the Ottoman millet system in Will Kymlicka, "Two Models of Pluralism and Tolerance," *Analyse and Kritik,* forthcoming.

15. United States v. Carolene Products Co. 304 U.S. 144 (1938). For a sophisticated elaboration of Stone's idea of discrete and insular minorities, see John Hart Ely, *Democracy and Distrust* (Cambridge, Mass.: Harvard University Press, 1980), 76, 148–49, 151–53, 160–61.

16. Cf. John Locke, *A Letter concerning Toleration*, ed. J. H. Tully (Indianapolis: Hackett Publishing Company, 1983), 26–28. Locke argues that governments should only be concerned with the "civil interests" of their citizens and such interests are "confined to the cares of things of this World, and hath nothing to do with the World to come."

17. Cf. Immanuel Kant, "What Is Enlightenment?" in *Kant: Selections*, ed. L. W. Beck (New York: The MacMillan Company, 1988), 462–67. Kant argues for religious freedom but not on the grounds that religious beliefs are a private concern with which the public and the state have no business. Instead, Kant claims that the process of enlightenment by which individuals develop intellectual independence will be blocked unless people are free in "the public use" of their reason (463). This freedom must include the freedom to apply their reason in a public manner to religious matters. (466) It is interesting to note that in this essay, Kant is invoking much the same consideration that Mill took essential to the cause of liberty under the phrase "the permanent interests of man as a progressive being." See John Stuart Mill, *On Liberty*, ed. C. V. Shields (Indianapolis: Bobbs-Merrill, 1956), 14.

18. 15. Hume argues that a mitigated form of skepticism helps to combat dogmatism and instill modesty and tolerance. See David Hume, *An Enquiry concerning Human Understanding*, ed. E. Steinberg (Indianapolis: Hackett Publishing Company, 1977), 111. Regarding the idea that some forms of skepticism can lead to intolerance, see Richard Tuck, "Skepticism and Toleration in the Seventeenth Century," in *Justifying Toleration*, ed. Susan Mendus (New York: Cambridge University Press, 1988), 21–27.

19. Kant regarded reason as the ultimate tribunal before which all claims must be brought, but his view has been—and continues to be—rejected by many. "Our age is, in especial degree, the age of criticism, and to criticism everything must submit. Religion through its sanctity, and law-giving through its majesty, may seek to exempt

themselves from it. But they then awaken just suspicion, and cannot claim the sincere respect which reason accords only to that which has been able to sustain the test of free and open examination" (Immanual Kant, *Critique of Pure Reason*, trans. N. K. Smith [New York: St, Martin's Press, 1965], 9).

20. Samuel Scheffler, *Human Morality* (New York: Oxford University Press, 1992), 122.

21. Nagel, *Equality*, 14–15.

17

Socratic Intolerance and Aristotelian Toleration

Evelyn M. Barker

Classical philosophers generally did not consider tolerance either a private virtue or a public good; nor did ancient Greek communities tolerate philosophers who offended traditional religion and popular institutions. Thus there was "ancient philosophical intolerance" in a double sense—that of ancient philosophers themselves toward their philosophical and popular opposition, and that of ancient societies toward philosophers living in their midst. Communities on occasion did honor their citizen philosophers: Empedocles was asked to rule in Akragas; Pythagoras, Parmenides, Anaxagoras, and Protagoras drew up laws at the invitation of fellow citizens. In several cases, however, the philosophers' lawmaking proved so unpopular they were run out of town.

I. F. Stone claims that the Athenian democratic state was exceptional among ancient societies in having a "principle of free speech" that made it tolerant of dissent. According to Stone, the Athenians' conviction and execution of Socrates for impiety was an aberration provoked by Socrates' own intolerance.[1] In the first part of this chapter I challenge the historical accuracy of Stone's claims. I interpret Stone's impatience with Socrates as that of a modern liberal whose tolerance is based on the ethical relativism Socrates opposes. Since it seems to me that Socratic intolerance is acceptable, in the second part of this chapter I develop a classical justification of toleration I find in Aristotle, one which accommodates the absolutist ethics of Socratic intolerance.

COULD SOCRATES HAVE APPEALED TO AN ATHENIAN PRINCIPLE OF FREE SPEECH?

Socrates was indeed intolerant: He taxed his fellow citizens with not living a good life, implying that they were hypocrites or of dubious character because they could not formulate acceptable abstract principles to justify their actions and beliefs. His successors furthered this tradition, insisting that a good life requires an ethic based on knowledge about the nature of things, in the belief that an individual's mistaken world view translates into defective moral character and conduct.

The freedom of the Athenian democratic state, however, did not encompass anything comparable to our modern liberal conception of a principled acceptance of diverse value systems and world views. Stone's thesis is anachronistic in assigning to Athenian democracy his modern liberal ideology. Ironically, Stone unfairly "blames the victim," who actually upholds the principle of free speech. Socrates' address to the jury implies that philosophic questioning, no matter how unpopular, is necessary for the common good of the Athenian democratic state in which the values of the many—wealth, power, and bodily pleasure—otherwise go unchallenged.

The prosecution of Socrates for impiety is only the most egregious instance of democratic Athens' intolerance. Anaxagoras was the first philosopher the Athenians prosecuted. Aristotle left Athens after the death of Alexander, because of an indictment for impiety, and even circumspect Protagoras decamped on being charged with atheism. The popular politician Alcibiades lost favor and was convicted of impiety for what a tolerant society might believe a prank, the mutilation of cult statues during a night of drunken revelry. Stone dismisses these instances. But his contention that there was no Athenian "witch hunt" against philosophers does not prove the contrary, the existence of an Athenian "principle of free speech" protecting philosophers.[2]

Stone maintains that Socrates' arrogant tone of moral superiority angered the Athenian jury and that he did not present his case properly. Stone outlines a speech which, he claims, would have won Socrates' acquittal. It appeals to the democratic state's alleged "principle of free speech," arguing that even though Athenians dislike what Socrates says and does, they should hold fast to their liberal tradition of tolerance. Athenians not only should let him off, but should let him continue his inquiries so as to be true to their own democratic ideals.[3]

The Socratic address which Plato recounts does appeal to Athenian laws, some of which Socrates thought to be expressions of rationally grounded universal and eternal laws, as well as some Socrates thought misguided. The principle of free speech is not among them, as Stone observes. Stone maintains that Plato's intolerant political ideology causes his silence on this point and that of Socrates as well. But Aristotle's *Politics* makes no mention of a principle of free speech as a feature of democracy, nor does his *Constitution of Athens*.[4] Aristotle does speak of the oligarchy of Carthage granting relative freedom of speech to its poor people in its assembly, noting this privilege is not found in other constitutions: "When the kings introduce business in the assembly, they do not merely let the people sit and listen to the decisions that have been taken by their rulers, but the people have the sovereign decision and anybody who wishes may speak against the proposals introduced, a right that does not exist under other constitutions."[5] Thus all three men, familiar with Athenian politics, fail to recognize an Athenian democratic ideal of free speech.

We have a fourth unimpeachable source to prove that their silence on this point is historically sound: Pericles' funeral oration indicates that Athenian toleration would not extend to Socrates' philosophic activities. Pericles does commend the tolerance of the citizens toward one another: "There is no exclusiveness in our private intercourse, we are not suspicious of one another, nor angry with our neighbor if he does what he likes; we do not put on sour looks at him which though harmless are not pleasant."[6] But this tolerant attitude concerns actions in private life. Pericles immediately continues by explaining what Athens expects of its citizens in *public* life:

> While we are thus unconstrained in our private intercourse, a spirit of reverence pervades our public acts; we are prevented from doing wrong by respect for authority and for the laws, having an especial regard to those which are ordained for the protection of the injured as well as to those unwritten laws which bring upon the transgressor of them the reprobation of the general sentiment.

Pericles praises the model Athenian for participating in the deliberations of the assembly, thereby fulfilling his privilege and responsibility as a member of a democratic community: "An Athenian citizen does not neglect the state because he takes care of his own household; and even those of us who are engaged in business have a very fair idea of politics. We alone regard a man who takes no interest in public affairs, not as a harmless, but as a useless character; and if few of us are originators, we are all sound judges of a policy."[7]

Thus the toleration practiced by Athenians did not extend to behavior that did not conform to the norms of democratic citizenship, or threatened the existence of a *democratic political* society: What Socrates was accused of, and the charge he defends himself against, is that he corrupted Athenian youth by encouraging activities which would not make them good citizens of a democratic state.

Socrates admits he intentionally refrained from taking his place in the assembly, a dereliction of civic duty for which Stone excoriates him.[8] Stone attributes Socrates' refusal to attend the assembly to a preference to save his own soul. But in Plato's *Apology* Socrates excuses himself on the grounds of personal safety: "For the truth is, that no man who goes to war with you or any other multitude, honestly striving against the many lawless and unrighteous deeds which are done in a state, will save his life; he who will fight for the right, if he would live even for a brief space, must have a private station and not a public one."[9] He provides an example that happened "in the days of the democracy," when he declined an order to arrest Leon the Salaminian, concluding, "Now do you really imagine that I could have survived all these years, if I had led a public life, supposing that like a good man I had always maintained the right and had made justice, as I ought, the first thing?"

If Socrates is correct on this point, Stone's thesis of principled Athenian toleration of dissenting speech is undercut. Socrates in the assembly would surely have opposed the popular imperialist goals of the democratic state of which Pericles boasts in these words: "For we have compelled every land and every sea to open up a path for our valor, and have every where planted eternal memorials of our friendship and of our enmity." If Socrates' life really would have been at risk for openly criticizing popular democratic imperialistic ventures, as Plato recounts, there could not have been a firm Athenian democratic principle that would have protected him had he dissented publicly in the Assembly.

Xenophon confirms that "influential men threatened him" on the occasion (described in *Apology* 32bc) he did participate in the Assembly, when he rejected the motion against the Athenian commanders at the battle of Arginusae: "He thought it more important to keep his oath than wrongfully to curry favor with the people and defend himself against intimidation."[10]

Socrates' claim of personal danger is not his only justification for not participating in democratic policy making. Socrates maintains at length that he *substitutes* philosophic inquiry with his fellow citizens for participation in assembly deliberations as his unique contribution to the Athenian common good. In so doing, he removes his philosophizing from the private domain, where Athenian democratic freedom allowed people to do what they pleased. By philosophizing in the public domain, Socrates makes dialectic a political activity not protected by Athenian tolerance. He consciously begins his public ministry by questioning politicians and other distinguished citizens, raising the issue of their competence for managing the state's affairs.

In saying his questioning is enjoined by an oracle, Socrates connects his activity with politics as well as with religion. The Athenian state regularly prefaced laws and decrees with a dedication to an appropriate deity, and a citizen demonstrated trustworthiness and seriousness of purpose by an oath to the gods. The effect, if not the purpose, of Socrates' philosophic encounters with his fellow citizens was to undermine their allegiance to a democratic form of government. Not only did he refuse personally to engage in democratic decision making, but his philosophizing discredited the authority of those initiating policy and the Athenian citizen's capacity for judgment. He spurs his admirers either to oppose democracy, like Charmides, or to follow his example in holding aloof from politics, like Plato.

Socrates takes pride in not taking money for his philosophy "lessons," unlike the Sophists, with whom he was often assimilated. But that does not help his case with the Athenians. The Sophists' fees proved that they were engaging in private consensual transactions, while Socrates' free discussions appear a political agenda subversive of democratic institutions. Thus his Athenian prosecutors were deadly serious in their insistence that he abandon his public philosophical inquiries, for according to Socrates' own account it appears a political threat to the common good of a democratic community, not a personal eccentricity.

Athenian toleration is not a matter of principle but has two quite other grounds. First, it is a grace of Athenian life, a flower of the freedom of popular self-government. Second, frankness of speech is a means to effective popular deliberation in the assembly. Stone rightly emphasized that the Athenian democracy made Peitho, the goddess of persuasion, a central deity of the democratic state. If Socratic speech appears to threaten democratic institutions or the common good of a democratic state, however, no fundamental principle of free speech shelters it. By boasting he should be rewarded with public honors rather than convicted, Socrates reenforces his basic argument that speech of principled dissent from goals of the democratic majority operates for the common good of the Athenian democratic society and should be tolerated. But classical Athenians were not ready for this democratic principle.

Plato appeared to understand this. In contrast to Socrates, he withdrew entirely from public political life, founding a school, a private institution, in order to carry out his philosophical inquiries. The philosophical writings that he presented publicly were in the new literary form of a dialogue. Athenians read and admired them as beautiful literature, rather than taking them as serious political tracts. Thus his philosophical activity was clearly within the shelter of Athenian tolerance in private life. Aristotle and other philosophers prudently followed Plato's strategy of founding schools for carrying on philosophical pursuits in Athens.

ARISTOTLE'S JUSTIFICATION OF TOLERATION

Sophists, because of their relativism, are sometimes said to endorse tolerance as a value. But they by no means preached toleration, although they might themselves have practiced it. Protagoras, for example, counseled hearers that they could live successfully and argue best by knowing the mores of their own community, abiding by them, and appealing to them in defense of their private actions and public proposals.

It is in Aristotle one may discern a classical basis for democratic toleration both in private and in public life. His philosophical justification of toleration is interesting because it does not, like the modern view, rest on ethical relativism or on philosophical pluralism. Thus it accommodates the absolute ethics of Socratic philosophical intolerance. Aristotle's justification of toleration rests on two pillars of his philosophy: (1) the doctrine of the mean applied to political life; and (2) his conception of "political friendship."

In the first book of *Politics* Aristotle asserts a principle of hierarchical rule of higher over lower, asserting that the soul properly rules the body despotically, while the intellect exercises aristocratic domination over the appetites. To the soul of a state correspond citizen functions that fulfill justice and virtue generally, including the military; to its body, those producing wealth and material necessities.[11] In accord with his principle of despotic hierarchical rule, Aristotle recommends that the best states exclude from citizenship those who pursue the bodily interests of the state—farmers, businessmen, artisans, manual workers, sailors. But this autocratic stance is mitigated in Aristotle's pragmatic approach to politics, which recommends that a political system should be designed for the majority of human beings.

> What is the best constitution and what is the best life for the majority of states and the majority of men? We have in mind men whose standard of virtue does not rise above that of ordinary people, who do not look for an education that demands either great natural ability or a large private fortune, who seek not an ideally perfect constitution, but, first a way of living in which as many as possible can join, and, second, a constitution within the compass of the greatest number of cities.[12]

In a large part of the *Politics*, Aristotle analyses oligarchy and democracy, the defective political forms in which the interests of the bodily parts of the state and the numerical majority predominate. His recommendations on how these defective political forms can work effectively are particularly applicable to current political and social conditions. What is needed for a viable community is "a system of government which the people involved will accept, and feel able to operate."[13]

Aristotle presents a powerful case for more inclusive forms of government like democracy, although he technically calls them "defective." He is, in a sense, a political pluralist, for he stresses that any form of government in which rulers consciously pursue the good of all in the community, rather than the good of the ruling faction, is just.[14] The practical aim of "constitutional government" is "to include within the political community as many diverse and conflicting interests and abilities as possible." Polity, the least desirable of the three correct forms, "is the most inclusive and stable of constitutions because it blends the principles of democracy and oligarchy that, between them, include the most people and are the source of the most explosive and prevalent of conflicts, namely, rich versus poor."[15]

Aristotle stresses that a democracy needs to have a method of deliberation about matters of common interest. A good democratic state is one in which policies win support not from an absolute numerical majority, but from a majority composed from different segments of the community, rich and poor, nobles, farmers, craftsmen. Such broad based support requires discussion between members of differing groups in the community, who would have varying value priorities.[16]

Aristotle criticizes Socrates' dictum in the *Republic*, "It is best that the state should be as much of a unity as possible."[17] A community requires a variety of talents to provide a good life for its citizens and thus must countenance a diversity of individuals of varying life styles. He maintains that philosophical unity in ethical belief is not requisite for the harmony and stability of a community. He invokes his doctrine of the mean in judging satisfactory even the deviant political forms of democracy and oligarchy so long as they do not go to extremes:

> There is one thing that must not be overlooked, though it often is in constitutions that deviate from the norm—the principle of the middle way. . . . Some people, believing that their own view of goodness is the only right one, push that view to extremes. They fail to realize that a nose which deviates from perfection by being either hooked or snub is still an excellent nose and looks like one as well; but if the process is carried to excess, first it will lose the proportion which belongs to this part of the body and finally it will not look like a nose at all, because of the extreme to which either the hook or the snub has been pushed . . . Both oligarchy and democracy may be tolerably good, though they deviate from the standard of perfection; but if one carries either of them to excess, first the constitution will become worse and finally hardly even a constitution at all.[18]

Aristotle's image of the functional and attractive even if imperfect nose suggests that an ethic other than the absolute one he favors may also be effective in guiding individuals toward a good life, so long as it stays within reasonable bounds and avoids vice. Similarly in *Nichomachean Ethics* Aristotle clearly places philosophic wisdom and moral virtue higher than honor, money, and bodily pleasure as human ends, yet discusses in detail how one may rightly pursue honor, money, and bodily pleasure.

Thus, instead of philosophical unity in principles and value priorities recommended by Plato's *Republic*, Aristotle puts forward the ideal of unanimity, agreement on practical steps to be taken by the community: "A city is unanimous when men have the same opinion about what is to their interest, and choose the same actions, and do what they have resolved in common. It is about things to be done, therefore, that people are said to be unanimous, and among these, about matters of consequence and in which it is possible for both or all parties to get what they want."[19]

In order to achieve such unanimity debate should center on means to be instituted and strive for agreement on particular outcomes satisfactory to all, rather than ultimate principles. Thus, one seeks a no-win/no-lose policy acceptable to individuals of different persuasions, rather than the triumph of principle or political faction. Aristotle calls such unanimity "political friendship." Political friendship makes tolerance a value for every sort of community, but it is particularly applicable to a democratic one in which freedom is espoused as a political goal. It does not require citizens to be united in moral or political ideology, only that they should be ready to reach consensus on particular actions to institute commonly recognized goods. The purpose is to obtain outcomes all agree to be good and avert those generally recognized as bad, rather than the victory of an abstract conception of justice.

He emphasizes the value of friendship in achieving stability and harmony in the wider political community, pointing out that where friendship makes citizens recognize each other's good, justice is not so primary and indispensable. From Aristotle's "political friendship" one may develop an "unprincipled" philosophical basis for tolerance. Affection for particular others who are our intimates makes us tolerant of them, for we prize them in their individuality, even when we do not share their values or approve their life style on philosophical grounds. We also tolerate those with whom we join in work ventures, entertainment, or religious or philanthropic endeavors because we value both the goal and our shared activities with them. Going one step further, we tolerate the views of those with whom we share citizenship in a particular democratic community where the common good affects each citizen's good, and the good of each includes the common good.

Thus toleration need not require a belief in the equal acceptability of diverse ethics or world views. Modern liberal tolerance based on ethical pluralism sometimes betrays antipathy toward a morality not grounded in "scientific rationality," or one which does not express acceptance of ethical pluralism. It seems more genuinely democratic to have plural grounds for tolerance in a society, rather than demanding pluralism as a matter of philosophical or political principle.

I would like to end with some kind words for philosophic intolerance of the kind practiced by ancient philosophers such as Socrates. One who believes another's ethical conceptions mistaken and based on a false world view often does not simply acquiesce in others' life style or beliefs, but opposes them. While this activity usually makes others uncomfortable, it does not cause them harm, nor need it be oppression or discrimination. Rather, it often shows concern for the well-being of friends and fellow citizens and respect for their minds. This Socratic philosophical intolerance seems to me to be something we can and should tolerate, unlike the ancient Athenians.

NOTES

1. I. F. Stone, *The Trial of Socrates* (New York: Anchor Books, 1989).

2. Ibid., chapter 18.

3. Ibid., chapters 14–16.

4. Aristotle, *Politics* 3.2. Aristotle stresses freedom as the fundamental principle of democratic polities in general, describing it as "doing what one likes," and connecting it with political self-rule or "rule by turns."

5. Ibid., 1273a.10–14.

6. As reported in Thucydides, *History of the Peloponnesian War* 2.37–39.

7. Ibid., 38.

8. Stone, *The Trial of Socrates*, chapter 3.

9. Plato, *Apology* 31d, 32e.

10. "Memoirs of Socrates," in *Xenophon Conversations of Socrates*, trans. Hugh Tredennick and Robin Waterfield (London: Penquin Books, 1990), 1.

11. Aristotle, *Politics* 4.4.

12. Ibid., 1.2.

13. Ibid., 4.1.1288b–1289a.

14. Ibid., 3.6.

15. W. R. Newell, "Monarchy in Aristotle's *Politics*," in *Essays on the Foundations of Aristotelian Political Science*, ed. Carnes Lord and David K. O'Connor (Berkeley: University of California, 1991), 204 n. 17.

16. Aristotle, *Politics* 3.2, 4.14, 6.3.

17. Ibid., 2.2.

18. Ibid., 5.9.

19. Aristotle, *Nichomachean Ethics* 9.6.

Carnap's Principle of Tolerance

Stephen F. Barker

INTRODUCTION

Nowadays in our society much attention is given to the importance of tolerance. We are more concerned than our forebearers were about the diversity of ethnic, religious, cultural, and other groups within society, and we preach to one another far more than they did about how everyone ought to practice toleration of these diversities. Philosophers too have begun to give increasing attention to tolerance and toleration and to conflicting views as to their justification.[1]

There is a certain view of tolerance which has entered quite deeply into the thinking of many liberal-minded people in the twentieth century. According to this view, it is the unjustifiability of ordinary moral and value judgments which justifies tolerance as an overarching principle.

Those who take this view notice that widely divergent moral and value judgments often get made, especially by individuals whose backgrounds are diverse; and they hold that there is no way of proving any of these judgments to be more correct than other contrary ones. This leads them to a skeptical or negative attitude regarding ordinary moral and value judgments (which, when made with firmness, they consider to be "judgmental"). Because they regard ordinary moral and value judgments with suspicion, they conclude that one ought not to insist upon one's own judgments to the exclusion of others'; instead, one ought to tolerate everyone's judgments. They conclude that the obligation to be tolerant is a universal principle whose standing is superior to and independent of any specific morality or value outlook.[2] The idea is that it is proper for reasonable people to differ greatly in their specific value-outlooks, because of their differing ethnic, religious, and cultural backgrounds, none of these being any more correct than any other; all people, however, just for this reason, should recognize the obligation to be tolerant and are blameworthy when they violate it by behaving or thinking intolerantly.

Possibly it will be thought that such a viewpoint is so obviously unsound that it is a waste of time to discuss it.[3] That is too optimistic, I think. Unfortunately, the view has had a compelling fascination for many people, including a variety of lively philosophers.[4] For that reason I believe it is worth discussing. I propose to approach it through examining a version of this position that was developed by Rudolf Carnap.

Carnap made a striking attempt to affirm a principle of tolerance within logic and philosophy and to make it a higher-level obligation, a sort of meta-principle. All inquirers ought to agree to it, he thought, regardless of how much they diverge as regards other statements they make. Moreover, his justification for this principle of tolerance depends on his belittling appraisal of all ordinary claims in logic and philosophy. Thus there is a structural parallel between Carnap's view about tolerance in philosophical inquiry and the position mentioned above concerning tolerance in personal and social ethics: in each case we have a negative appraisal of claims in a certain area which is put forward as a proposed justification for tolerance in that area. The fact that Carnap was thinking more of tolerance toward diverse forms of logic than of tolerance toward diversities in social practices only tends to make his viewpoint all the more overarchingly general. If Carnap were right in his reasoning in favor of tolerance in logic and philosophy, this would surely have important implications concerning tolerance in the social and political realms.

Carnap's attempt is challenging and instructive, not because his version of the position is ultimately defensible, but rather because the sharp paradoxes to which it leads bring out clearly for us the difficulties of trying to treat tolerance as such a higher level principle.

LOGICAL SYNTAX

Carnap was a central and influential member of the movement that came to be called logical positivism. His book *The Logical Syntax of Language*,[5] first published in 1934, was one of the central texts of that movement (it has been viewed by some as Carnap's masterwork[6]). When Carnap spoke of "logical syntax," he meant to be talking about rules of language. His goal was to outline a general account of languages of every kind, though his emphasis was on how to construct artificial languages, rather than on how to describe natural languages. (He seems to have assumed that once we grasp the nature of artificial languages, this will explain natural languages, which will differ only in being more crude and less clear.) Carnap was especially concerned with the construction of artificial languages for mathematical logic and natural science, because he regarded these fields as paradigms of respectable thinking.

In *The Logical Syntax of Language* Carnap takes a stand concerning philosophy that is in line with the over-all outlook of logical positivism. He sharply rejects the view of most traditional philosophers, according to whom philosophy was supposed to discover very general and fundamental truths about the nature of reality. According to Carnap there is no special type of nontrivial truth discoverable through philosophical reflection.[7] Empirical truths are the only substantive truths there are, and these are the province of natural science. The principles of logic and mathematics are worth studying, too, but are expressive merely of symbolic conventions.

Carnap's diagnosis is that traditional philosophers have imagined they were raising substantive questions about the ultimate nature of reality, but were mistaken in this. Metaphysics is not a kind of arm-chair science. Metaphysical questions either are "pseudo-questions" (i.e., meaningless, not genuine questions at all) or they are covertly questions about logical syntax (purely verbal questions about grammar, or about the choice of a word). Traditional philosophers have been led into these misunderstandings because of their failure to grasp the nature of logical syntax. Once clarity is achieved concerning it, Carnap holds that these metaphysical confusions will evaporate, and there will no longer be any motivation for confused philosophical writings. (Carnap regards Heidegger's writing as an extreme example of such confusion.[8])

If philosophy is to differ both from natural science and from logic and mathematics, and if philosophy is to avoid talking metaphysical nonsense, what then is there for philosophy to do? The intellectually respectable task for philosophy, Carnap answers, is that it should frankly become the study of logical syntax. It is to concern itself with characterizing the rules of language in general, and of course it may also study the rules of specific languages.

In 1934 Carnap thought that the only rules of language needing to be discussed were syntactical rules (that is, rules which mention only signs and sign combinations). He distinguished between two kinds of syntactical rules: formation rules and transformation rules. The formation rules characterize those sign combinations which are well formed and therefore can count as sentences in the language. The transformation rules characterize which sign combinations are derivable in the language from which others; that is, they constitute the inferential structure of the language.

We should notice that the usual manner of organizing inferential transformations in a language involves selecting a group of "primitive sentences" (or postulates), which are to be the basis from which other sentences (theorems) are to be derived. In languages of pure logic and mathematics, Carnap expects that these primitive sentences will all be analytic (which seems to mean that they are to be treated as true simply because the transformation rules say so, and not for any other reason). In languages for natural science, however, he expects empirical sentences to predominate among the primitive ones (there the transformation rules in effect will tell us to be guided by sense experience). Thus, when Carnap speaks of a language, he means a logical system comprising both a grammatical scheme for constructing well-formed sentences and also a scheme that picks out specific sentences to be asserted as postulates and theorems.[9]

ARBITRARINESS AND TOLERANCE

Central to Carnap's view of language was the view that the rules of language are arbitrary and conventional, never true or false, valid or invalid, correct or incorrect. In principle, then, no particular choice as to which rules to adopt is any more right than any other.

This view of linguistic rules certainly is plausible as regards the grammatical rules: any given criteria of what it is for expressions to be well formed always could be modified in ways which would not need to make the scheme inoperable. Thus, for instance, having started to discuss a subject in English, we could switch to French or Italian instead, or to Esperanto, or to some new artificial language we have invented; and, in principle, we should be able to carry on our discussion. There is no a priori reason why we ought to use any particular grammar and vocabulary, nor are there empirical reasons that narrowly constrain this choice. However, notice that Carnap formulates the point in a sweeping manner, so as to suggest also that there are no real reasons why any selection of postulates and theorems is better than any other; and our suspicions may well be alerted by this formulation.

Closely associated with Carnap's view of linguistic rules as arbitrary is the so-called linguistic theory of the a priori, a view of analytic propositions which was widely adopted by the logical positivists, under the inspiration of Wittgenstein's *Tractatus*.[10] According to this view, it is merely because of arbitrary rules of language that analytic propositions have the truth values they have; therefore, their truth values are conventional and could be changed at will. This is supposed to explain how analytic propositions can have truth values while lacking any subject matter to which they need correspond.

It is this linguistic theory of the a priori which, I believe, leads Carnap to advance what he calls the "principle of tolerance." He states the principle as follows: "It is not our business to set up prohibitions, but to arrive at conventions."[11] He goes on to add, as a subsidiary formulation, "In logic, there are no morals."[12] And he explains this as meaning that "everyone is at liberty to build up his own logic, i.e. his own language, as he wishes."[13] Carnap speaks of this principle as expressing a "tolerant attitude."[14] The point seems to be that because the notion of correctness has no relevance to choices of rules and postulates in language systems, those who study logical syntax ought to adopt a policy of toleration regarding divergent choices.[15]

One would like to have had from Carnap a fuller account of what his philosophical motives were for saying what he says about tolerance. Also, one would like to have heard more from him about what he intends the principle of tolerance to mean, and about how he would try to justify it. As it is, his discussion is brief, and we have to interpret him as best we can.

PROBLEMS WITH THE PRINCIPLE

At first blush, Carnap's principle of tolerance seems to say that anyone may set up a language system in any way. Let us consider the principle in this version, before noticing the exceptions to it that Carnap later introduces.

Carnap's principle is *permissive* in form. Its grammar indicates that it is not intended descriptively; that is, Carnap is not saying that people do set up languages any way they please; rather, he is saying that when they do so they are within the limits of the permissible.

To say that it is permissible to set up language in any way surely is equivalent to saying that people never deserve censure for setting up languages as they please. A corrollary of this would be that others are *forbidden* to censure those who set up languages as they please. Thus we could reformulate Carnap's principle in the perhaps clearer form of a prohibition: "Everyone is forbidden to censure those who set up languages as they please."

What kind of permissions and prohibitions are we dealing with here? Are they *moral* permissions and prohibitions? If so, Carnap would be saying that all ways of setting up language systems are morally blameless, and any censure of them up is morally blameworthy. Can we really suppose, though, that Carnap is talking about what is morally permitted and morally blameworthy? There are difficulties with such an interpretation.

For one thing, Carnap has said, "In logic there are no morals." This seems to imply that no moral judgments can be relevant to logic. Yet Carnap pretty clearly intends that the principle of tolerance is somehow to belong to logic, for he gives it a central position in his exposition of logic. Thus an inconsistency for Carnap results if we interpret the principle of tolerance as a moral principle.

Another aspect of the difficulty is that Carnap holds not merely that in logic there are no morals; also he holds, in a certain sense, that there are no morals in morals, either. For him, there are no morals anywhere. This view comes out most explicitly in his *Philosophy and Logical Syntax* of 1935,[16] where he compares moral judgments to "lyrical cries." Carnap takes over from Wittgenstein the view that moral judgments never have any truth values and thus always are nonsensical pseudo-statements. Wittgenstein had thought, however, that some such pseudo-statements were *important* nonsense, deeply significant to life; but Carnap shows no sympathy for that notion and regularly treats nonsense in a dismissive manner.[17] Thus, in trying to interpret Carnap's principle of tolerance, we encounter a paradox: Carnap puts it forward as something important, and the principle certainly sounds like a moral judgment; yet if it is moral in character it must be nonsense, according to Carnap's view of moral judgments; and Carnap does not think nonsense should be taken seriously.[18] Thus Carnap's position seems less than coherent.

We might try to interpret the principle of tolerance as dealing not with *moral* permission and prohibition but rather with some sort of *intellectual* permission and prohibition. Yet what could this mean?

If we agree with traditional philosophers that there are laws of logic which are true in a more than merely conventional sense, then we can hold that these laws ought to govern how the rules of language are to be set up. This would give us a basis for talking about permissions and prohibitions. We could say that these laws establish standards of intellectual probity *permitting* anyone to set up any linguistic system which conforms to these logical laws and *prohibiting* other people from criticizing this.

Such an interpretation will not suit Carnap, however. It is part of his position in *The Logical Syntax of Language* that logic does not involve truths that amount to anything more than arbitrary linguistic conventions. He does not at all want to say, as most traditional philosophers since Aristotle have said, that there are logical truths not established by us, to which our thinking has an intellectual obligation to conform. Thus, the attempt to substitute intellectual permissions and prohibitions for moral ones in our interpretation of Carnap leaves his position still unsatisfactory.

EXCEPTIONS TO THE PRINCIPLE

So far, we have been speaking as though Carnap's principle of tolerance did sweepingly permit all language systems, as its initial wording suggests.

When we look more fully into his text, however, we find that Carnap did not really intend the permission to be nearly so sweeping.

One exception to generalized tolerance does get introduced almost immediately after Carnap has stated the principle of tolerance. He says of a person choosing a set of linguistic rules: "All that is required of him is that, if he wishes to discuss it, he must state his methods clearly, and give syntactical rules instead of philosophical arguments."[19] That is, Carnap's tolerance is limited; he does demand clear rules, clearly stated, from anyone who uses language. As we have already seen, Carnap regards metaphysicians as especially prominent sinners against the demand for clarity, and he sharply censures their uses of language.[20]

Also, Carnap's tolerance does not extend to those who set up rules of language in ways that lead to logical contradictions. Thus he says Frege committed two major *errors* in establishing a language for mathematical logic.[21] Here, I take it, by speaking of "errors" Carnap is definitely not adopting a tolerant attitude toward this aspect of Frege's work, but is censuring it.

Carnap's principle of tolerance, as he originally stated it, seemed to say that people may set up whatever language systems they please, but now we find him making these two major exceptions to his decree. How are these exceptions to be understood?

Those of us who are not Carnapians may consider it easy to justify censuring unclarity and inconsistency. With regard to unclarity, the point would seem to be that those who express themselves unclearly are troublemakers; they waste our time and befuddle us. Such activity as theirs ought not to be tolerated, because it is intellectually (and sometimes morally) harmful; we make this value judgment in a spirit of censure, not in a tolerant spirit. Similarly, those who set up rules which permit contradictions to arise within their systems deserve censure, because contradictions are necessarily false; theorems within a system ought all to be true. Carnap himself really cannot describe matters in these terms, however.

First, consider Carnap's rejection of unclarity. He prescribes that people who discuss language ought to do so clearly. Yet his prescription presupposes the judgment that clarity is valuable. As we have seen, Carnap's teaching is that all value judgments are nonsensical, and that the nonsensical is not to be taken seriously. If this were right, then his own prescription could not deserve to be taken seriously (although just possibly it would come close enough to making sense so that it could be accused of falling under its own ban). Thus, Carnap is trying to issue a serious demand for clarity when, by his own lights, the demand is not to be taken seriously. Carnap is not entitled to invoke the normal assumption that clarity really is valuable, and so his laying down of a prescription against unclarity fails to be coherent.

Carnap also gets into trouble with regard to the second type of exception which he wants to make to his principle of tolerance. He censures others who have supposedly committed *errors* when they set up their rules of language in ways that yield theorems of the form "*p & -p.*" Yet from his own point of view it is merely conventional that such theorems are reckoned *false*; they are not false in any substantive way. He has no right, from his own standpoint, to censure those who permit some of their theorems to exhibit this particular pattern of signs.[22] Thus Carnap is not in a position to defend coherently his exceptions to the principle of tolerance.

INTERNAL VERSUS EXTERNAL QUESTIONS

Carnap further developed his postion in a later, related paper, "Empiricism, Semantics, and Ontology,"[23] and his advocates may think that the difficulties just noted are resolved there. In that paper Carnap introduced a distinction between "internal questions" and "external questions" concerning existence, as these may arise for language systems capable of expressing mathematics and science.

Internal questions are supposed to be those which can be settled within the framework of a system, merely by appeal to the rules of the system. Thus internal questions are not problematic, because there are definite procedures for settling what their answers are. Carnap counts as internal all ordinary questions as to what things exist, when these are asked within the "framework of things." The latter seems to be the sort of language system in which the scientific world view is commonly expressed. Presumably, Carnap's reason for classifying questions about what ordinary things exist as internal is because he thinks their answers will be theorems of the scientific system, derivable via its rules. He says that these ordinary questions about what there is involve an empirical, nonmetaphysical concept of reality.

However, external questions are supposed to be questions not posed within the framework of any specified system. They are posed from outside, asking how a given system is related to what there "really" is. For example, suppose a traditional philosopher, considering a system whose theorems purport to be about the external world, asks whether such a world really exists or asks whether a system purporting to refer to it is more correct than one which does not. Or suppose the philosopher, considering a system which purports to describe abstract entities such as numbers, asks whether there really are such entities. These will be external questions, according to Carnap, and the concept of 'reality' they employ is metaphysical. He seems to suppose that no system has rules determining answers to such metaphysical questions, so they are unsettleable. As theoretical questions, they therefore make no sense and are not to be taken seriously.

For Carnap, it is a corollary of this that other philosophers are mistaken when they suppose that using a language framework commits the user to a metaphysical doctrine. Carnap holds, for example, that one can do mathematics employing a language containing abstract entity names, without thereby being guilty of believing in abstract entities. His view seems to be that the using of any language can be innocent, but that entangling oneself in metaphysical pseudo-beliefs is blameworthy. In this article of 1950 Carnap does not emphasize his principle of tolerance, but one can see that he is continuing to welcome the use of divergent languages and is deploring the intolerance of philosophers who censure ways of speaking divergent from their own.

For our purposes, however, the principal change of emphasis in this article by Carnap lies in his pragmatic account of external questions. He holds, to be sure, that external questions have no correct or incorrect answers and therefore make no theoretical sense. However, he now urges, that they can be understood as "practical" questions which invite us to make decisions about what languages to use. Thus Carnap interprets the question, Are there really abstract entities? as a covert way of asking, Shall we employ a language containing abstract names? This latter question has no true or false answer, but our response to it does not have to be arbitrary. Carnap advises us to consider what our purposes are and to select those language frameworks which most effectively advance our purposes. Thus his basic appeal is to pragmatic usefulness.

How satisfactory is this restatement by Carnap of the situation? He is right, of course, that considerations of usefulness should be a factor in our decisions about what languages to employ. Yet does he provide a coherent account of how these considerations enter into such decisions?

The difficulty is that Carnap is juggling two opposing lines of thought. On the one hand, he has created the impression that in order for a question to be genuine, it has to have an answer determined by the rules of the linguistic framework within which it is asked. Yet, on the other hand, he claims that these practical questions about the pragmatic utility of language frameworks somehow are to be taken seriously, although there is no linguistic framework within which they arise.[24] These two lines of thought clash.

To the extent that Carnap regards these pragmatic issues as external, he makes them sound like pseudo questions which have no criteria for their resolution and hence cannot be taken seriously. To the extent that he regards them as issues we can take seriously and can thoughtfully think through so as to move toward answers, he makes them sound like his internal questions, for he seems to be presupposing that criteria of utility are available, and we might have expected him to think that these must be embedded in a linguistic framework within which the questions are being asked.

Carnap wants to find a place for these practical questions, yet he also wants to refuse them the status of internal questions. This does not work out satisfactorily, because his distinction between the external and the internal has not been drawn in such a way as to enable it to carry the load he wants to impose on it. Thus the 1950 reformulation of his position fails to surmount difficulties of the same type that undermined his 1934 version.

CONCLUSION

Carnap is led to his principle of tolerance by his view that philosophical statements are not to be taken seriously. Since he thinks none of them says anything of substance, he concludes that tolerance toward all of them is the proper attitude. Thus he thinks that tolerance emerges as a higher level principle, made firm by the infirmity of what is to be tolerated.

Serious difficulties infect Carnap's position. His principle of tolerance is itself a philosophical statement (and an ethical one), so his wish that we take it seriously is at odds with his own view of such statements. Moreover, when he decrees that unclarity and inconsistency are not to be tolerated, these exceptions themselves are arbitrary, on his principles. These problems are representative of the type of difficulty likely to affect any theory which seeks to justify tolerance on the basis of a negative appraisal of the types of statements that are to be tolerated.

In contrast to that approach, we will do better to regard tolerance as itself morally valuable. Some of us might take it to be an intrinsic value, while others of us might see it as an instrumental value serving to promote other more basic moral values. Then, if we are to hold that diversities of belief and behavior ought to be tolerated in some given area of life, we should be claiming that the policy of toleration either is intrinsically better or else that it yields better results there than do its alternatives. That is, we should be willing to make and take seriously value judgments concerning alternative outcomes, if we are to have a coherent case in favor of tolerance.

NOTES

1. See, for example, John Horton and Susan Mendus, eds., *Aspects of Toleration: Philosophical Studies* (London: Methuen, 1985); Susan Mendus and David Edwards, eds., *On Toleration* (Oxford: Clarendon Press, 1987); and John Horton and Peter Nicholson, eds., *Toleration: Philosophy and Practice* (Aldershot, England: Avebury, 1992).

2. This, of course, is not the view of classical liberal thinkers such as Locke and Mill. They, on the whole, sought to justify policies of toleration by appeal to their good consequences, thereby making the obligation to tolerate derivative from ordinary value judgments, which they did not radically question.

3. Glen Newey seems to suggest as much in his *"Fatwa* and Fiction: Censorship and Toleration," in ed. John Horton and Peter Nicholson, *Toleration: Philosophy and Practice* (Aldershot, England: Avebury, 1992), 92.

4. For example, see J.-P. Sartre, "Existentialism Is a Humanism," in *Existentialism from Dostoievsky to Sartre*, ed. Walter Kaufmann (New York: New American Library, 1975), 346.

5. Rudolf Carnap, *The Logical Syntax of Language* (Patterson, N.J.: Littlefield, Adams & Co., 1959).

6. Yehoshua Bar-Hillel, "Remarks on Carnap's Logical Syntax of Language," in *The Philosophy of Rudolph Carnap,* ed. Paul A. Schilpp (LaSalle, Ill.: Open Court, 1963), 520.

7. On this point, Carnap was of course influenced by Wittgenstein's *Tractatus.*

8. Carnap's discussion of Heidegger occurs in his "The Elimination of Metaphysics through Logical Analysis of Language," in *Logical Positivism*, ed. A. J. Ayer (Glencoe, Ill.: The Free Press, 1959), section 5. This article was originally published as "Uberwindung der Metaphysik durch Logische Analyse der Sprache," *Erkenntnis* 2 (1932).

In this article Carnap declares severely that "metaphysicians are musicians without musical ability." (80).

9. Within a year or two after publishing *The Logical Syntax of Language*, Carnap decided that his view of linguistic rules as wholly syntactical had been too narrow. The work of the Polish logicians, especially Alfred Tarski, convinced him that semantical rules also need to be included (semantical rules speak about how signs are correlated with nonlinguistic objects). In spite of this major shift in his view of rules, Carnap kept intact his identification of a language with a logical system based on a set of rules.

10. Ludwig Wittgenstein, *Tractatus Logico—Philosophicus* (London: Routledge & Kegan Paul, 1922).

Wittgenstein's linguistic theory of the a priori in the *Tractatus* presupposed that there are elementary propositions which merely describe directly verifiable empirical facts, and that all other propositions are truth-functional compounds of these elementary propositions. According to this view, necessary truths must all be truth-functional tautologies, and necessary falsehoods must all be truth-functional contradictions. The theory is that such tautologies and contradictions merely reflect the conventional rules governing the words or symbols that serve as truth-functional connectives. This is supposed to be why these propositions "say nothing," and why their truth values can be assertained a priori.

The logical positivists downplayed this implausible presupposition concerning the truth-functional structure of language, but continued to affirm its supposed consequence, the emptiness and conventionality of all propositions knowable a priori.

An especially lively statement of the linguistic theory of the a priori is offered by Hans Hahn in his "Logic, Mathematics and Knowledge of Nature," in *Twentieth-Century Philosophy: The Analytic Tradition*, ed. Morris Weitz (New York: The Free Press, 1966), 220-235. This is a translation of sections 1 through 4 of Hahn's *Logik, Mathematik und Naturerkennen* (Wein: Gerold & Company, 1933).

11. Carnap, *Logical Syntax*, 51.

12. Ibid., 52.

13. Ibid.

14. Ibid.

[15] Against my attempt to explain the principle of tolerance on the basis of the linguistic theory of the a priori, it might be objected (a) that Carnap in *The Logical Syntax of Language* does not explicitly say that he is embracing the linguistic theory of the a priori; and (b) in a much later writing (Schilpp, *Philosophy of Rudolph Carnap*, 915–16) Carnap explicitly denied holding a linguistic theory of logical truth and criticizes that theory effectively.

Nevertheless, my view is that we must interpret Carnap of *The Logical Syntax of Language* as essentially committed to a linguistic theory of the a priori. Such a theory was strongly circulating among his fellow logical positivists, and I can see no way of understanding why he wrote as he did about tolerance, unless he was embracing this theory.

16. Rudolf Carnap, *Philosophy and Logical Syntax* (London: Psyche Miniatures, 1935).

17. That is, Carnap is uniformly censorious of those whom he thinks guilty of misleading themselves and others by employing linguistic usages that appear to make sense, but really do not. Presumably, he did not object to frankly nonsensical use of language, as in nonsense poetry; and certainly he did not object to music, which he thinks has no cognitive content, but does not purport to have any.

18. In "Carnap's Intellectual Autobiography" (Schilpp, *Philosophy of Rudolph Carnap*, 9) he does declare that his view "led at no time to a nihilistic attitude toward moral questions." We must accept this report, of course, and conclude that Carnap did take seriously the everyday ethical problems he confronted. The general drift of his meta-ethical views is nihilistic, however; that is, if one were both to think through the implications of Carnap's non-cognitive theory of ethics and to continue to accept it, one would be driven to a nihilistic attitude toward moral issues.

19. Carnap, *Logical Syntax*, 52.

20. It is interesting to speculate what Carnap's response would have been if Heidegger had concocted a clear set of linguistic rules characterizing his use of

expressions such as "das Nichts" and had added them as an appendix to *Was Ist Metaphysik*. Would Carnap genially have accepted that as making Heidegger's work scientifically respectable? Or would he have abandoned tolerance and censured Heidegger's rules?

21. Schilpp, *Philosophy of Rudolph Carnap*, 138. Russell, in his theory of types, showed how to avoid these errors, Carnap supposes.

22. Someone will say that when theorems like this appear in a system, then every well-formed formula will be a theorem, destroying the usefulness of the system.

To this there are various replies. (a) That is so for many systems, but need not be so for all. The supposedly disastrous result could always be forestalled by adding a rule to the effect that when any expression p has been derived as a theorem, one is not permitted thereafter to derive $-p$ as well. Then we could have p & $-p$ as a theorem without having all well-formed formulas as theorems. (b) To say that a system becomes useless when all well-formed formulas are theorems is to make a dubious value judgment. Some of the purposes of logic and mathematics might be ill-served by such a system, but those are not the only possible purposes.

23. Rudolf Carnap, "Empiricism, Semantics, and Ontology," *Revue Internationale de Philsophie* 11 (January 1950): 20–40.

24. Notice how suspicious is the claim that there can be no such linguistic framework. Elsewhere Carnap recognizes situations in which one language (a metalanguage) can speak about another language (an object language). So one would have thought that we could have linguistic frameworks within which we could describe and compare the degrees of utility of various other linguistic frameworks; and in that case the so-called practical questions of which Carnap speaks would be internal rather than external questions.

Perhaps Carnap would try to reply that what makes these practical questions external is that we have not yet set up a language system in which to discuss them, though we could do so. That reply seems quite unclear, however; what is Carnap's evidence that no such system has been set up, and indeed what are his criteria for telling whether a language system has been set up?

Contributors

Andrew Altman is Associate Professor of Philosophy at the George Washington University. He is the author of *Arguing About Law: An Introduction to Legal Philosophy* (Wadsworth, 1996) and *Critical Legal Studies: A Liberal Critique* (Princeton, 1990). Professor Altman received his Ph.D. from Columbia University and has been a Liberal Arts Fellow at the Harvard Law School. Currently, he is working on issues of race, racism, and the law.

Evelyn M. Barker is a professor *emerita* at University of Maryland Baltimore County, where she has been a faculty member since 1966. She received her Ph.D. in philosophy from Harvard University, and has also taught at Wells College, Mount Holyoke College and University College of the University of Maryland. The author of *Everyday Reasoning* (Prentice-Hall, 1981), she edited Ralph Barton Perry's *The Humanity of Man* (Braziller, 1956), and has published articles on Aristotle, phenomenology and medical ethics.

Stephen F. Barker is professor of philosophy at the Johns Hopkins University in Baltimore. His areas of interest include the theory of knowledge, the history of modern philosophy, and applied ethics. He has written *Induction and Hypothesis, Philosophy of Mathematics,* and *The Elements of Logic.* Also he was an editor of *The Legacy* of *Logical Positivism,* of *Thomas Reid: Critical Interpretations,* of *Respect for Life in Medicine, Philosophy and the Law,* and of *John Wisdom's Proof and Explanation.*

David Cain is Distinguished Professor of Religion at Mary Washington College. Author-photographer of *An Evocation of Kierkegaard/En Fremkaldelse af Kierkegaard,* a "coffee-table Kierkegaard" (forthcoming from Reitzels Forlag, Copenhagen, December, 1996), he has published numerous articles on Kierkegaard. Other special interests, in addition to dialogue among religions, are Dostoevsky, theodicy, atonement, religion and literature, and the films of Federico Fellini and Giulietta Masina. The lecture version of the present article (November, 1993) he dedicated in gratitude to the beauty of the work of Fellini, who died 31 October, 1993, and of Masina, whose death followed, 23 March, 1994. He is an ordained minister in the United Church of Christ.

Robert Paul Churchill received his Ph.D. degree in philosophy from The Johns Hopkins University. He is Professor of Philosophy at The George Washington University and Executive Director of the Society for Philosophy in the Contemporary World. In addition to his textbooks on logic and the edited collection, *The Ethics of Liberal Democracy,* he has published articles on a wide variety of topics, including altruism, genocide, pacifism, the theory and practice of nonviolence, Just War theory, national defense policy, Gandhi, and Vaclav Havel. He is presently working on a book tentatively titled *Complicity with Evil: A Philosophical Examination of Social and Behavioral Explanations of Human Cruelty.*

Gertrude D. Conway is presently a Professor of Philosophy at Mount Saint Mary's College in Emmitsburg, Maryland. After completing her Ph.D. at Fordham University, she was a member of the faculty at Shiraz (formerly Pahlavi) University in Iran. Her scholarly work focuses on twentieth century philosophy, especially Wittgenstein and Hermeneutics. She is the author of *Wittgenstein on Foundations* (Humanities Press International, 1989). Her current scholarship focuses on philosophical issues tied to the problem of crosscultural understanding and dialogue.

Richard H. Dees is an associate professor of philosophy and a member of the core faculty of women's studies at Saint Louis University. He has published essays on contextual models of political justification and on the moral and political thought of David Hume in such journals as the *Journal of the History of Philosophy, Philosophy and Phenomemological Research, and the Canadian Journal of Philosophy.* He is currently working on a book on trust and the justification of toleration.

John Donovan is Associate Professor of Philosophy and Director of the Honors Program at Mr. St. Mary's College. He earned his Ph.D. in Philosophy from Georgetown University. His areas of academic specialization are the Philosophy of Religion and German Idealism. He is the author of *Doing and Don'ting—A Workbook in Moral Identity,* several articles on Thomas Merton, and a study of Nietzsche entitled "The Uses and Abuses of Nietzsche in History." His current project is a study of the origins of the Philosophy of Religion as a discipline independent of confessional theology.

Edwin C. George lectures on philosophy and religion for the University of Hawaii and other schools in the area. He is currently writing a dissertation on Kierkegaard.

Gordon Graham is Regius Professor of Moral Philosophy at the University of Aberdeen in Scotland. He is the author of many papers and several books, including most recently *Ethics and International Affairs* (Blackwell) and *The Shape of the Past: A Philosophical Approach to History* (Oxford University Press).

Jeff Jordan is an Associate Professor of Philosophy at the University of Delaware. He is the editor of *Gambling on God: Essays on Pascal's Wager* (1994), and co-editor of *Faith, Freedom, and Rationality* (1996). Jordan is also the author of twenty articles, primarily in the areas of philosophy of religion and sociopolitical philosophy.

Edward Langerak is Professor of Philosophy at St. Olaf College, where he has taught since 1970. He has authored several articles on the subjects of tolerance and personal commitment in a pluralistic society, including "Theism and Toleration," forthcoming in Blackwells *Companion to Philosophy of Religion*. He has co-authored *Christian Faith, Health, and Medical Practice,* which is forthcoming in its second edition (Eerdmans Publishing Co.).

John McCumber is present Professor of Philosophy and German and Jean Lane Professor of Humanities at Northwestern University. He has taught at the University of Michigan—Dearborn and the Graduate Faculty, New School for Social Research. He is the author of numerous articles concerning the history of philosophy and of two books, *Poetic Interaction: Language, Freedom, Reason,* and *The Company of Words: Hegel, Language and Systematic Philosophy.*

Seyyed Hossein Nasr was born in Iran. He studied in America where he received his B.S. degree in physics from the Massachusetts Institute of Technology and his M.A. and Ph.D. degrees in the history of science and learning with a concentration in Islamic science, from Harvard University. From 1958–79, he was Professor of Philosophy at Tehran University. During 1968–72, he also served as the Dean, Faculty of Letters from 1970–71, he served as Vice-Chancellor at Tehran University. From 1972–75 Dr. Nassar served as the Chancellor (President) of Aryamehr University. In 1974, he founded the Iranian Academy of Philosophy and served as its first president until 1979. In 1979, he became Professor of Islamic Studies at Temple University, and is now University Professor of Islamic Studies at the George Washington University.

Robert Cummings Neville holds the Ph.D. in philosophy from Yale University and is currently professor of philosophy, religion, and theology at Boston University where he is also the dean of the School of Theology. He has been president of the American Academy of Religion, the Metaphysical Society of America, and the International Society for Chinese Philosophy. Among his fourteen books are *The Cosmology of Freedom, The Puritan Smile,* and *The High Road Around Modernism,* all of which deal with themes in political philosophy.

William O'Meara earned his Ph.D. in Philosophy from Loyola University in Chicago, 1969. He is presently Professor of Philosophy at James Madison University. His publications include articles on George Herbert Mead, Whitehead, Alan Gewirth, Marx, and Husserl, and he edited with his colleagues at JMU a reader in introduction to Philosophy *The Continuing Quest*. He has also directed a number of grants from the Virginia Foundation for the Humanities and Public Policy, producing programs for public television and public radio.

J. B. Schneewind currently teaches philosophy at Johns Hopkins University. He has written *Sidgwick's Ethics and Victorian Moral Philosophy* (1977) and a history of modern moral philosophy, *The Invention of Autonomy* (forthcoming). He was President of the Eastern Division of the American Philosophical Association in 1995–1996.

Index

A

Abraham, 46, 50, 95, 131
Ackerman, Bruce, 202, 207, 209
Afghanistan, 30
After Virtue, 152, 153, 182
Akragas, 246
Alcibiades, 247
Alexander, 247
Algeria, 29
Allah, 105
Allen, Woody, 86
Alley, Robety, 209
Altarity, 66
America (*see also* United States), 49,
  53, 139; American Civil War, 145;
  American politics, 111; American
  society, 145
Americans, 55, 136, 138, 147, 224
Ames, William, 8
Amish, 203
Anaxagoras, 246, 247
Anderson, Benedict, 243
Anglican, 155
Anglicans (*see also* Episcopalians),
  150, 151
*Anti-Oedipus: Capitalism and
  Schizophrenia*, 184, 185

Apology, 249, 254
Aquinas, Thomas, 95, 107
Aquinas: Selected Political Writings,
  107
Arabs, 29, 50
Arblaster, Anthony, 207
Arendt, Hannah, 209
Arginusae, 249
*Argument of the Letter concerning
  Toleration, Briefly Consider'd and
  Answer'd*, 151, 152
Aristotelian, xvi, 22, 23, 81, 88, 91;
  Aristotelian categories, 17
Aristotelianism, 146
Aristotle, xv, xvi, 16–27, 87–89, 90,
  93, 158, 165, 199, 202, 247, 248,
  251–53, 254, 255, 261
Aryan, 128
Asia, 115
*Aspects of Toleration: Philosophical
  Studies*, 121, 124, 153, 154, 207,
  227, 265
atheism, 247
atheists, xiii, 6, 7
Athenian, 246–50; Athenian politics,
  248
Athenians, 250, 254
Athens, 247, 248